Hydroponicalley
grows

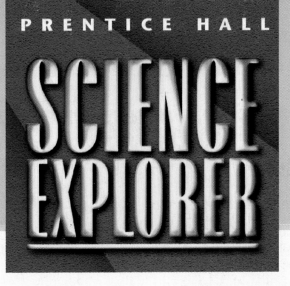

PRENTICE HALL

SCIENCE EXPLORER

Motion, Forces, and Energy

Needham, Massachusetts
Upper Saddle River, New Jersey
Glenview, Illinois

Motion, Forces, and Energy

Book-Specific Resources

Student Edition
Annotated Teacher's Edition
Teaching Resources with Color Transparencies
Consumable and Nonconsumable Materials Kits
Guided Reading Audiotapes
Guided Reading Audio CDs
Guided Reading and Study Workbook
Guided Reading and Study Workbook, Teacher's Edition
Lab Activity Videotapes
Science Explorer Videotapes
Science Explorer Web Site at **www.phschool.com**

Program-Wide Resources

Computer Test Bank Book with CD-ROM
How to Assess Student Work
How to Manage Instruction in the Block
Inquiry Skills Activity Book
Integrated Science Laboratory Manual
Integrated Science Laboratory Manual, Teacher's Edition
Interactive Student Tutorial CD-ROM
Prentice Hall Interdisciplinary Explorations
Probeware Lab Manual
Product Testing Activities by Consumer Reports™
Program Planning Guide
Reading in the Content Area with Literature Connections
Resource Pro® CD-ROM (Teaching Resources on CD-ROM)
Science Explorer Videodiscs
Standardized Test Preparation Book
Student-Centered Science Activity Books
Teacher's ELL Handbook: Strategies for English Language Learners

Spanish Resources

Spanish Student Edition
Spanish Guided Reading Audio CDs with Section Summaries
Spanish Guided Reading Audiotapes with Section Summaries
Spanish Science Explorer Videotapes

Science Explorer Student Editions

From Bacteria to Plants
Animals
Cells and Heredity
Human Biology and Health
Environmental Science
Inside Earth
Earth's Changing Surface
Earth's Waters
Weather and Climate
Astronomy
Chemical Building Blocks
Chemical Interactions
Motion, Forces, and Energy
Electricity and Magnetism
Sound and Light

ISBN 0-13-054097-8
3 4 5 6 7 8 9 10 04 03 02

Cover: Carnival ride at the Del Mar Fair, Del Mar, California

Program Authors

Michael J. Padilla, Ph.D.
Professor
Department of Science Education
University of Georgia
Athens, Georgia

Michael Padilla is a leader in middle school science education. He has served as an editor and elected officer for the National Science Teachers Association. He has been principal investigator of several National Science Foundation and Eisenhower grants and served as a writer of the National Science Education Standards.

As lead author of *Science Explorer,* Mike has inspired the team in developing a program that meets the needs of middle grades students, promotes science inquiry, and is aligned with the National Science Education Standards.

Ioannis Miaoulis, Ph.D.
Dean of Engineering
College of Engineering
Tufts University
Medford, Massachusetts

Martha Cyr, Ph.D.
Director, Engineering Educational Outreach
College of Engineering
Tufts University
Medford, Massachusetts

Science Explorer was created in collaboration with the College of Engineering at Tufts University. Tufts has an extensive engineering outreach program that uses engineering design and construction to excite and motivate students and teachers in science and technology education.

Faculty from Tufts University participated in the development of *Science Explorer* chapter projects, reviewed the student books for content accuracy, and helped coordinate field testing.

Book Author

Peter Kahan
Former Science Teacher
Dwight-Englewood School
Englewood, New Jersey

Contributing Writers

Mark Illingworth
Teacher
Hollis Public Schools
Hollis, New Hampshire

Thomas R. Wellnitz
Science Teacher
The Paideia School
Atlanta, Georgia

Reading Consultant

Bonnie B. Armbruster, Ph.D.
Department of Curriculum and Instruction
University of Illinois
Champaign, Illinois

Interdisciplinary Consultant

Heidi Hayes Jacobs, Ed.D.
Teacher's College
Columbia University
New York, New York

Safety Consultants

W. H. Breazeale, Ph.D.
Department of Chemistry
College of Charleston
Charleston, South Carolina

Ruth Hathaway, Ph.D.
Hathaway Consulting
Cape Girardeau, Missouri

Tufts University Program Reviewers

Behrouz Abedian, Ph.D.
Department of Mechanical Engineering

Wayne Chudyk, Ph.D.
Department of Civil and Environmental Engineering

Eliana De Bernardez-Clark, Ph.D.
Department of Chemical Engineering

Anne Marie Desmarais, Ph.D.
Department of Civil and Environmental Engineering

David L. Kaplan, Ph.D.
Department of Chemical Engineering

Paul Kelley, Ph.D.
Department of Electro-Optics

George S. Mumford, Ph.D.
Professor of Astronomy, Emeritus

Jan A. Pechenik, Ph.D.
Department of Biology

Livia Racz, Ph.D.
Department of Mechanical Engineering

Robert Rifkin, M.D.
School of Medicine

Jack Ridge, Ph.D.
Department of Geology

Chris Swan, Ph.D.
Department of Civil and Environmental Engineering

Peter Y. Wong, Ph.D.
Department of Mechanical Engineering

Content Reviewers

Jack W. Beal, Ph.D.
Department of Physics
Fairfield University
Fairfield, Connecticut

W. Russell Blake, Ph.D.
Planetarium Director
Plymouth Community Intermediate School
Plymouth, Massachusetts

Howard E. Buhse, Jr., Ph.D.
Department of Biological Sciences
University of Illinois
Chicago, Illinois

Dawn Smith Burgess, Ph.D.
Department of Geophysics
Stanford University
Stanford, California

A. Malcolm Campbell, Ph.D.
Assistant Professor
Davidson College
Davidson, North Carolina

Elizabeth A. De Stasio, Ph.D.
Associate Professor of Biology
Lawrence University
Appleton, Wisconsin

John M. Fowler, Ph.D.
Former Director of Special Projects
National Science Teacher's Association
Arlington, Virginia

Jonathan Gitlin, M.D.
School of Medicine
Washington University
St. Louis, Missouri

Dawn Graff-Haight, Ph.D., CHES
Department of Health, Human Performance, and Athletics
Linfield College
McMinnville, Oregon

Deborah L. Gumucio, Ph.D.
Associate Professor
Department of Anatomy and Cell Biology
University of Michigan
Ann Arbor, Michigan

William S. Harwood, Ph.D.
Dean of University Division and Associate Professor of Education
Indiana University
Bloomington, Indiana

Cyndy Henzel, Ph.D.
Department of Geography and Regional Development
University of Arizona
Tucson, Arizona

Greg Hutton
Science and Health Curriculum Coordinator
School Board of Sarasota County
Sarasota, Florida

Susan K. Jacobson, Ph.D.
Department of Wildlife Ecology and Conservation
University of Florida
Gainesville, Florida

Judy Jernstedt, Ph.D.
Department of Agronomy and Range Science
University of California, Davis
Davis, California

John L. Kermond, Ph.D.
Office of Global Programs
National Oceanographic and Atmospheric Administration
Silver Spring, Maryland

David E. LaHart, Ph.D.
Institute of Science and Public Affairs
Florida State University
Tallahassee, Florida

Joe Leverich, Ph.D.
Department of Biology
St. Louis University
St. Louis, Missouri

Dennis K. Lieu, Ph.D.
Department of Mechanical Engineering
University of California
Berkeley, California

Cynthia J. Moore, Ph.D.
Science Outreach Coordinator
Washington University
St. Louis, Missouri

Joseph M. Moran, Ph.D.
Department of Earth Science
University of Wisconsin–Green Bay
Green Bay, Wisconsin

Joseph Stukey, Ph.D.
Department of Biology
Hope College
Holland, Michigan

Seetha Subramanian
Lexington Community College
University of Kentucky
Lexington, Kentucky

Carl L. Thurman, Ph.D.
Department of Biology
University of Northern Iowa
Cedar Falls, Iowa

Edward D. Walton, Ph.D.
Department of Chemistry
California State Polytechnic University
Pomona, California

Robert S. Young, Ph.D.
Department of Geosciences and Natural Resource Management
Western Carolina University
Cullowhee, North Carolina

Edward J. Zalisko, Ph.D.
Department of Biology
Blackburn College
Carlinville, Illinois

Teacher Reviewers

Stephanie Anderson
Sierra Vista Junior High School
Canyon Country, California

John W. Anson
Mesa Intermediate School
Palmdale, California

Pamela Arline
Lake Taylor Middle School
Norfolk, Virginia

Lynn Beason
College Station Jr. High School
College Station, Texas

Richard Bothmer
Hollis School District
Hollis, New Hampshire

Jeffrey C. Callister
Newburgh Free Academy
Newburgh, New York

Judy D'Albert
Harvard Day School
Corona Del Mar, California

Betty Scott Dean
Guilford County Schools
McLeansville, North Carolina

Sarah C. Duff
Baltimore City Public Schools
Baltimore, Maryland

Melody Law Ewey
Holmes Junior High School
Davis, California

Sherry L. Fisher
Lake Zurich Middle School North
Lake Zurich, Illinois

Melissa Gibbons
Fort Worth ISD
Fort Worth, Texas

Debra J. Goodding
Kraemer Middle School
Placentia, California

Jack Grande
Weber Middle School
Port Washington, New York

Steve Hills
Riverside Middle School
Grand Rapids, Michigan

Carol Ann Lionello
Kraemer Middle School
Placentia, California

Jaime A. Morales
Henry T. Gage Middle School
Huntington Park, California

Patsy Partin
Cameron Middle School
Nashville, Tennessee

Deedra H. Robinson
Newport News Public Schools
Newport News, Virginia

Bonnie Scott
Clack Middle School
Abilene, Texas

Charles M. Sears
Belzer Middle School
Indianapolis, Indiana

Barbara M. Strange
Ferndale Middle School
High Point, North Carolina

Jackie Louise Ulfig
Ford Middle School
Allen, Texas

Kathy Usina
Belzer Middle School
Indianapolis, Indiana

Heidi M. von Oetinger
L'Anse Creuse Public School
Harrison Township, Michigan

Pam Watson
Hill Country Middle School
Austin, Texas

Activity Field Testers

Nicki Bibbo
Russell Street School
Littleton, Massachusetts

Connie Boone
Fletcher Middle School
Jacksonville Beach, Florida

Rose-Marie Botting
Broward County School District
Fort Lauderdale, Florida

Colleen Campos
Laredo Middle School
Aurora, Colorado

Elizabeth Chait
W. L. Chenery Middle School
Belmont, Massachusetts

Holly Estes
Hale Middle School
Stow, Massachusetts

Laura Hapgood
Plymouth Community Intermediate School
Plymouth, Massachusetts

Sandra M. Harris
Winman Junior High School
Warwick, Rhode Island

Jason Ho
Walter Reed Middle School
Los Angeles, California

Joanne Jackson
Winman Junior High School
Warwick, Rhode Island

Mary F. Lavin
Plymouth Community Intermediate School
Plymouth, Massachusetts

James MacNeil, Ph.D.
Concord Public Schools
Concord, Massachusetts

Lauren Magruder
St. Michael's Country Day School
Newport, Rhode Island

Jeanne Maurand
Glen Urquhart School
Beverly Farms, Massachusetts

Warren Phillips
Plymouth Community Intermediate School
Plymouth, Massachusetts

Carol Pirtle
Hale Middle School
Stow, Massachusetts

Kathleen M. Poe
Kirby-Smith Middle School
Jacksonville, Florida

Cynthia B. Pope
Ruffner Middle School
Norfolk, Virginia

Anne Scammell
Geneva Middle School
Geneva, New York

Karen Riley Sievers
Callanan Middle School
Des Moines, Iowa

David M. Smith
Howard A. Eyer Middle School
Macungie, Pennsylvania

Derek Strohschneider
Plymouth Community Intermediate School
Plymouth, Massachusetts

Sallie Teames
Rosemont Middle School
Fort Worth, Texas

Gene Vitale
Parkland Middle School
McHenry, Illinois

Zenovia Young
Meyer Levin Junior High School (IS 285)
Brooklyn, New York

PRENTICE HALL SCIENCE EXPLORER

Contents

Motion, Forces, and Energy

Activities

Inquiry Activities

CHAPTER PROJECT

Opportunities for long-term inquiry

DISCOVER

Exploration and inquiry before reading

Sharpen your Skills

Practice of specific science inquiry skills

TRY THIS

Reinforcement of key concepts

Skills Lab

In-depth practice of inquiry skills

Real-World Lab

Everyday application of science concepts

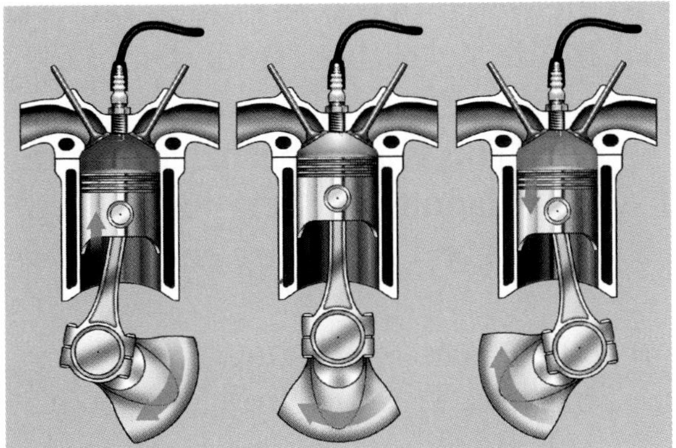

EXPLORING

Visual exploration of concepts

Interdisciplinary Activities

Math Toolbox

Science and History

Science and Society

Connection

UNDERSTANDING NATURE'S DESIGNS

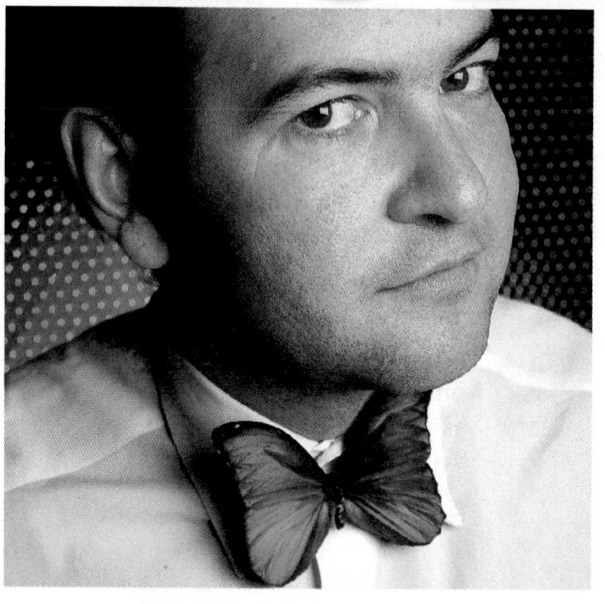

Engineer and Scientist Ioannis Miaoulis
Dr. Miaoulis was born in Greece and grew up there. He then came to the United States to study. He is now a professor of mechanical engineering and Dean of the School of Engineering at Tufts University in Medford, Massachusetts.

Fish in a tank glide under the watchful eye of a video camera. Inside a glass box, spiders spin webs in the wind from a powerful fan. "This is a biomechanics laboratory," says Professor Ioannis Miaoulis (YAHN is my OW lis). "What we study is how animals and plants use energy, motion, and forces."

Miaoulis walks over to a network of earthen tunnels built between two panes of glass. The structure looks like a toy ant farm, but it has a tube for blowing air over the top. Miaoulis explains:

"This is a cross section of a prairie-dog burrow. There are two entrance holes. One hole is flat, while the other one is built up and rounded. Biologists were wondering why. They thought the prairie dogs wanted a good view, but then why not make both holes high and rounded and get a good view from both?"

TALKING WITH IOANNIS MIAOULIS

Miaoulis and his students are learning the likely reason. Wind blowing over a flat surface moves more slowly, because it doesn't have to travel as far as the same breeze going over a rounded surface. "Slow air means high pressure across here" — Miaoulis points to the flat hole. "Fast air going over the rounded hole means low pressure. High pressure here, low pressure there. The holes' shape moves air through the burrow—in the flat hole and out the rounded one. It's prairie-dog air conditioning."

Q *How did you get started in science?*

A I grew up in Athens, Greece. It's a congested and polluted city, but my school was in the woods and I could do things outdoors. I got to love nature. I dug out anthills to see how they were inside. I found the places where turtles laid their eggs. In the summers, we lived near the ocean and every day I'd go fishing and snorkeling. I got to know each rock underwater. I didn't even know what a scientist was then, but I was observing and thinking through things because I wanted to catch more fish. If the flow of water was in this direction, where would be a good place for the fish to hang out? I was observing flow patterns to see where, how, and why fish build their nests. I still do it, in part to catch them, because I still like fishing. But now I do it to observe them, to figure them out. I was always curious.

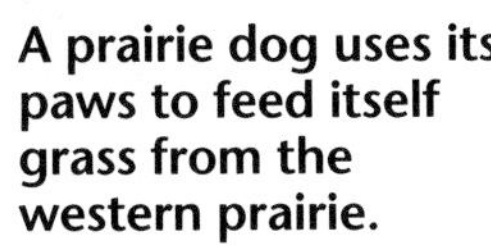

A prairie dog uses its paws to feed itself grass from the western prairie.

Air moves through a prairie dog hole that can be more than four meters deep. Side pockets are for nesting and food storage.

How Prairie-Dog Air Conditioning Works

1. **Air moves over the flat hole.**
2. **Air moves faster over the rounded hole. Fast-moving air creates a large pressure drop.**

Air flows from an area of high pressure to an area of low pressure. The difference in pressure between the two holes pushes air through the prairie dogs' burrow, creating a breeze.

Butterfly wings are studied under bright lights to learn how evenly they absorb heat.

A microscopic view of a butterfly wing shows the many thin, overlapping layers that collect heat from the sun.

Q ***You teach engineering. Is that different from science?***

A Well, I enjoyed doing things with my hands, taking things apart and seeing how they worked, building things and making them work. I found that what I enjoyed about studying was learning science and then doing something with it. And that's engineering. I try to discover something about an animal that nobody ever understood before. Then I'll use that information to design something that will make people's lives easier.

Q ***How have you used nature in your engineering designs?***

A Here's an example. I got interested in how heat travels in the chips that make computers work.

> **"What we study is how animals and plants use energy, motion, and forces."**

They're made in very thin layers or films, thinner than one-hundredth the thickness of your hair. Sometimes, if chips don't heat evenly, they fall apart when you try to make them. I wondered if any plants or animals had solved that problem—using thin films to control how heat was absorbed or reflected. We looked for animals that bask or lie in the sun, or for animals and insects that depend on the warmth of the sun.

Why is a maple seed shaped as it is?
A seed tends to detach when the wind is blowing.
Because of its winglike shape, the seed spirals slowly to the ground. So, in the wind, it travels away from the tree.
A seed that falls away from the roots and shade of the parent tree has a better chance to grow.

If you touch a butterfly, you get a dust on your fingers. When I was little I used to catch butterflies and didn't really understand what the dust was. If you slice those "dust" particles, you find that they are made of many layers. These thin films are little solar collectors. Butterflies can change the amount of heat they catch. They just change the angle at which they hold the thin films on their wings up to the sun. Large areas of butterfly wings heat evenly. So we're looking at the layers on butterfly wings to learn how to make computer chips that will transfer heat more evenly.

Q ***How do you come up with the questions you ask?***

A It depends. Sometimes it's simply by observing things. If you see a maple seed with wings falling in a fancy way, you might not even think twice about it. But if you start observing and appreciating nature, you start asking questions about how things work. Why would it help the tree to have a seed that could be blown by the wind? I can combine my love of nature from when I was small with what I've learned of science and engineering.

Maple seeds can fall to the ground any time from May to early fall.

In Your Journal

Do you, too, have "a questioning eye"? Miaoulis carefully observes plants and animals and asks himself questions about them. Quietly observe some animals in your environment (pets, insects, birds) for 15 or 20 minutes. Then write down four "how" or "why" questions about the movement and speed of the animals. For example, why does a frog have a stop-and-start movement?

CHAPTER 1

Motion

www.phschool.com

Describing and Measuring Motion

Discover **How Fast and How Far?**
Try This **Sunrise, Sunset**
Skills Lab **Inclined to Roll**

Integrating Earth Science

Slow Motion on Planet Earth

Discover **How Slow Can It Flow?**
Sharpen Your Skills **Predicting**
Real-World Lab **Stopping on a Dime**

Acceleration

Discover **Will You Hurry Up?**

PROJECT 1

Speeds à la Carte

Imagine that you have traveled thousands of miles to visit the tropics of South America. Suddenly, vivid reds and blues brighten the green of the rain forest as a group of macaws swoop down and perch above you in a nut tree. They squawk at each other as they crack nuts with their powerful jaws and eat the meat. In a few minutes they spread their wings to take off, and vanish from sight. The macaws cracking nuts, flapping their wings, and flying through the forest are all examples of motion. Your plane flight to South America is another.

In this chapter, you will learn how to describe and measure motion. You will find examples of motion and describe how fast different objects move. You will measure the speeds of various common moving things.

Your Goal To identify several examples of motion and measure how fast each one moves. You will arrange your results from slowest to fastest.

Your project must

- include careful distance and time measurements
- use your data to calculate the speed of each example
- provide display cards that show data, diagrams, and calculations
- follow the safety guidelines in Appendix A

Get Started Brainstorm with a group of your classmates several examples of motion. For example, you might consider a feather falling, your friend riding a bicycle, or the minute hand moving on a clock. Which examples will be easy to measure? Which will be more challenging?

Check Your Progress You'll be working on this project as you study this chapter. To keep your project on track, look for Check Your Progress boxes at the following points.

Section 1 Review, page 25: Create a data table.

Section 3 Review, page 38: Repeat measurements and make calculations.

Wrap Up At the end of the chapter (page 41), you will compare the speeds recorded by the class.

These red-and-green macaws live in the Amazon River basin in Peru.

SECTION 1

Describing and Measuring Motion

DISCOVER

ACTIVITY

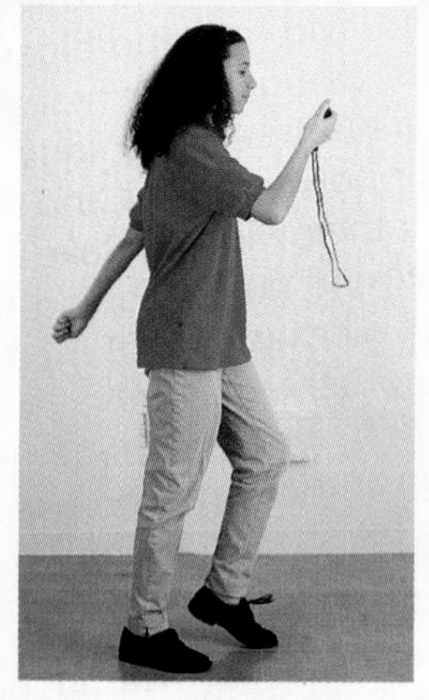

How Fast and How Far?

1. Find out how long it takes you to walk 5 meters at a normal pace. Record your time.
2. Now find out how far you can walk in 5 seconds if you walk at a normal pace. Record your distance.
3. Repeat Steps 1 and 2, walking slower than your normal pace. Then repeat Steps 1 and 2, walking faster than your normal pace.

Think It Over

Inferring What is the relationship between the distance you walk, the time it takes you to walk, and your walking speed?

GUIDE FOR READING

- **When is an object in motion?**
- **How can you find the speed and velocity of an object?**

Reading Tip **Before you read, rewrite the headings in the section as questions. As you read, look for answers.**

It's three o'clock and school is over! You hurry out of class to enjoy the bright afternoon. A light breeze is blowing. A few clouds are lazily drifting across the sky, and colorful leaves float down from the trees. Two birds fly playfully over your head. A bunch of frisky squirrels chase one another up a tree. You spend a few minutes with some friends who are kicking a ball around. Then you head home.

Does anything strike you about this afternoon scene? It is filled with all kinds of motion: blowing, drifting, fluttering, flying, and chasing. There are simple motions and complicated motions, motions

▼ Gray squirrels

Figure 1 Whether or not an object is in motion depends on the reference point you choose. *Comparing and Contrasting Which people are moving if you compare them to the escalator? Which people are moving if you compare them to Earth?*

that are over in a moment, and motions that continue all afternoon. How else can you describe all of these examples of motion? There is actually a great deal to understand about how and why all these things move as they do. In this section, you will learn how scientists describe and measure motion.

Recognizing Motion

Deciding if an object is in motion isn't as easy as it sounds. For example, you are probably sitting as you read this paragraph. Are you moving? Other than your eyes blinking and your chest moving up and down, you would probably say that you (and this book) are not moving. An object is in **motion** when its distance from another object is changing. Since the distance between you and this book is not changing, you conclude that neither you nor the book is moving.

At the same time that you think you are sitting still, you are actually moving about 30 kilometers every second. At that speed, you could travel from New York City to Los Angeles in about 2 minutes! You are moving because you are on planet Earth, which is orbiting the sun. Earth moves about 30 kilometers every second, so you and everything else on Earth are moving at that speed as well.

Whether an object is moving or not depends on your point of view. If you compare the books on a desk to the floor beneath them, they are not moving.

Figure 2 Both the Hubble Space Telescope and the astronaut are actually moving rapidly through space. But compared to the Hubble Space Telescope, the astronaut is not moving and can therefore complete necessary repairs.

But if you compare them to the sun, the books are moving quite rapidly. Earth and the sun are different reference points. A **reference point** is a place or object used for comparison to determine if something is in motion. **An object is in motion if it changes position relative to a reference point.** You assume that the reference point is stationary, or not moving.

If you have ever been on a slow-moving train, you know that you may not be able to tell the train is moving unless you look out the window. A nearby building is a good reference point, and a glance at it will tell you if you and the train are moving. But it is important to choose your reference point carefully. Have you ever been in a school bus stopped right next to another school bus? Suddenly, you think your bus is moving backward. When you look out the window on the other side, you find that your bus isn't moving at all. Actually, the other bus is moving forward! Your bus seemed to be moving backward because you used the other bus as a reference point. You assumed your reference point was stationary. But in fact, your reference point—the other bus—was really moving.

Sunrise, Sunset

ACTIVITY

Earth rotates as it moves around the sun. But to you, the sun appears to move.

1. Choose a spot from which you can observe the sky throughout one day.
2. From the same spot, observe the sun at 6 to 8 different times during the day. **CAUTION:** *Be careful not to look directly at the sun.* Describe its position by comparing it with things around you, such as trees and buildings.
3. Draw a diagram showing the sun's positions throughout the day.

Observing What reference point(s) did you use? Did the sun appear to move when compared with those reference points? Did it really move?

Describing Distance

INTEGRATING MATHEMATICS

To describe motion further, you need to use units of measurement. Whether you realize it or not, you use units, or standard quantities, all the time. You might, for example, measure 2 cups of milk for a recipe, swim 100 yards after school, or buy 3 pounds of fruit at the store. Cups, yards, and pounds are all units.

Scientists all over the world use the same system of units so that they can communicate information clearly. This system of measurement is called the **International System of Units,** or in French, Système International (SI). SI is a system based on the number ten. This makes calculations with the system relatively easy.

The basic SI unit of length is the **meter** (m). A meter is a little longer than a yard. The Eiffel Tower in Figure 3 is measured in meters. To measure the length of an object smaller than a meter, scientists use the metric unit called the centimeter (cm). The prefix *centi-* means "one hundredth." A centimeter is one hundredth of a meter, so there are 100 centimeters in a meter. The beautiful butterfly in Figure 3 is measured in centimeters. For even smaller lengths, the millimeter (mm) is used. The prefix *milli-* means "one thousandth," so there are 1,000 millimeters in a meter. In the International System, long distances are measured in kilometers (km). The prefix *kilo-* means "one thousand." There are 1,000 meters in a kilometer.

SI units are also used to describe quantities other than length. You can find more information about SI units in the Skills Handbook on page 204 of this textbook.

Checkpoint *What unit would you use to describe the width of your thumb?*

Math TOOLBOX

Converting Units

When you convert one metric unit to another, you must move the decimal point.

1. How many millimeters are in 14.5 meters? You are converting from a larger unit to a smaller one, so you multiply. There are 1,000 millimeters in a meter. To multiply by 1,000, move the decimal to the right three places.

   14.500 m = 14,500. mm

   There are 14,500 mm in 14.5 m.

2. Convert 1,200 centimeters to meters. You are converting from a smaller unit to a larger one, so you divide (move the decimal to the left).

   1,200. cm = 12.00 m

   1,200 cm equals 12 m.

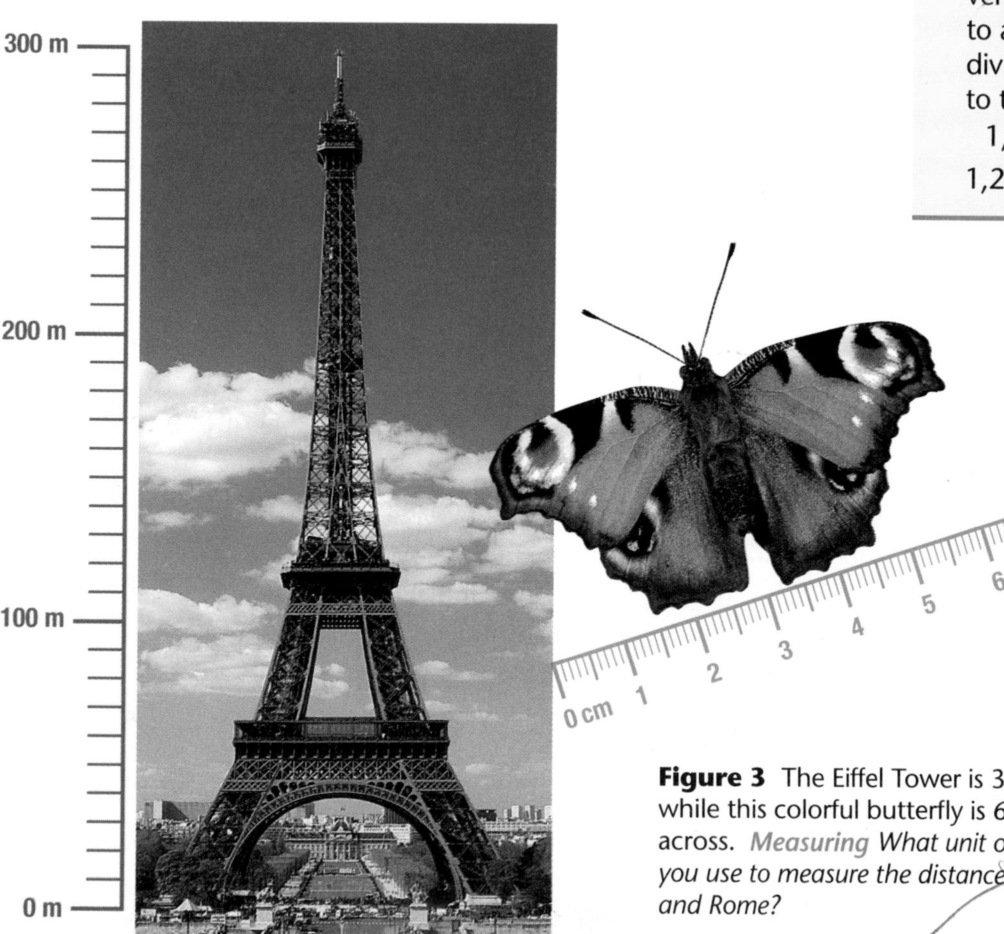

Figure 3 The Eiffel Tower is 300 meters tall, while this colorful butterfly is 6.1 centimeters across. *Measuring* *What unit of length would you use to measure the distance between Paris and Rome?*

Social Studies **CONNECTION**

Does speed affect the shape of cities? Because people want to travel quickly, they live close to major transportation routes—highways and railroads. Thus a city often looks like a hub with spokes coming out of it along the transportation routes.

In Your Journal

People prefer not to travel more than one hour from home to work. The table shows a city's travel routes.

Route	Average Speed
Highway 1	75 km/h
Highway 2	55 km/h
Blue Rail	60 km/h
Red Rail	75 km/h
Main Street	35 km/h

Along which two routes would you expect to find people living farther from the center of the city? Explain why. Draw a map of what you think this city might look like.

Calculating Speed

Scientists use SI units to describe the distance an object travels. A car, for example, might travel 90 kilometers. An ant might travel 2 centimeters. If you know the distance an object travels in a certain amount of time, you know the speed of the object. To be more exact, the **speed** of an object is the distance the object travels per unit of time. Speed is a type of rate. A rate tells you the amount of something that occurs or changes in one unit of time.

To calculate the speed of an object, divide the distance the object travels by the amount of time it takes to travel that distance. This relationship can be written as follows.

$$\text{Speed} = \frac{\text{Distance}}{\text{Time}}$$

Speed measurements consist of a unit of distance divided by a unit of time. If you measure distance in meters and time in seconds, you express speed in meters per second (m/s). (The slash is read as "per.") If you measure distance in kilometers and time in hours, you express speed in kilometers per hour (km/h).

If a car travels 90 kilometers in one hour, the car is traveling at a speed of 90 km/h. An ant that moves 2 centimeters in one second is moving at a speed of 2 centimeters per second, or 2 cm/s. The ant is much slower than the car.

Constant Speed A ship traveling across the ocean may move at the same speed for several hours. Or a horse cantering across a field may keep a steady pace for several minutes. If so, the ship and the horse travel at constant speeds. If the speed of an object does not change, the object is traveling at a constant speed. When an object travels at a constant speed, you know that its speed is the same at all times during its motion.

Figure 4 This horse is cantering at a constant speed. ***Problem Solving*** *What information do you need to calculate the horse's speed?*

Figure 5 The cyclists do not travel at a constant speed throughout this cross-country race. *Comparing and Contrasting How does average speed differ from constant speed?*

If you know the distance an object travels in a given amount of time, you can use the formula for speed to calculate the object's constant speed. Suppose, for example, that the horse in Figure 4 is moving at a constant speed. Find the horse's speed if it canters 21 meters in 3 seconds. Divide the distance traveled, 21 meters, by the time, 3 seconds, to find the horse's speed.

$$\text{Speed} = \frac{21\text{ m}}{3\text{ s}} = 7\text{ m/s}$$

The horse's speed is 7 meters per second, or 7 m/s.

Average Speed Most objects do not move at constant speeds for very long. The cyclists in Figure 5, for example, change their speeds many times during the race. They might glide along on level ground, move more slowly as they climb steep inclines, and dash down hills. Occasionally, they stop to fix a tire.

Unlike the horse described earlier, you cannot use any one speed to describe the motion of the cyclists at every point during the race. You can, however, find the average speed of a cyclist throughout the entire race. To find the average speed, divide the total distance traveled by the total time.

Suppose a cyclist travels 32 kilometers during the first two hours of riding, and 13 kilometers during the next hour. The average speed of the cyclist during the trip is the total distance divided by the total time.

$$\text{Total distance} = 32\text{ km} + 13\text{ km} = 45\text{ km}$$

$$\text{Total time} = 2\text{ h} + 1\text{ h} = 3\text{ h}$$

$$\text{Average speed} = \frac{45\text{ km}}{3\text{ h}} = 15\text{ km/h}$$

The average speed of the cyclist is 15 kilometers per hour.

☑ *Checkpoint* *How do you calculate average speed?*

Describing Velocity

Knowing the speed at which something travels does not tell you everything about its motion. For example, if a weather forecaster announces that a severe storm is traveling at 25 km/h, would you prepare for the storm? Storms usually travel from west to east. If you live to the west of the storm and the storm is traveling to the east, you need not worry. But if you live to the east of the storm, take cover.

It is important to know not only the speed of the storm, but also its direction. **When you know both the speed and direction of an object's motion, you know the velocity of the object.**

The Speed of Transportation

The speed with which people can travel from one place to another has increased over the years.

1885

Benz Tricycle Car Introduced

This odd-looking vehicle was the first internal combustion (gasoline-powered) automobile sold to the public. Although it is an ancestor of the modern automobile, its top speed was only about 15 km/h—not much faster than a horse-drawn carriage.

1800 **1850**

1818

National Road Constructed

The speed of transportation has been limited largely by the quality of roadways. The U.S. government paid for the construction of a highway named the Cumberland Road. It ran from Cumberland, Maryland, to Wheeling, in present-day West Virginia. Travel by horse and carriage on the roadway was at a speed of about 11 km/h.

1869

Transcontinental Railroad

After more than six and a half years of work, railroad tracks from each side of the country met in Utah, just north of Great Salt Lake. Passengers could now travel across the United States by steam-powered trains. A cross-country trip took about a week at an average speed of 30 km/h.

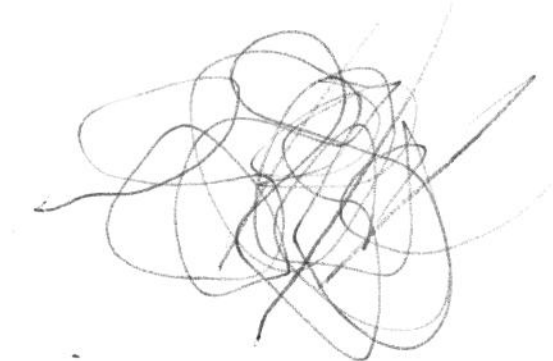

Speed in a given direction is called **velocity**. If you know the velocity at which an object is moving, you know two different things about the object's motion—its speed and its direction. A weather forecaster may give the speed of the storm as 25 km/h, but you don't know its velocity unless you know that the storm is moving 25 km/h eastward.

Air traffic controllers must keep very close track of the velocities of all of the aircraft under their control. These velocities change more often than the velocities of storm systems. An error in determining a velocity, either in speed or in direction, could lead to a collision.

In Your Journal

The distance between Wheeling, West Virginia, and Cumberland, Maryland, is 258 kilometers. How many hours would it take to travel this distance for each of the vehicles in the time line if they each traveled at the speed shown? Record your results on a bar graph.

1908

Ford Model T Mass-Produced

Between 1908 and 1927, over 15 million of these automobiles were sold. The Model T had a top speed of 65 km/h.

1956

Inauguration of the Interstate Highway System

The passage of the Federal Aid Highway Act established the Highway Trust Fund. This act allowed the construction of the Interstate and Defense Highways. Nonstop transcontinental auto travel became possible. Speed limits in many parts of the system were more than 100 km/h.

1900 **1950** **2000**

1936

***Pioneer Zephyr* Introduced**

The first diesel passenger train in the United States was the *Pioneer Zephyr*. The *Zephyr* set a long-distance record, traveling from Chicago to Denver at an average speed of 125 km/h for more than 1,633 km.

1983

TGV in Motion

First introduced in 1983, this French high-speed train now has a top speed of 300 km/h. On its route from Paris to Lyon, it averages 152.6 km/h.

EXPLORING Motion Graphs

Motion graphs provide an opportunity to analyze changes in distance and time.

FIRST DAY

Start with Enthusiasm.

The jogger travels at a constant speed of 170 m/min. The graph of constant speed is a slanted straight line. Notice that the speed is the same at every point on the graph. You can use the graph to analyze the jogger's motion. How far does the jogger run in 10 minutes? (1,700 m) How long does she run to travel 680 meters? (4 min)

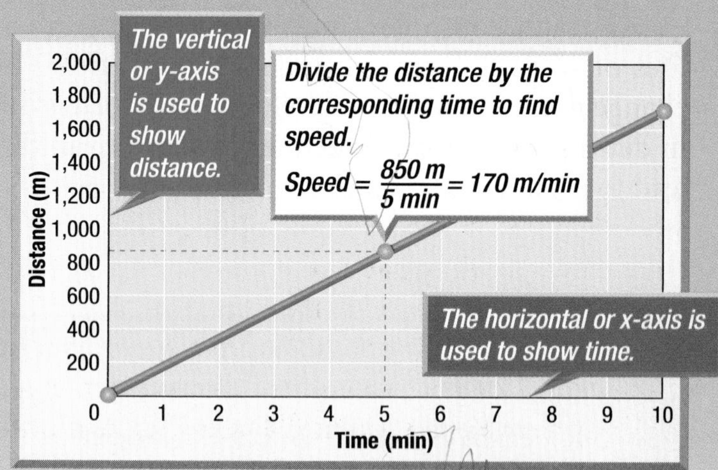

SECOND DAY

Take a Break.

The jogger again runs at a constant speed of 170 m/min, but she takes a break after running 850 m. The horizontal line shows that distance did not change during the break—thus there is no motion. What is the jogger's average speed if she ran a total distance of 1190 m? (119 m/min)

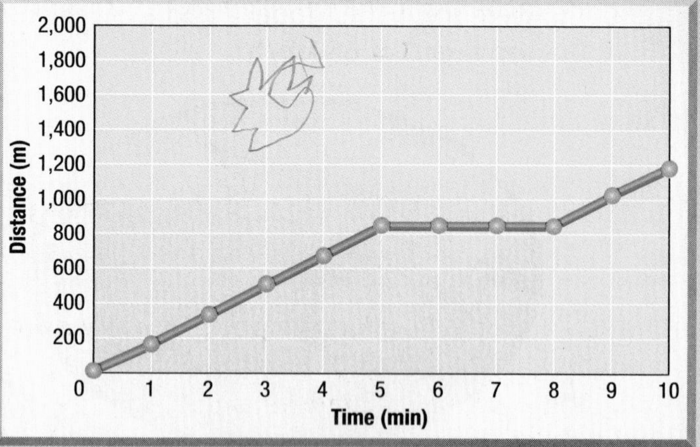

THIRD DAY

Slow Down.

As on the first day, the jogger runs at a constant speed, but this time she runs at a slower speed—100 m/min. Notice that the slant, or slope, of the graph is not as steep as it was on the first day. The steepness of the slope is related to the speed. The faster the speed, the steeper the slope. How far does the jogger run in 10 minutes on this day? (1,000 m)

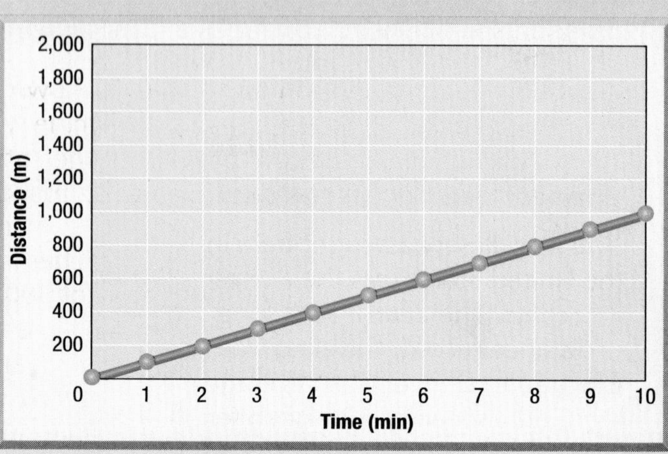

Stunt pilots make spectacular use of their control over the velocity of their aircraft. To avoid colliding with other aircraft, these skilled pilots must have precise control of both speed and direction. Stunt pilots use this control to stay in close formation while flying graceful maneuvers.

Figure 6 During a complicated maneuver an airplane's direction changes continuously, along with its speed.

Graphing Motion

You can show the motion of an object on a line graph in which you plot distance against time. A point on the graph represents the location of an object at a particular time. By tradition, time is shown on the x-axis and distance on the y-axis. A straight line (a line with a constant slant, or slope) represents motion at a constant speed. The steepness of the slope depends on how quickly or slowly the object is moving. The faster the motion, the steeper the slope, because the object moves a greater distance in a given amount of time. A horizontal line represents an object that is not moving at all. To see examples of how graphs represent motion, read about the jogger in *Exploring Motion Graphs* on page 24.

Section 1 Review

1. Why do you need a reference point to know if an object is moving?
2. What is the difference between an object's speed and an object's velocity?
3. A bamboo plant grows 15 centimeters in 4 hours. At what average speed does the plant grow?
4. **Thinking Critically Problem Solving** The distance traveled by two crawling babies is shown in the table. Graph the information and determine which baby moves at constant speed throughout the entire trip. What is that baby's speed? Describe the speed of the other baby.

Time (s)	**Baby Scott Distance** (m)	**Baby Sarah Distance** (m)
1	0.5	1
2	1	2
3	1.5	2.5
4	2	2.5
5	2.5	3.5

CHAPTER PROJECT 1

Check Your Progress

To measure each object's speed, you will need to know how far it moves in a certain amount of time. Create a data table to record your measurements and to show the speeds you calculate. Be sure to choose the best units for each speed measurement. To measure fast speeds, you may choose to measure distance in meters and time in seconds. For slower speeds you may choose to measure distance in centimeters or millimeters, and time in minutes or hours.

Skills Lab

Measuring

Inclined to Roll

In this lab, you will practice the skills of measuring time and distance to find the speed of a moving object.

Problem

How does the steepness of a ramp affect how fast an object moves across the floor?

Materials

skateboard
meter stick
protractor
masking tape
flat board, about 1.5 m long
small piece of sturdy cardboard
supports to prop up the board (books, boxes)
two stopwatches

Procedure

1. In your notebook, make a data table like the sample. Include space for five angles.
2. Lay the board flat on the floor. Using masking tape, mark a starting line in the middle of the board. Mark a finish line on the floor 1.5 m beyond one end of the board. Place a barrier after the finish line.
3. Prop up the other end of the board to make a slight incline. Use a protractor to measure the angle that the board makes with the ground. Record the angle in your data table.
4. Working in groups of three, have one person hold the skateboard so that its front wheels are even with the starting line. As the holder releases the skateboard, the other two students should start their stopwatches.
5. One timer should stop his or her stopwatch when the front wheels of the skateboard reach the end of the incline.
6. The second timer should stop his or her stopwatch when the front wheels reach the finish line. Record the times to the bottom of the ramp and to the finish line in the columns labeled Time 1 and Time 2.

DATA TABLE

Angle (degrees)	Trial Number	Time 1 (to bottom) (s)	Time 2 (to finish) (s)	Avg Time 1 (s)	Avg Time 2 (s)	Avg Time 2 – Avg Time 1 (s)	Avg Speed (m/s)
	1						
	2						
	3						
	1						
	2						
	3						
	1						
	2						

7. Repeat Steps 4–6 two more times. If your results for the three times aren't within 0.2 seconds of one another, carry out more trials.
8. Repeat Steps 3–7 four more times, making the ramp gradually steeper each time.
9. For each angle of the incline, complete the following calculations and record them in your data table.
   a. Find the average time the skateboard takes to get to the bottom of the ramp (Time 1).
   b. Find the average time the skateboard takes to get to the finish line (Time 2).
   c. Subtract the average Time 1 from the average Time 2.

Analyze and Conclude

1. How can you find the average speed of the skateboard across the floor for each angle of incline? Determine the average speed for each angle and record it in your data table.
2. Which is your manipulated variable and which is your responding variable in this experiment? Explain why. (For a discussion of manipulated and responding variables, see the Skills Handbook.)
3. On a graph, plot the speed of the skateboard (on the *y*-axis) against the angle of the ramp (on the *x*-axis). Connect the points on your graph.
4. What does the shape of your graph show about the relationship between the speed and the angle of the ramp?
5. **Think About It** Do you think your method of timing was accurate? Did the timers start and stop their stopwatches exactly at the appropriate points? How could the accuracy of the timing be improved?

Design an Experiment

A truck driver transporting new cars needs to roll the cars off the truck. You offer to design a ramp to help with the task. What measurements might you make that would be useful? Design an experiment to test your ideas.

SECTION 2 Slow Motion on Planet Earth

DISCOVER ACTIVITY

How Slow Can It Flow?

1. Put a spoonful of honey on a plate.
2. Lift one side of the plate just high enough that the honey is visibly flowing.
3. Reduce the angle of the plate a small amount so that the honey appears to be barely moving. Prop up the plate at this angle.
4. Using a ruler, place a piece of tape 4 cm from the bottom edge of the honey.
5. Time how long it takes the honey to flow to the tape. Use this information to calculate the speed of the honey.

Think It Over

Forming Operational Definitions How can you tell that an object is moving if it doesn't appear to be moving at first glance? Can you think of some other examples of motion that are too slow to see?

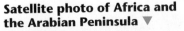

GUIDE FOR READING

- **How does the theory of plate tectonics describe the movement of Earth's continents?**

Reading Tip **Before you read, preview Figure 8, and describe what you think is happening.**

Have you ever noticed that Earth's landmasses resemble pieces of a giant jigsaw puzzle? It's true—take a look at a map of the world. The east coast of South America, for example, would fit nicely with the west coast of Africa. The Arabian Peninsula, as shown in the satellite photo below, would fit fairly well with the northeastern coast of Africa. Since the 1600s, people have wondered why Earth's landmasses look as if they would fit together. After all, land can't move—or can it?

What Are Earth's Plates?

Earth's rocky outer shell consists of broken pieces that fit together like a jigsaw puzzle. The upper layer of Earth consists of more than a dozen major pieces called **plates.** The boundaries between the plates are cracks in Earth's crust. The various plates are shown in Figure 7.

Scientists use this concept of plates to explain how landmasses have changed over time. **According to their explanation, known as the theory of plate tectonics, Earth's plates move ever so slowly in various directions.**

Satellite photo of Africa and the Arabian Peninsula ▼

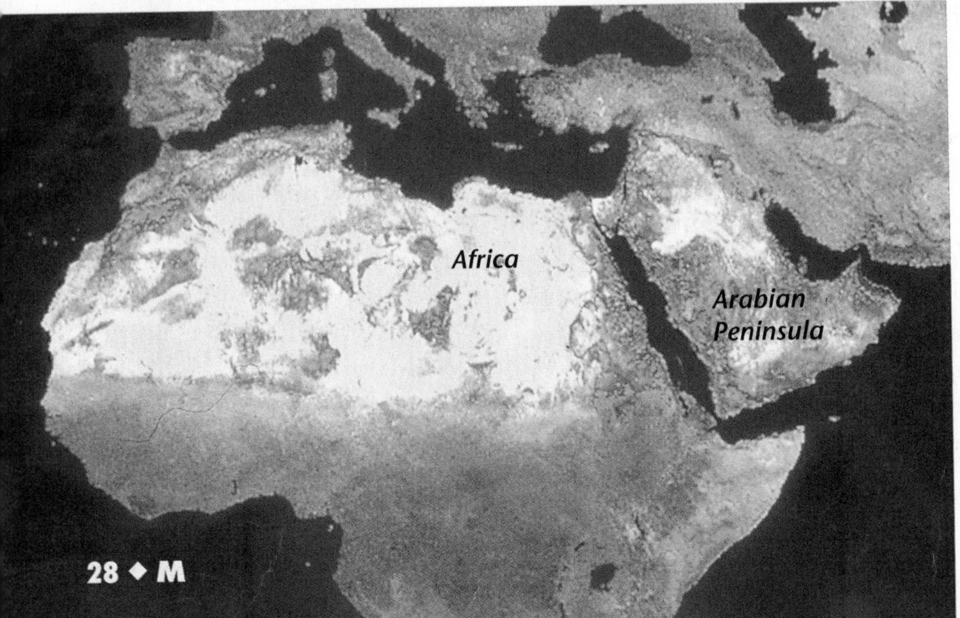

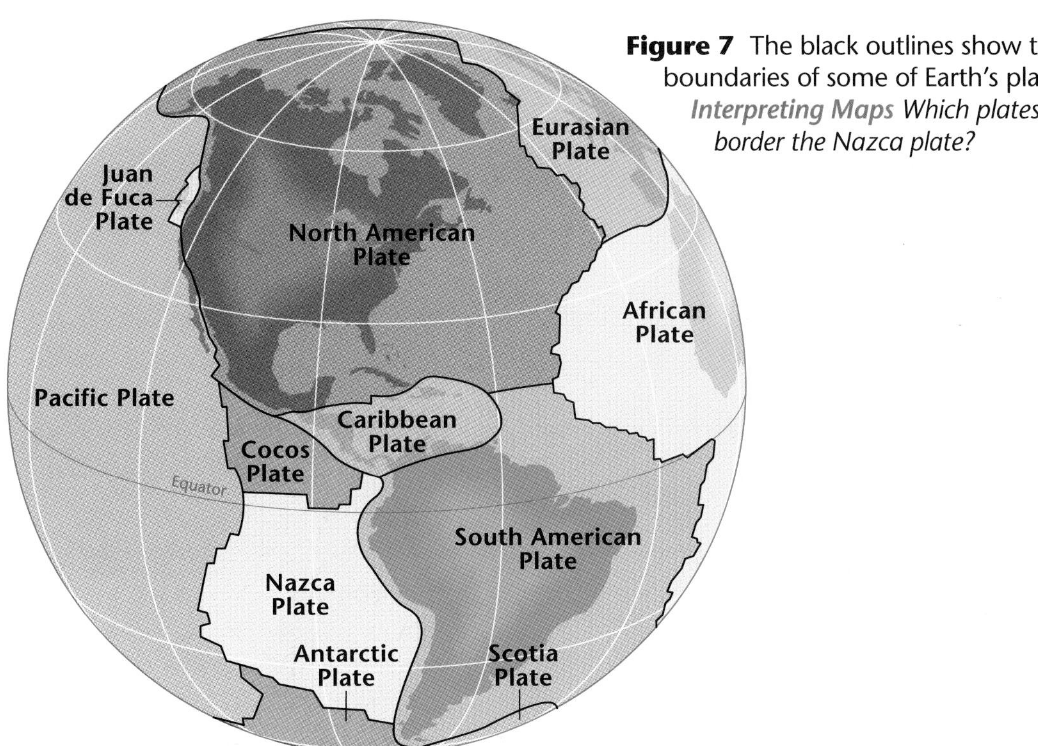

Figure 7 The black outlines show the boundaries of some of Earth's plates. *Interpreting Maps Which plates border the Nazca plate?*

Some plates pull away from each other, some plates push toward each other, and some plates slide past each other.

☑ *Checkpoint* ***What is the name scientists use for pieces of Earth's upper layer?***

How Fast Do Plates Move?

The speed with which Earth's plates move is very slow indeed. Some small plates can move as much as several centimeters per year, whereas others move only a few millimeters per year.

Knowing how far a plate moves in a certain amount of time enables scientists to calculate the average speed of the plate. This, in turn, enables scientists to explain how Earth's surface has changed over time. And it helps them to predict how it will change in the future. Figure 8 on pages 30–31 shows an estimate of how the continents have moved in the past and how they may move in the future.

Calculating Distance Suppose scientists study a particular plate over the course of a year. They find that the plate moves a distance of 5 centimeters. Thus the speed at which the plate moves is 5 centimeters divided by one year, or 5 cm/yr.

How can you use the speed of a plate to predict how far the plate will move in 1,000 years? To find distance, rearrange the speed formula to look like this: Distance = Speed × Time.

Predicting

ACTIVITY

Los Angeles, on the Pacific Plate, is slowly moving northwest. San Francisco, on the North American plate, is slowly moving southeast. These two cities are moving toward each other at a rate of about 5 cm/yr. If the two cities are now 554,000 m apart, how long will it take for the two cities to meet each other?

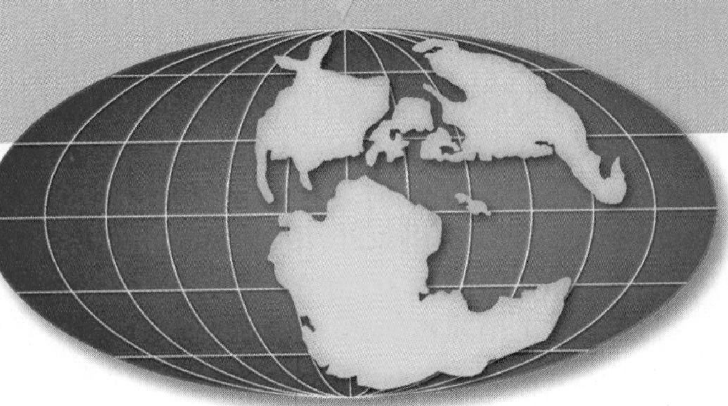

Figure 8 The shapes and positions of Earth's continents have changed greatly over time and will continue to change in the future. ***Interpreting Maps*** *Locate Australia on the map. How does its position change over time?*

This formula tells you to multiply the speed of the plate by the time during which the plate travels at that speed.

$$\text{Distance} = \frac{5\text{ cm}}{1\text{ yr}} \times 1{,}000\text{ yr} = 5{,}000\text{ cm}$$

The plate moves 5,000 centimeters in 1,000 years. Since 5,000 is a large number, try expressing this distance in meters. Recall that there are 100 centimeters in 1 meter, so you can divide by 100 by moving the decimal to the left two places.

$$5{,}000.\text{ cm} = 50.00\text{ m}$$

So in 1,000 years, which is well over ten average lifetimes, this plate moves only 50 meters. Walking at a brisk pace, you can probably travel the same distance in about 30 seconds!

Converting Units Suppose you want to know the speed of the plate in centimeters per day rather than centimeters per year. You can convert from one unit of measurement to another by using a conversion factor, a fraction in which the numerator and denominator are equal. In this example, 1 year is equal to 365 days. So you choose a conversion factor from these two possibilities.

$$\frac{1\text{ yr}}{365\text{ d}} = 1 \text{ or } \frac{365\text{ d}}{1\text{ yr}} = 1$$

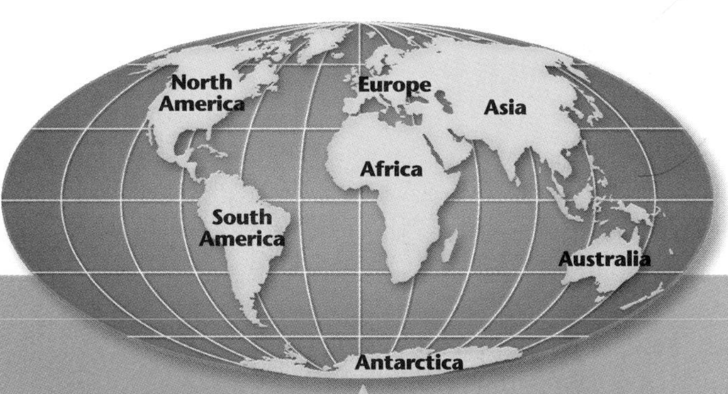

45 Million Years Ago

Present

100 Million Years From Now?

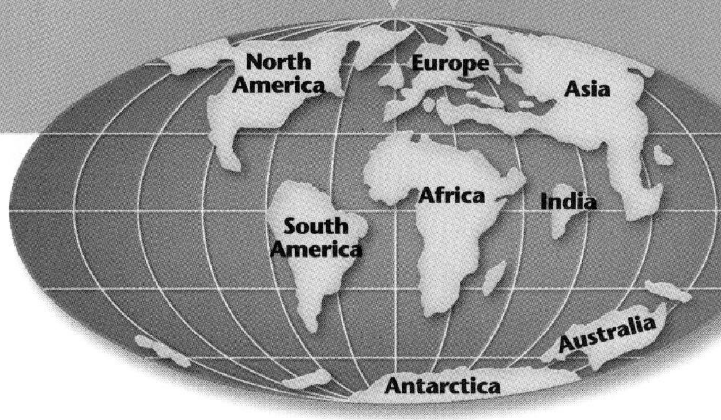

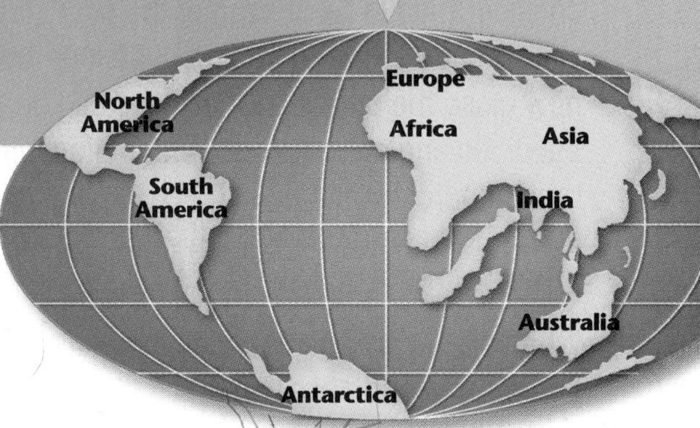

The conversion factor you need is the one that will allow you to cancel the years units. This factor is the one that has years in the numerator.

$$\frac{5\ cm}{1\ yr} \times \frac{1\ yr}{365\ d} = 0.0137\ cm/d$$

So you can describe the speed of this plate as 5 centimeters per year or as 0.0137 centimeters per day.

Section 2 Review

1. What is the theory that explains the slow movement of continents on Earth's surface?
2. Give two reasons why you don't notice the land moving beneath you. (*Hint*: Remember reference points.)
3. Suppose you are studying the motion of one of Earth's plates. What units would you probably use to describe its speed? Explain why.
4. **Thinking Critically Problem Solving** A certain plate moves 5 mm in 100 days. What is its speed in mm/d? What is its speed in mm/yr?

Science at Home

Have each member of your family measure the length of the white part at the end of one fingernail. Write down the results (and which finger you used) and mark your calendar for a date in exactly three weeks. On that day, measure the new length of the white part of the same fingernail. Then calculate the speed, in millimeters per day, at which your fingernail grew. Discuss with your family how your results compare with the typical speed with which continents move.

Real-World Lab

You and Your Community

Stopping on a Dime

The school has decided to put in a new basketball court in a small area between two buildings. Safety is an important consideration in the design of the court. You and your friends volunteer to find out experimentally how close the out-of-bounds lines can be to the buildings and still allow players to stop without running into a wall.

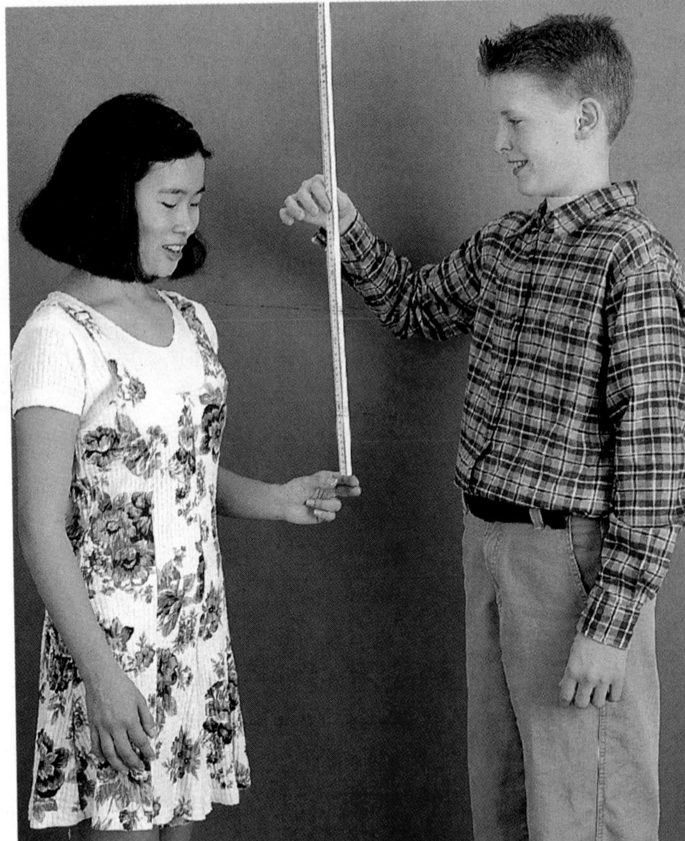

Problem

What is the distance needed between an out-of-bounds line and a wall so that a player can stop before hitting the wall?

Skills Focus

measuring, calculating, inferring

Materials

wooden meter stick
tape measure
2 stopwatches or watches with second hands

Procedure

Part I Reaction Time

1. Have your partner suspend a wooden meter stick, zero end down, between your thumb and index finger, as shown. Your thumb and index finger should be about 3 cm apart.
2. Your partner will drop the meter stick without giving you any warning. You will try to grab it with your thumb and index finger.
3. Note the level at which you grabbed the meter stick and use the chart shown to determine your reaction time. Record the time in the class data table.
4. Reverse roles with your partner and repeat Steps 1 through 3.

Reaction Time

Distance (cm)	Time (s)	Distance (cm)	Time (s)
15	0.175	25	0.226
16	0.181	26	0.230
17	0.186	27	0.235
18	0.192	28	0.239
19	0.197	29	0.243
20	0.202	30	0.247
21	0.207	31	0.252
22	0.212	32	0.256
23	0.217	33	0.260
24	0.221	34	0.263

CLASS DATA TABLE			
Student Name	Reaction Time (s)	Running Time (s)	Stopping Distance (m)

Part II Stopping Distance

5. On the school field or in the gymnasium, mark off a distance of 25 m. **CAUTION:** *Be sure to remove any obstacles from the course.*
6. Have your partner time how long it takes you to run the course at full speed. After you pass the 25-m mark, come to a stop as quickly as possible and remain standing. You must not slow down before the mark.
7. Have your partner measure the distance from the 25-m mark to your final position. This is the distance you need to come to a complete stop. Enter your time and distance into the class data table.
8. Reverse roles with your partner. Enter your partner's time and distance into the class data table.

Analyze and Conclude

1. How can you calculate the average speed of the student who ran the 25-m course the fastest? Find this speed.
2. Multiply the speed of the fastest student (calculated in Question 1) by the slowest reaction time listed in the class data table. Why would you be interested in this product?
3. Add the distance calculated in Question 2 to the longest stopping distance in the class data table. What does this total distance represent?
4. Explain why it is important to use the fastest speed, the slowest reaction time, and the longest stopping distance in your calculations.
5. What other factors should you take into account to get results that apply to a real basketball court?
6. **Apply** Suppose the distance between the out-of-bounds line and the wall in a playground or gymnasium is, according to your calculations, too short for safety. Suggest some strategies that could be used (other than moving the wall) for making that playground safer.

Getting Involved

Visit a local playground and examine it from the viewpoint of safety. Use what you learned about stopping distance as one of your guidelines, but also try to identify other potentially unsafe conditions. Write a letter to the department of parks or to the officials of your town informing them of your findings.

SECTION 3

Acceleration

DISCOVER

ACTIVITY

Will You Hurry Up?

1. Measure 10 meters in an area in which you can walk freely. Mark the distance with a piece of masking tape.
2. Walk the 10 meters in such way that you keep moving faster throughout the entire distance. Have a partner time you.
3. Repeat Step 2, but try to walk the 10 meters in less time than you did before. Try it again, but this time walk it in twice the amount of time as the first. Remember that you must keep speeding up throughout the entire 10 meters.

Think It Over

Inferring How is the change in your speed related to the time in which you walk the 10-meter course?

GUIDE FOR READING

- **What happens to the motion of an object as it accelerates?**
- **How is acceleration calculated?**

Reading Tip **As you read, list the three different types of acceleration. Then give several examples of each.**

The pitcher winds up. She throws. The ball speeds to the batter and, *crack*—off the bat it goes. It's going, it's going, it's gone—a home run!

Before landing, the ball went through several changes in motion. It started moving when it left the pitcher's hand, sped up, stopped when it hit the bat, changed direction, sped up again, and eventually slowed down. Most examples of motion involve similar changes. In fact, it is rare for any motion to stay the same for very long. You can describe changes in motion in much the same way as you did when you learned how to describe motion in terms of speed and velocity.

Acceleration in Science

Consider a car stopped at a red light. When the light changes to green, the driver of the car gently steps on the accelerator. As a result, the car speeds up, or accelerates. In everyday language, *acceleration* means "the process of speeding up."

Acceleration has a more precise definition in science. **Acceleration** is the rate at which velocity changes. Recall that velocity has two components (speed and direction). Acceleration involves a change in either of these components. **In science, acceleration refers to increasing speed, decreasing speed, or changing direction.**

Figure 9 The batter accelerates the softball as she hits it. *Relating Cause and Effect How does the motion of the ball change?*

Increasing Speed Any time the speed of an object increases, the object experiences acceleration. Can you think of examples of acceleration? A softball accelerates when the pitcher throws it, and again when a bat hits it. A car that begins to move from a stopped position or speeds up to pass another car is accelerating.

People can experience acceleration as well. The runners in Figure 10 increase their speed to sprint down the track. A figure skater will accelerate as he speeds up before jumping into the air. Similarly, a gymnast might accelerate as she runs into a tumbling routine. You accelerate as you speed up to catch the bus for school.

Decreasing Speed Just as objects can speed up, they can also slow down. Motion in which speed decreases is also considered acceleration in science. This change in speed is sometimes called deceleration, or negative acceleration.

Can you think of examples of deceleration? A softball decelerates as it rolls to a stop. A car decelerates when it comes to a stop at a red light. A jet decelerates as it lands on an aircraft carrier. The diver in Figure 10 decelerates when traveling through the water.

Changing Direction A car on a highway may be traveling at constant speed. Thus you may be tempted to conclude that it is not accelerating. Recall, however, that velocity involves *both* speed and direction. Therefore, an object can be accelerating even if its speed is constant. The car, for example, will be accelerating if it follows a gentle curve in the road or changes lanes. The skaters in Figure 10 accelerate as they round the turns on the track.

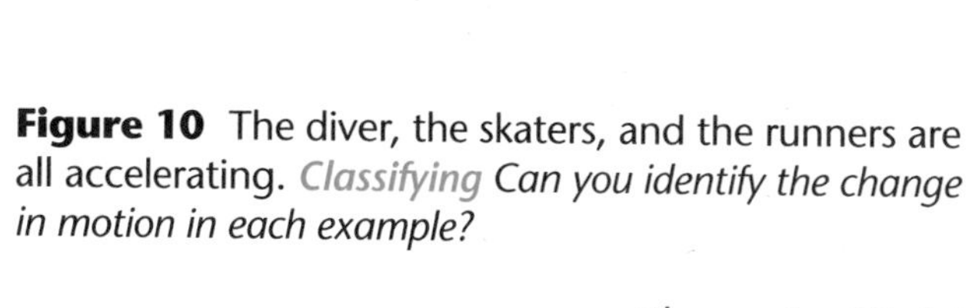

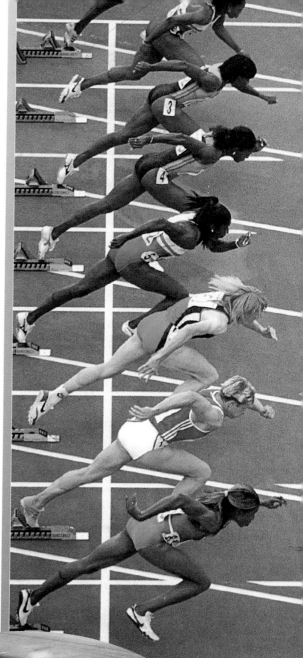

Figure 10 The diver, the skaters, and the runners are all accelerating. *Classifying Can you identify the change in motion in each example?*

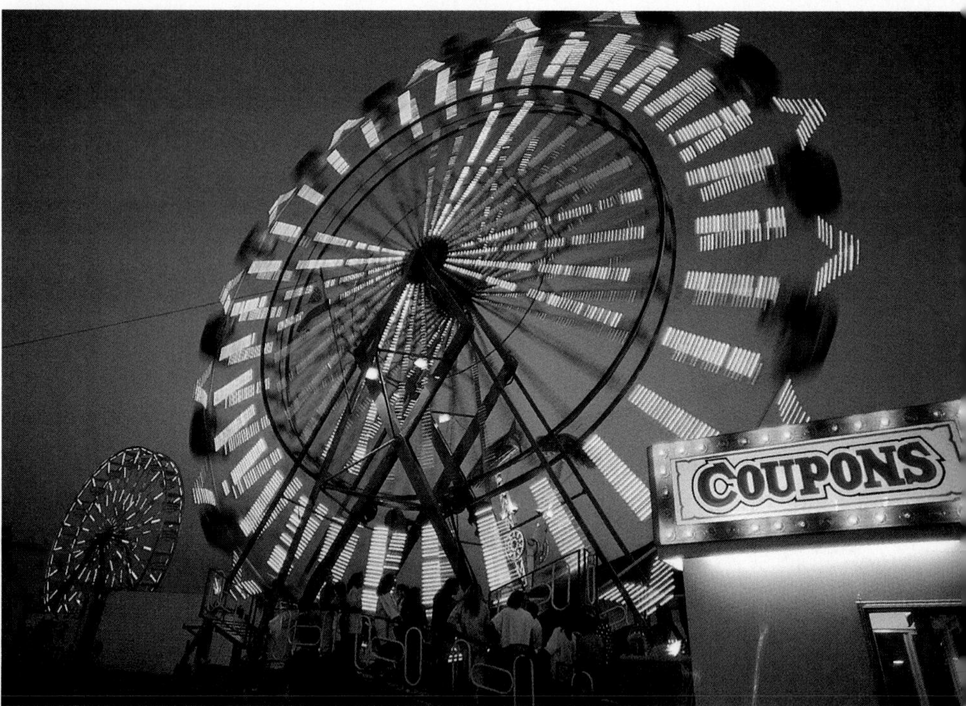

Figure 11 The Ferris wheel is accelerating because it is changing direction. *Making Generalizations What path does the Ferris wheel follow?*

Many objects continuously change direction without changing speed. The simplest example of this type of motion is circular motion, or motion along a circular path. The seats on the Ferris wheel accelerate because they move in a circle.

INTEGRATING SPACE SCIENCE In a similar way, the moon accelerates because it is continuously changing direction. Just as Earth revolves around the sun, the moon revolves around Earth. Another object that continuously accelerates is an artificial satellite orbiting Earth.

Checkpoint ***How is it possible for a car to be accelerating if its speed is a steady 65 km/h?***

Calculating Acceleration

Acceleration describes the rate at which velocity changes. **To determine the acceleration of an object, you must calculate the change in velocity during each unit of time.** This is summarized by the following formula.

$$\text{Acceleration} = \frac{\text{Final velocity} - \text{Initial velocity}}{\text{Time}}$$

If velocity is measured in meters/second and time is measured in seconds, the unit of acceleration is meters per second per second. This unit is written as m/s^2. This unit may sound peculiar at first. But acceleration is the change in velocity per unit of time and velocity is the change in distance per unit of time. Therefore, acceleration has two units of time. Suppose velocity is measured in kilometers/hour and time is measured in hours. Then the unit of acceleration becomes kilometers per hour per hour, or km/h^2.

If the object's speed changes by the same amount during each unit of time, the acceleration at any time during its motion is the same. If, however, the acceleration varies, you can describe only the average acceleration.

For an object moving without changing direction, the acceleration of the object is the change in its speed during one unit of time. Consider, for example, a small airplane moving on a runway. The speed of the airplane at the end of each of the first 5 seconds of its motion is shown in Figure 12.

To calculate the acceleration of the airplane, you must first subtract the initial speed (0 m/s) from the final speed (40 m/s). This gives the change in speed, 40 m/s. Then divide the change in speed by the time, 5 seconds. The acceleration is 40 m/s divided by 5 seconds, which is 8 m/s^2.

The acceleration tells you how the speed of the airplane in Figure 12 changes during each second. Notice that after each interval of one second, the speed of the airplane is 8 m/s greater

Change in Speed Over Time

Time (s)	Speed (m/s)
0	0
1	8
2	16
3	24
4	32
5	40

Figure 12 The speed of the airplane increases by the same amount each second.

Sample Problem

A roller coaster car rapidly picks up speed as it rolls down a slope. As it starts down the slope, its speed is 4 m/s. But 3 seconds later, at the bottom of the slope, its speed is 22 m/s. What is its average acceleration?

You know the initial velocity and final velocity of the car, and the length of time during which its velocity changed. You are looking for its acceleration.

$$\text{Acceleration} = \frac{\text{Final velocity} - \text{Initial velocity}}{\text{Time}}$$

Substitute and solve.

$$\text{Acceleration} = \frac{22 \text{ m/s} - 4 \text{ m/s}}{3 \text{ s}}$$

$$\text{Acceleration} = \frac{18 \text{ m/s}}{3 \text{ s}}$$

$$\text{Acceleration} = 6 \text{ m/s}^2$$

Think about it. The answer is reasonable. If the car's velocity increases by 6 m/s each second, its velocity will be 10 m/s after one second, 16 m/s after two seconds, and 22 m/s after three seconds.

Practice Problems

1. A car advertisement states that a certain car can accelerate from rest to 90 km/h in 9 seconds. Find the car's average acceleration.
2. An eagle accelerates from 15 m/s to 22 m/s in 4 seconds. What is the eagle's average acceleration?

Changes in Speed and Distance Over Time		
Time (s)	Speed (m/s)	Distance (m)
0	0	0
1	10	5
2	20	20
3	30	45
4	40	80
5	50	125

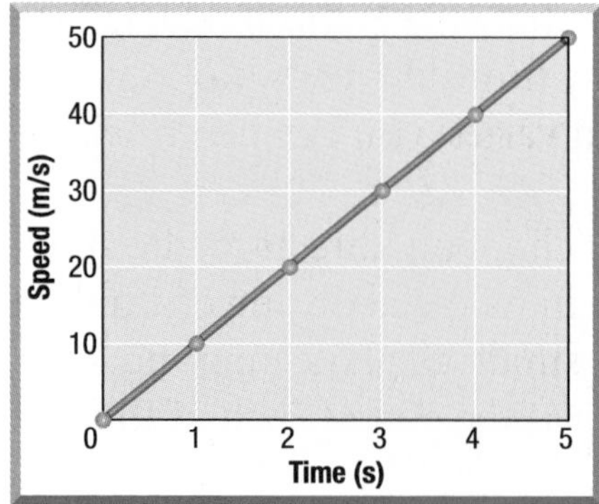

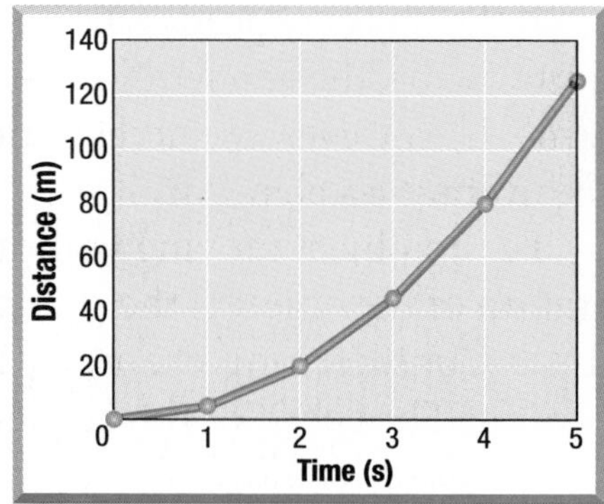

Figure 13 These graphs plot the motion of an accelerating object. *Predicting How would the slope of the speed and time graph change if the object were accelerating more rapidly? More slowly? What do you think the graph of a decelerating object would look like?*

than during the previous interval. So after one second, its speed is 8 m/s. After two seconds, its speed is 8 m/s + 8 m/s, or 16 m/s, and so on. Since the acceleration of the airplane does not change during the 5 seconds, you can use this formula for any time interval during the five seconds. Try it.

Graphing Acceleration

You can use a graph to analyze the motion of an object that is accelerating. Figure 13 shows the data for an object that is accelerating at 10 m/s^2. The graph showing speed versus time is a slanted straight line. The straight line shows that acceleration is constant. For every increase of one second, the speed increases by 10 m/s. Thus the graphed line rises the same amount each second. If the object accelerated by a different amount each second, the graph would not be a straight line.

The graph of distance versus time is a curved line. This tells you that the distance traveled by the accelerating object varies each second. As the speed increases, the graph curves upward.

Section 3 Review

1. What three kinds of change in motion are called acceleration? Give an example of each.
2. What formula is used to calculate acceleration?
3. A horse trots around a large circular track, maintaining a constant speed of 5 m/s. Is the horse accelerating? Explain.
4. **Thinking Critically Problem Solving** A car is creeping down a deserted highway at 1 m/s. Sometime later, its speed is 25 m/s. This could have happened if the car accelerated at 3 m/s^2 for 8 seconds. Is this the only way the increase in speed could have happened? Explain.

Check Your Progress

CHAPTER PROJECT 1

You can improve the accuracy of your speed estimations by repeating measurements and by using averaged data. Make all your calculations in an organized, step-by-step manner. Prepare display cards that show how you calculated each speed.

CHAPTER 1 STUDY GUIDE

Describing and Measuring Motion

Key Ideas

- The motion of an object is determined by its change of position relative to a reference point.
- Speed is the distance an object travels in one unit of time. If an object moves at constant speed, its speed can be determined by dividing the distance it travels by the time taken. If an object's speed varies, then dividing distance by time gives you the object's average speed.
- When you state both the speed of an object and the direction in which it is moving, you are describing the object's velocity.
- The slope of a distance-time graph represents speed. The steeper the slope, the faster the speed.

Key Terms

motion
reference point
International System of Units (SI)
meter
speed
velocity

Slow Motion on Planet Earth

INTEGRATING EARTH SCIENCE

Key Idea

- The plates that make up Earth's outer layer move very slowly, only centimeters per year, in various directions.

Key Term

plate

Acceleration

Key Ideas

- Acceleration is the rate at which velocity changes. It involves increasing speed, decreasing speed, or changing direction.
- Acceleration can be calculated by dividing the change in velocity by the amount of time it took that change to occur.

Key Term

acceleration

Organizing Information

Concept Map Copy the concept map about motion onto a separate sheet of paper. Then complete it and add a title. (For more on concept maps, see the Skills Handbook.)

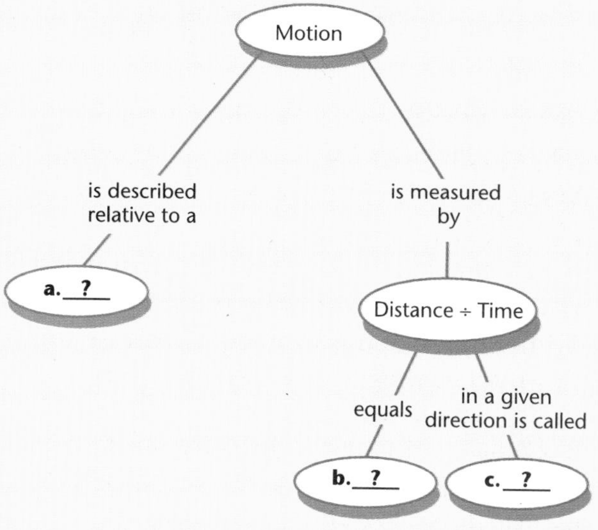

Reviewing Content

For more review of key concepts, see the Interactive Student Tutorial CD-ROM.

Multiple Choice

Choose the letter of the best answer.

1. A change in position with respect to a reference point is
   a. acceleration. b. velocity.
   c. direction. d. motion.
2. To find the average speed of an object,
   a. add together its different speeds and divide by the number of speeds.
   b. divide the distance it travels by the time taken to travel that distance.
   c. divide the time it takes to travel a distance by the distance traveled.
   d. multiply the acceleration by the time.
3. If you know a car travels 30 km in 20 minutes, you can find its
   a. acceleration. b. average speed.
   c. direction. d. graph.
4. A child on a merry-go-round is accelerating because the child
   a. is moving relative to the ground.
   b. does not change speed.
   c. is moving relative to the sun.
   d. is always changing direction.
5. If you divide the increase in an object's speed by the time taken for that increase, you are determining the object's
   a. acceleration. b. constant speed.
   c. average speed. d. velocity.

True or False

If the statement is true, write true. If it is false, change the underlined word or words to make the statement true.

6. In a moving elevator, you are not moving from the reference point of the <u>elevator</u>.
7. The graph of distance versus time for an object moving at constant speed is a <u>curve</u>.
8. The upper layer of Earth is made of pieces called <u>reference points</u>.
9. Acceleration is a change in speed or <u>direction</u>.
10. The distance an object travels in one unit of time is called <u>acceleration</u>.

Checking Concepts

11. Suppose you walk toward the rear of a moving train. Describe your motion as seen from a reference point on the train. Then describe it from a reference point on the ground.
12. Which has a greater speed, a hawk that travels 600 meters in 60 seconds or a tiny warbler that travels 60 meters in 5 seconds? Explain.
13. You have a motion graph for an object that shows distance and time. How does the slope of the graph relate to the object's speed?
14. How can you tell if an object is moving if its motion is too slow to see?
15. An insect is on a compact disc that is put into a compact disc player. The disc spins around and the insect hangs on for dear life. Is the insect accelerating? Explain why or why not.
16. **Writing to Learn** Suppose that one day some of the things that usually move very slowly start to go faster, while some things that usually move quickly slow to a snail's pace. Write a description of some of the strange events that might occur during this weird day. Include a few actual speeds as part of your description.

Thinking Critically

17. **Making Generalizations** Suppose you make two measurements. One is the time that a car takes to travel a city block. The other is the time the car takes to travel the next city block. From these measurements, explain how you decide if the car is moving at a steady speed or if it is accelerating.
18. **Problem Solving** Two drivers start at the same time to make a 100-km trip. Driver 1 takes 2 hours to complete the trip. Driver 2 takes 3 hours, but stops for an hour at the halfway point. Which driver had a greater average speed for the whole trip? Explain.
19. **Applying Concepts** A family takes a car trip. They travel for an hour at 80 km/h and then for 2 hours at 40 km/h. Find the average speed. (*Hint:* Remember to consider the total distance and the total amount of time.)

Applying Skills

Use the illustration of the motion of a ladybug to answer Questions 20–22.

20. Measuring Measure the distance from the starting line to line B, and from line B to the finish line. Measure to the nearest tenth of a centimeter.

21. Calculating Starting at rest, the ladybug accelerated to line B and then moved at constant speed until she reached the finish line. If she took 2.5 seconds to move from line B to the finish line, calculate her constant speed during that time.

22. Interpreting Data The speed you calculated in Question 21 is also the speed the ladybug had at line B (at the end of her acceleration). If she took 2 seconds to accelerate from the start line to line B, what is her acceleration during that time?

Performance Assessment

CHAPTER PROJECT 1

Project Wrap Up Organize your display cards so that they are easy to follow. Remember to put a title on each card stating the speed that was being measured. Place them in order from the slowest speed to the fastest. Then display your cards to your class. Compare your results with those of other students.

Reflect and Record When you measured the same speed more than once, were the data always the same? Explain. What factors make measuring a speed difficult?

Test Preparation

Use these questions to prepare for standardized tests.

Study the graph. Then answer Questions 23–27.

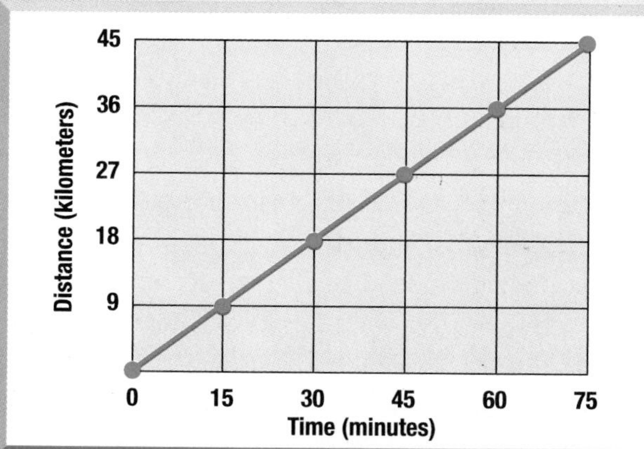

23. What would be the best title for this graph?
a. Train at Rest
b. Train Moving at Constant Acceleration
c. Train Moving at Constant Speed
d. Train Slowing to a Stop

24. During each 15-minute interval, the train travels a distance of
a. 9 kilometers. **b.** 18 kilometers.
c. 36 kilometers. **d.** 45 kilometers.

25. According to the graph, how long does it take for the train to travel 27 kilometers?
a. 15 minutes **b.** 30 minutes
c. 45 minutes **d.** 1 hour

26. What is the train's speed?
a. 9 km/h **b.** 18 km/h
c. 36 km/h **d.** 72 km/h

27. After 75 minutes, the train stops for 5 minutes to pick up passengers. How would the graph look during this period?
a. The line would slant downward.
b. The line would be horizontal.
c. The line would be broken.
d. The line would stop at a point and continue from the same point once the train begins to move again.

CHAPTER 2

Forces

WEB ACTIVITY www.phschool.com

SECTION 1 The Nature of Force

Discover What Changes Motion?
Try This Around and Around
Skills Lab Forced to Accelerate

SECTION 2 Force, Mass, and Acceleration

Discover How Do the Rocks Roll?

SECTION 3 Friction and Gravity

Discover Which Lands First?
Try This Spinning Plates
Sharpen Your Skills Calculating
Real-World Lab Sticky Sneakers

PROJECT 2

Newton Scooters

A strong kick sends the soccer ball soaring toward the goal. The goalie does his best to stop the ball. Both the kicker and the goalie exert forces on the ball to change its motion. In this chapter you will learn how forces change all kinds of motion. You will find that there are forces acting on the ball even when it is soaring through the air.

In this chapter, you will learn how Newton's three basic laws of motion govern the relationship of forces and motion. You will use Newton's third law to build a scooter. Unlike the soccer ball, the scooter must move without being kicked!

Your Goal To design and build a vehicle that is powered only according to Newton's third law of motion.

Your vehicle must

- move forward by pushing back on something
- not be powered by any form of electricity or use gravity in order to move
- travel a minimum distance of 1.5 meters
- be built following the safety guidelines in Appendix A

Get Started Brainstorm possible designs for your vehicle, but be careful not to lock yourself into a single idea. Remember that a car with wheels is only one type of vehicle. Try to think of ways to recycle household materials to build your vehicle.

Check Your Progress You'll be working on this project as you study this chapter. To keep your project on track, look for Check Your Progress boxes at the following points.

Section 2 Review, page 54: Determine factors that will affect the acceleration of your vehicle.

Section 3 Review, page 61: Draw a diagram of your proposed design.

Section 4 Review, page 69: Construct your vehicle and identify the force that propels it.

Wrap Up At the end of the chapter (page 75), demonstrate how your vehicle moves.

Both the kicker and the goalie use forces to control the motion of the soccer ball.

SECTION 1 The Nature of Force

DISCOVER — ACTIVITY

What Changes Motion?

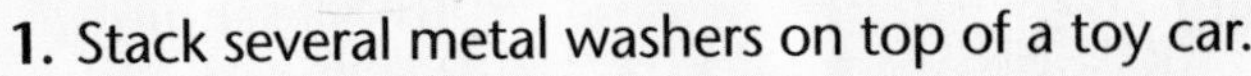

1. Stack several metal washers on top of a toy car.

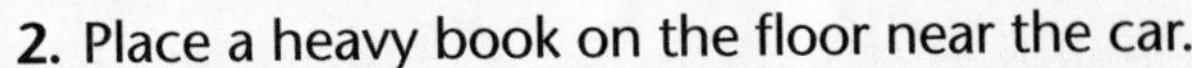

2. Place a heavy book on the floor near the car.
3. Predict what will happen to both the car and the washers if you roll the car into the book. Test your prediction.

Think It Over

Observing What happened to the car when it hit the book? What happened to the washers? What might be the reason for any difference between the motions of the car and the washers?

GUIDE FOR READING

- **How are balanced and unbalanced forces related to motion?**
- **What is Newton's first law of motion?**

Reading Tip **As you read, use your own words to define each boldfaced word.**

An arrow soars through the air to its distant target. A long jumper comes to a sudden stop in a cloud of sand. You kick a soccer ball around your opponent. There is some type of motion involved in each of these activities. But why does each object move as it does? What causes an object to start moving, stop moving, or change direction? The answer is a force. In each of these activities, a force is exerted on, or applied to, an object.

What Is a Force?

In science the word *force* has a simple and specific meaning. A **force** is a push or a pull. When one object pushes or pulls another object, you say that the first object is exerting a force on the second object. You exert a force on a pen when you write, on a book when you lift it, and on a zipper when you pull it.

You exert a force on a pebble when you skim it across a pond, on a wagon when you pull it, and on a nail when you hammer it into a piece of wood.

Like velocity and acceleration, forces are described not only by how strong they are, but also by the *direction* in which they act. If you push on a door, you exert a force in a different direction than if you pull on the door.

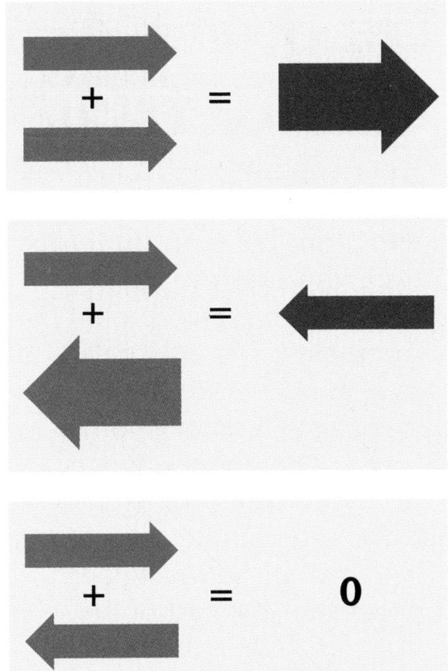

Figure 1 Two forces can combine so that they add together (top), or subtract from each other (center). They may also cancel each other (bottom).

Unbalanced Forces

Suppose you need to push a heavy box across a floor. When you push on the box, you exert a force on it. If a friend helps you, the total force exerted on the box is the sum of your force plus your friend's force. When two forces act in the same direction, they add together.

Figure 1 uses arrows to show the addition of forces. The head of each arrow points in the direction of a force. The width of each arrow tells you the strength of a force. A wider arrow shows a greater force. (When forces are shown in this book, the strength of a force will usually be shown by the width of an arrow.)

When forces act in opposite directions, they also add together. However, you must pay attention to the direction of each force. Adding a force acting in one direction to a force acting in the opposite direction is the same as adding a positive number and a negative number. So when two forces act in opposite directions, they combine by subtraction. If one force is greater than the other force, the overall force is in the direction of the greater force.

Figure 2 The arrow, the jumper, and the soccer ball are all in motion. *Making Generalizations What makes an arrow fly through the air to its target, a long jumper thud to a stop, and a soccer ball change direction?*

Language Arts CONNECTION

You have learned that *net force* means "overall force." Have you heard the term *net profit?* Here, the adjective *net* describes the total amount of money left over after paying all expenses. For example, suppose you sell popcorn at a sports event to raise money for a class trip. Your *net profit* is the amount of money that is left after you subtract your expenses—the cost of the popcorn kernels, butter, salt, bags, and posters.

In Your Journal

Can you think of another meaning for the word *net?* Many words have more than one meaning. Here are just a few: *spring, pound, bat, bowl,* and *row.* Think of two meanings for each word. Use at least two of these words in sentences that show their different meanings. Add more words to the list.

You can see what happens when the students in the center of the next page exert unequal forces in opposite directions.

In any situation, the overall force on an object after all the forces are added together is called the **net force.** When there is a net force acting on an object, the forces are said to be unbalanced. **Unbalanced forces** can cause an object to start moving, stop moving, or change direction. **Unbalanced forces acting on an object will change the object's motion.** In other words, an unbalanced force will cause an object to accelerate. For example, if two unequal forces acting in opposite directions are applied to a box, the box will accelerate in the direction of the greater force.

Balanced Forces

Forces exerted on an object do not always change the object's motion. Consider the forces involved when the dogs in Figure 3 pull on a stocking in opposite directions. Even though there are forces acting on it, the motion of the stocking does not change. While one dog exerts a force on the stocking in one direction, the other dogs exert an equal force on the stocking in the opposite direction.

Equal forces acting on one object in opposite directions are called **balanced forces.** One force is exactly balanced by the other force. **Balanced forces acting on an object will not change the object's motion.** When you add equal forces exerted in opposite directions, the net force is zero. You can also see how balanced forces cancel in the example at the bottom of the next page. The box does not move at all.

☑ *Checkpoint* ***Which cause change in motion—balanced forces or unbalanced forces?***

Figure 3 These dogs are exerting a great deal of force, but they aren't moving. *Applying Concepts What would happen if one of the dogs pulled harder? Explain why.*

EXPLORING Combined Forces

What happens when two friends push on the same object? The forces they exert combine in different ways, depending on the directions in which they push.

UNBALANCED FORCES IN THE SAME DIRECTION

When two forces act in the same direction, the net force is the sum of the two individual forces. The box moves to the left.

UNBALANCED FORCES IN OPPOSITE DIRECTIONS

When forces act in opposite directions, the net force is the difference between the two forces. The box moves to the right.

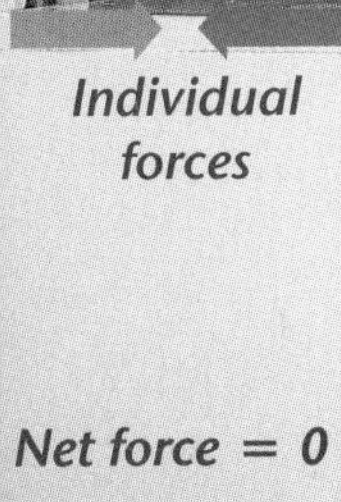

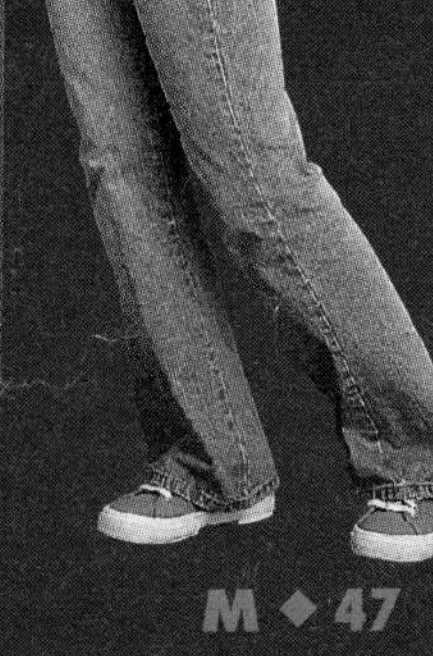

BALANCED FORCES IN OPPOSITE DIRECTIONS

When two equal forces act in opposite directions, they cancel each other out. The box doesn't move.

Around and Around

ACTIVITY

An object moving in a circle has inertia.

1. Tape one end of a length of thread (about 1 m) to a table tennis ball.
2. Suspend the ball in front of you and swing it in a horizontal circle. Keep the ball about 2 or 3 cm above the floor.
3. Let go of the thread and observe the direction in which the ball rolls.
4. Repeat this several times, letting go of the thread at different points.

Inferring At what point do you need to let go of the thread if you want the ball to roll directly away from you? Toward you? Draw a diagram as part of your answer.

Newton's First Law of Motion

The ancient Greeks observed that objects have natural resting places. Objects move toward those places. A rock falls to the ground. A ball rolls to the bottom of a hill. Once an object is in its natural resting place, it cannot move by itself. For an object to start moving, a force has to act on it.

Inertia In the early 1600s, the Italian astronomer Galileo Galilei questioned the idea that a force is needed to keep an object moving. He suggested that once an object is in motion, no push or pull is needed to keep it moving. Force is needed only to change the motion of an object. But whether it is moving or at rest, every object resists any change to its motion. This resistance is called inertia. **Inertia** (in UR shuh) is the tendency of an object to resist change in its motion.

You may have observed this yourself. A puck that rides on a cushion of air in an "air-hockey" game glides along quite freely once you push it. Similarly, a tennis ball flies through the air once you hit it with a racket. In both cases, the object continues to move even after you remove the force.

Galileo's ideas paved the way for the English mathematican Sir Isaac Newton. Newton discovered the three basic laws of motion in the late 1600s. The first of Newton's three laws of motion restates Galileo's idea. **Newton's first law of motion states that an object at rest will remain at rest, and an object that is moving at constant velocity will continue moving at constant velocity unless acted upon by an unbalanced force.** Newton's first law of motion is also called the law of inertia.

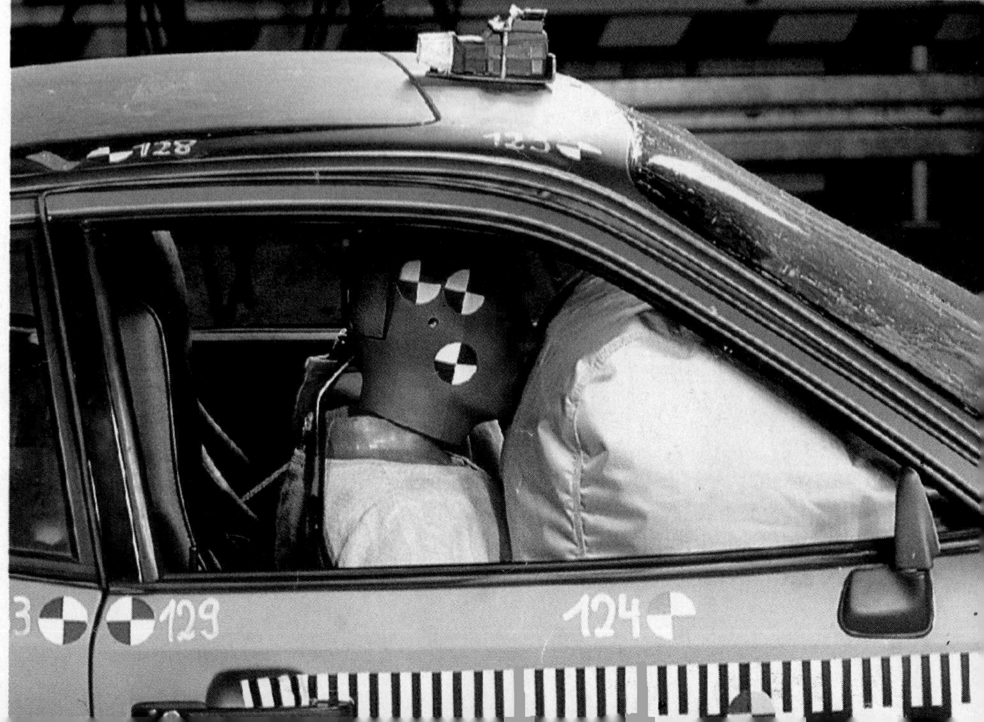

Figure 4 These crash-test dummies weren't wearing safety belts. ***Relating Cause and Effect*** *What caused them to move forward even after the car stopped?*

Inertia explains many common events. For example, if you are in a car that stops suddenly, inertia causes you to continue moving forward. The crash test dummies in Figure 4 don't stop when the car does. Passengers in a moving car have inertia. Therefore a force is required to change their motion. That force is exerted by the safety belt. If the safety belt is not worn, that force may be exerted by the windshield instead!

Figure 5 The two jars have the same volume, but very different masses.

Mass Which is more difficult to move, a jar of pennies or a jar of plastic foam "peanuts"? Obviously, the jar of pennies is harder to move. What is the difference between the jar of pennies and the jar of plastic peanuts? After all, you can see in Figure 5 that both jars occupy the same amount of space, and so have the same volume. The difference is the amount of mass each one has. **Mass** is the amount of matter in an object. The jar of pennies has more mass than the jar of plastic peanuts.

The SI unit of mass is the kilogram (kg). A small car might have a mass of 1,000 kilograms. A bicycle without a rider might have a mass of about 10 kilograms, and a student might have a mass of 45 kilograms. You describe the mass of smaller objects in terms of grams (1 kilogram = 1,000 grams). The mass of a nickel is about 5 grams.

The amount of inertia an object has depends on its mass. The greater the mass of an object, the greater its inertia. Mass, then, can also be defined as a measure of the inertia of an object.

Section 1 Review

1. What are the differences in how balanced and unbalanced forces affect motion?
2. What is inertia? How is it involved in Newton's first law of motion?
3. Two children who are fighting over a toy pull on it from opposite sides. The result is a stand-off. Explain this in terms of the net force.
4. **Thinking Critically** **Applying Concepts** Draw a diagram in which two forces acting on an object are unbalanced and a diagram in which two balanced forces act on an object. Use arrows to show the forces.

Science at Home

Fill a paper cup with water. Cover the cup with an index card and place a coin or paper clip in the center of the index card. Challenge your family members to move the coin from the card to the cup without touching the coin or holding on to the card. If they cannot think how to do it, show them how. Hold the cup and use your finger to flick the card with a sharp sideways force. The force doesn't have to be very strong, but it must be sharp. Explain what happens to the coin in terms of inertia.

Skills Lab

Interpreting Data

Forced to Accelerate

In this lab, you will practice the skill of interpreting data as you explore the relationship between force and acceleration.

Problem

How is the acceleration of a skateboard related to the force that is pulling it?

Materials

skateboard
string
masking tape
meter stick
stopwatch
spring scale, 5 N
several bricks or other large mass(es)

Procedure

1. Attach a loop of string to a skateboard. Place the bricks on the skateboard.
2. Using masking tape, mark off a one-meter distance on a level floor. Label one end "Start" and the other "Finish."
3. Attach a spring scale to the loop of string. Pull it so that you maintain a force of 2.0 N. Be sure to pull with the scale straight out in front. Practice applying a steady force to the skateboard as it moves.
4. Copy the data table into your notebook.
5. Find the smallest force needed to pull the skateboard at a slow, constant speed. Do not accelerate the skateboard. Record this force on the first line of the table.
6. Add 0.5 N to the force in Step 5. This will be enough to accelerate the skateboard. Record this force on the second line of the table.
7. Have one of your partners hold the front edge of the skateboard at the starting line. Then pull on the spring scale with the force you found in Step 6.
8. When your partner says "Go" and releases the skateboard, maintain a constant force until the skateboard reaches the finish line. A third partner should time how long it takes the skateboard to go from start to finish. Record the time in the column labeled Trial 1.
9. Repeat Steps 7 and 8 twice more. Record your results in the columns labeled Trial 2 and Trial 3.
10. Repeat Steps 7, 8, and 9 using a force 1.0 N greater than the force you found in Step 5.
11. Repeat Steps 7, 8, and 9 twice more. Use forces that are 1.5 N and 2.0 N greater than the force you found in Step 5.

DATA TABLE

Force (N)	Trial 1 Time (s)	Trial 2 Time (s)	Trial 3 Time (s)	Avg Time (s)	Avg Speed (m/s)	Final Speed (m/s)	Acceleration (m/s^2)

Analyze and Conclude

1. For each force you used, find the average of the three times that you measured. Record the average in your data table.
2. Find the average speed of the skateboard for each force. Use this formula:

   Average speed = 1 m ÷ Average time

   Record this value for each force.
3. To obtain the final speed of the skateboard, multiply each average speed by 2. Record the result in your data table.
4. To obtain the acceleration, divide each final speed you found by the average time. Record the acceleration in your data table.
5. Make a line graph. Show the acceleration on the *y*-axis and the force on the *x*-axis. The *y*-axis scale should go from zero to about 1 m/s^2. The *x*-axis should go from zero to 3.0 newtons.
6. If your data points seem to form a straight line, draw a line through them.
7. Your first data point is the force required for an acceleration of zero. How do you know the force for an acceleration of zero?
8. According to your graph, how is the acceleration of the skateboard related to the pulling force?
9. **Think About It** Which variable is the manipulated variable? Which is the responding variable?

Design an Experiment

Design an experiment to test how the acceleration of the loaded skateboard depends on its mass. Think about how you would vary the mass of the skateboard. What quantity would you need to measure that you did not measure in this experiment? Do you have the equipment to make that measurement? If not, what other equipment would you need?

Force, Mass, and Acceleration

DISCOVER

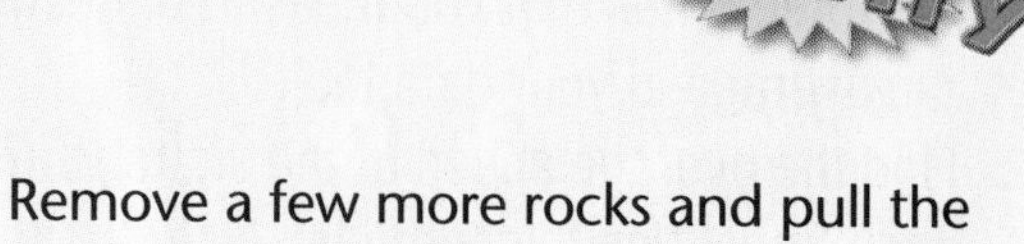

How Do the Rocks Roll?

1. Place several small rocks in a toy dump truck. Hook a spring scale to the bumper of the truck.
2. Practice pulling the truck with the spring scale so that the reading on the scale stays constant.
3. Pull the truck with a constant force and observe its motion. Then remove a few rocks from the truck and pull it again with the same force.
4. Remove a few more rocks and pull the truck again. Finally, empty the truck and observe how it moves with the same constant force.

Think It Over

Observing How did changing the mass of the loaded truck affect its motion?

GUIDE FOR READING

- **How are force and mass related to acceleration?**

Reading Tip **As you read, use your own words to describe the relationship among force, mass, and acceleration.**

On a sunny afternoon you are baby-sitting for two boys who love wagon rides. You soon find that they enjoy the ride most if you accelerate quickly. They shout "Faster, faster!" and after a few minutes you sit down in the wagon to catch your breath. The smaller boy takes a turn pulling, but finds that he can't make the wagon accelerate nearly as fast as you can. How is the acceleration of the wagon related to the force pulling it? How is the acceleration related to the mass of the wagon?

Newton's Second Law of Motion

Newton's second law of motion explains how force, mass, and acceleration are related. **The net force on an object is equal to the product of its acceleration and its mass.** The relationship

among the quantities force, mass, and acceleration can be written in one equation.

$$Force = Mass \times Acceleration$$

People often refer to this equation itself as Newton's second law of motion.

As with any equation, you must pay attention to the units of measurement. When acceleration is measured in meters per second per second (m/s^2) and mass is measured in kilograms, force is measured in kilograms × meters per second per second ($kg{\cdot}m/s^2$). This long unit is called the newton (N), in honor of Isaac Newton. One **newton** equals the force required to accelerate one kilogram of mass at 1 meter per second per second.

$$1\ N = 1\ kg \times 1\ m/s^2$$

A student might have a mass of 40 kilograms. Suppose she is walking, and accelerates at 1 m/s^2. You can easily find the force exerted on her by substituting mass and acceleration into the equation. You find that 40 kilograms × 1 m/s^2 is 40 newtons.

Sometimes you may want to write the relationship among acceleration, force, and mass in a different form.

$$Acceleration = \frac{Force}{Mass}$$

This form is found by rearranging the equation for Newton's second law.

Sample Problem

A 52-kg water-skier is being pulled by a speedboat. The force causes her to accelerate at 2 m/s^2. Calculate the net force that causes this acceleration.

Analyze. You know the acceleration and the mass. You want to find the force.

Write the equation. $Force = Mass \times Acceleration$

Substitute and solve. $Force = 52\ kg \times 2\ m/s^2$

$Force = 104\ kg \times m/s^2 = 104\ kg{\cdot}m/s^2$

$Force = 104\ N$

Think about it. The answer tells you that a force of 104 N is required to accelerate the water-skier. This is not a large force, but it does not include the force that overcomes friction.

Practice Problems

1. What is the net force on a 1,000-kg elevator accelerating at 2 m/s^2?
2. What net force is needed to accelerate a 55-kg cart at 15 m/s^2?

Changes in Force and Mass

How can you increase the acceleration of the wagon? Look again at the equation for acceleration: Acceleration = Force ÷ Mass. One way to increase acceleration is by changing the force. According to the equation, acceleration and force change in the same way. An increase in force causes an increase in acceleration. So to increase the acceleration of the wagon, you can increase the force you use to pull it. You can pull harder.

Another way to increase acceleration is to change the mass. According to the equation, acceleration and mass change in opposite ways. This means that an increase in mass causes a decrease in acceleration. It also means that a decrease in mass causes an increase in acceleration. So to increase the acceleration of the wagon, you can decrease its mass. Instead of you, the boys should ride in the wagon.

Figure 6 The acceleration of an object depends on the force acting on it and the object's mass.

Section 2 Review

1. What three quantities are related in Newton's second law of motion? What is the relationship among them?
2. When the net force on an object increases, how does the object's acceleration change?
3. Suppose you know the acceleration of a shopping cart as it rolls down a supermarket aisle. You want to find the net force with which it was pushed. What other information do you need in order to find the force?
4. **Thinking Critically** **Problem Solving** Suppose you doubled the force acting on an object. In what way could you change its mass to keep its acceleration unchanged?

CHAPTER PROJECT 2

Check Your Progress

The vehicle for your project will need to accelerate from a resting position. From Newton's second law of motion, you know that Acceleration = Force ÷ Mass. This means you have two ways of increasing acceleration: increasing force or decreasing mass. How can you either increase the force acting on your vehicle or decrease its mass?

SECTION 3
Friction and Gravity

DISCOVER

Which Lands First?

Do you think a quarter will fall more quickly than a dime? More quickly than a nickel? Record your predictions and find out!

1. Place a dime, a nickel, and a quarter along the edge of a desk.
2. Put a ruler behind the coins. Line it up with the edge of the desk.
3. Keeping the ruler parallel to the edge of the desk, push all three coins over the edge at the same time. Observe any time difference when the coins land.

Think It Over

Predicting Did you see a pattern in the time the coins took to fall? Use your observations about the coins to predict whether a soccer ball will fall more quickly than a marble. Will a pencil fall more quickly than a book? How can you test your predictions?

GUIDE FOR READING

- **What factors determine the friction force between two surfaces?**
- **How does mass differ from weight?**
- **What is the law of universal gravitation?**

Reading Tip **As you read, compare and contrast friction and gravity.**

What happens if you push a book slowly across your desk and then stop pushing? Will it keep moving? Without actually pushing a book, you can predict that it will come to a stop. Now think about lifting a book above your desk and letting it go. Again, without actually dropping the book, you can predict that it will fall. In both of these situations, you first exert a force to change the motion of a book, and then you remove the force.

According to Newton's first law of motion, the book's motion changes only if unbalanced forces act on it. A force should not be necessary to keep the book moving at a constant speed. So why does the book stop sliding after you push it? And why does the book fall back to the ground once you stop exerting a force to hold it up?

From Newton's first law of motion, we know that in each case other forces must be acting on the book. Two other forces do indeed act on the book. When the book slides, the force of friction causes it to slow to a stop. When the book falls, the force of the gravity causes it to accelerate downward. In this section you will learn that these two forces affect nearly all motion.

Friction

When you push a book across a table, the surface of the book rubs against the surface of the table. In the same way, the skin of a firefighter's hands rubs against the polished metal pole as she slides down. Although surfaces may seem quite smooth, they actually have many irregularities. When two surfaces rub, the irregularities of one surface get caught on those of the other surface. The force that one surface exerts on another when the two rub against each other is called **friction.**

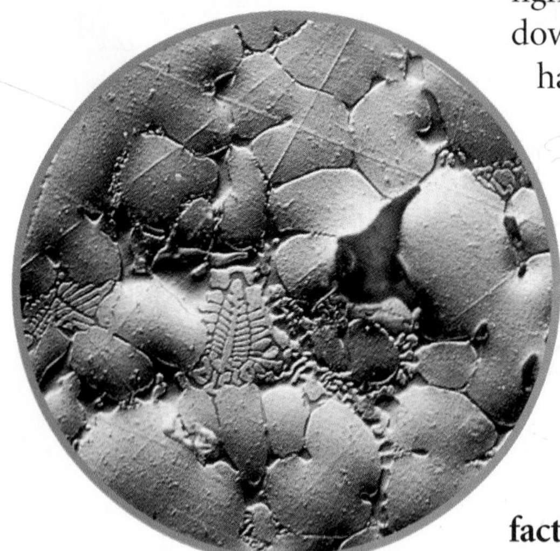

Figure 7 If you look at a polished metal surface under a special microscope, you'll find that it is actually quite rough. *Predicting What would a rough surface look like?*

The Nature of Friction Friction acts in a direction opposite to the object's direction of motion. Without friction, the object would continue to move at constant speed forever. Friction, however, opposes motion. Eventually friction will cause an object to come to a stop.

The strength of the force of friction depends on two factors: the types of surfaces involved and how hard the surfaces push together. Rough surfaces produce greater friction than smooth surfaces. The skiers in Figure 8 get a fast ride because there is very little friction between their skis and the snow. The reindeer would not be able to pull them easily over a rough surface such as sand. The force of friction also increases if the surfaces push harder against each other. If you rub your hands together forcefully, there is more friction than if you rub your hands together lightly.

Figure 8 These reindeer can't fly. But they can give an exciting ride to the two Finlanders on skis.

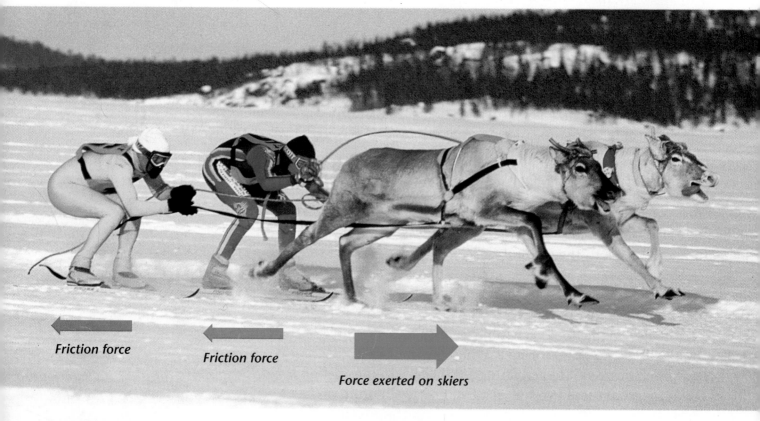

Figure 9 Friction enables these students to draw on the pavement. Friction also enables the metalworker to smooth a metal surface. *Inferring* *How can you tell that the grinder is producing heat?*

Is Friction Useful or Not? Is friction necessarily a bad thing? No—whether or not friction is useful depends on the situation. You are able to walk, for example, because friction acts between the soles of your shoes and the floor. Without friction your shoes would only slide across the floor, and you would never move forward. An automobile moves because of friction between its tires and the road. Thanks to friction you can light a match and you can walk on a sidewalk.

Friction is so useful that at times people want to increase it. If you are walking down a snow-covered hill, you might wear rubber boots or spread sand to increase the friction and slow you down. Ballet dancers spread a sticky powder on the soles of their shoes so that they do not slip on the dance floor.

Controlling Friction There are different kinds of friction. When solid surfaces slide over each other, the kind of friction that occurs is called **sliding friction.** When an object rolls over a surface, the kind of friction that occurs is **rolling friction.** The force needed to overcome rolling friction is much less than the force needed to overcome sliding friction.

Ball bearings are one way of reducing friction between two surfaces. Ball bearings are small, smooth steel balls. The balls roll between rotating metal parts. The wheels of in-line skates, skateboards, and bicycles all have ball bearings. Many automobile parts have ball bearings as well.

The friction that occurs when an object moves through a liquid or a gas is called **fluid friction.** The force needed to overcome fluid friction is usually less than that needed to overcome sliding friction. The fluid keeps surfaces from making direct contact and thus reduces friction. The moving parts of machines are bathed in oil so that they can slide past each other with less friction.

☑ *Checkpoint* *What are two ways to reduce friction?*

Spinning Plates

ACTIVITY

Find out if the force of rolling friction is really less than the force of sliding friction.

1. Stack two identical pie plates together. Try to spin the top plate.
2. Now separate the plates and fill the bottom of one pie plate loosely with marbles.
3. Place the second plate in the plate with marbles.
4. Try to spin the top plate again. Observe the results.

Drawing Conclusions What applications are there for the rolling friction modeled in this activity?

Figure 10 As soon as they jump from their airplane, sky divers begin accelerating. *Predicting Will a sky diver with greater mass accelerate more quickly than a sky diver with less mass?*

Gravity

Friction explains why a book comes to a stop after it is pushed. But why does the same book fall to the ground if you lift it and let it go? Newton realized that a force acts to pull objects straight down toward the center of Earth. He called this force gravity. **Gravity** is the force that pulls objects toward each other.

Free Fall When the only force acting on a falling object is gravity, the object is said to be in **free fall.** An object in free fall accelerates as it falls. Do you know why? In free fall the force of gravity is an unbalanced force, and unbalanced forces cause an object to accelerate.

How much do objects accelerate as they fall? Near the surface of Earth, the acceleration due to the force of gravity is 9.8 m/s^2. This means that for every second an object is falling, its velocity increases by 9.8 m/s. Suppose that an object is dropped from the top of a building. Its starting velocity is 0 m/s. At the end of the first second of falling, its velocity is 9.8 m/s. After two seconds, its velocity is 19.6 m/s (9.8 m/s + 9.8 m/s). After 3 seconds the velocity is 29.4 m/s. The velocity continues to increase as the object falls.

While it may seem hard to believe at first, all objects in free fall accelerate at the same rate regardless of mass. If you do not believe that the rates are the same, look at the two balls in Figure 11A.

Figure 11 A. Two balls with different masses are dropped to the ground. In a vacuum they would fall at exactly the same rate, regardless of their masses. **B.** A special device is used to drop one ball vertically and throw another ball horizontally at the same time.

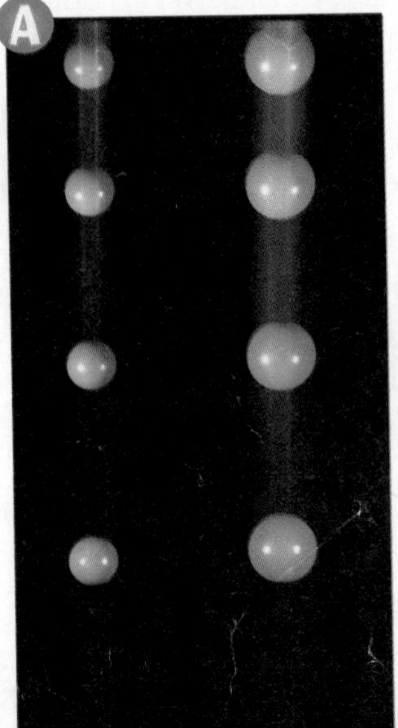

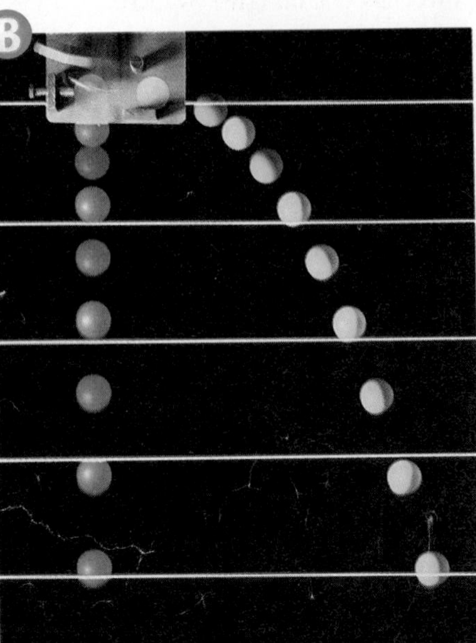

Projectile Motion Rather than dropping a ball straight down, what happens if you throw it horizontally? An object that is thrown is called a **projectile** (pruh JEK tul). Will a projectile land on the ground at the same time as an object dropped straight down?

An object that is simply dropped and one that is thrown horizontally are both in free fall. The horizontal motion of the thrown object does

not interfere with its free fall. Both objects will hit the ground at exactly the same time.

Air Resistance Despite the fact that all objects are *supposed* to fall at the same rate, you know that this is not always the case. For example, an oak leaf flutters slowly to the ground, while an acorn drops straight down. Objects falling through air experience a type of fluid friction called **air resistance.** Remember that friction is in the direction opposite to motion, so air resistance is an upward force. Air resistance is not the same for all objects. The greater the surface area of an object, the greater the air resistance. That is why a leaf falls more slowly than an acorn. In a vacuum, where there is no air, all objects fall with exactly the same rate of acceleration.

Air resistance increases with velocity. So as a falling object speeds up, the air resistance against it increases. Eventually, the air resistance equals the force of gravity. Remember that when forces are balanced, there is no acceleration. So although the object continues to fall, its velocity no longer increases. This velocity, the greatest velocity the object reaches, is called **terminal velocity**.

Figure 12 When air is present, air resistance exerts an upward force on objects. *Inferring The oak leaf and the acorn fall at the same rate in the vacuum tube on the right. Is there any air resistance?*

☑ *Checkpoint* ***At what rate does an object in free fall accelerate?***

Weight The force of gravity on a person or object at the surface of a planet is known as **weight.** When you step on a bathroom scale, you are determining the force with which Earth is pulling you. Do not confuse weight with mass! **Weight is a measure of the force of gravity on an object, and mass is a measure of the amount of matter in that object.**

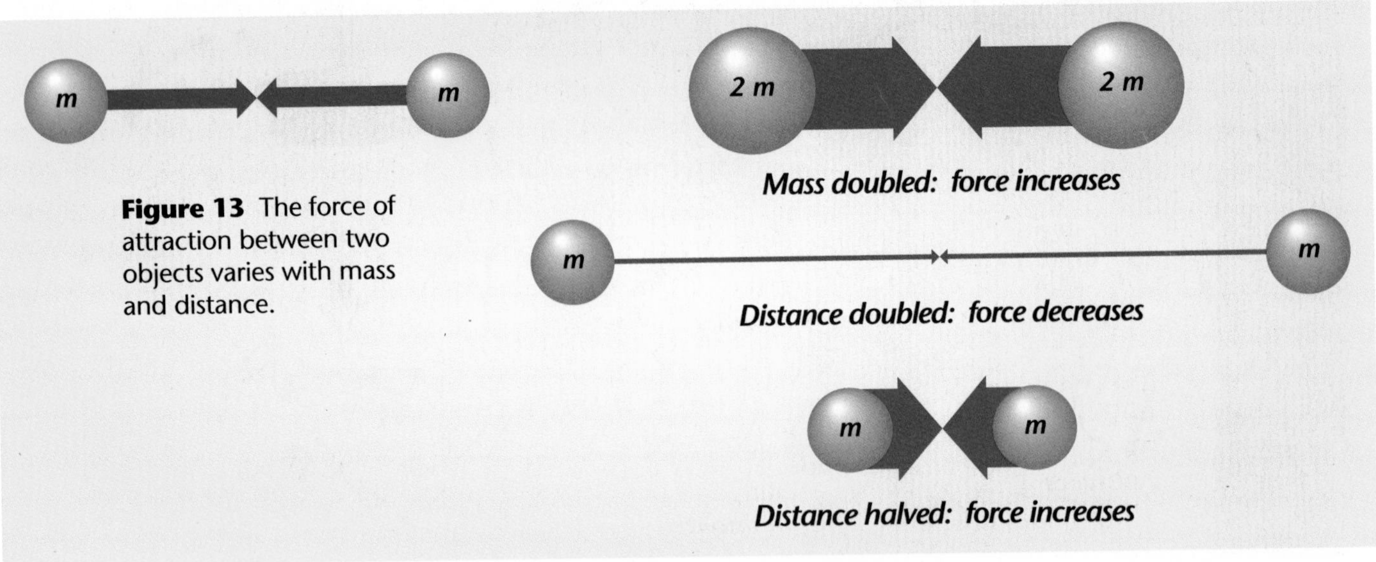

Figure 13 The force of attraction between two objects varies with mass and distance.

Since weight is a force, you can rewrite Newton's second law of motion, Force = Mass × Acceleration, to find weight.

Weight = Mass × Acceleration due to gravity

Weight is usually measured in newtons, mass in kilograms, and acceleration due to gravity in m/s^2. So a 50-kilogram person weighs 50 kg × 9.8 m/s^2 = 490 newtons on Earth's surface.

Universal Gravitation

Newton realized that Earth is not the only object that exerts a gravitational force. Instead, gravity acts everywhere in the universe. Gravity is the force that makes an apple fall to the ground. It is the force that keeps the moon orbiting around Earth. It is also the force that keeps all the planets orbiting around the sun.

What Newton discovered is now called the law of universal gravitation. **The law of universal gravitation states that the force of gravity acts between all objects in the universe.** Any two objects in the universe, without exception, attract each other. This means that you are not only attracted to Earth, but you are also attracted to all the other objects around you! Earth and the objects around you are attracted to you as well.

Why don't you notice that the objects around you are pulling on you? After all, this book exerts a gravitational force on you. The reason is that the strength of the force depends on the masses of the objects involved. The force of gravity is much greater between you and Earth than between you and your book.

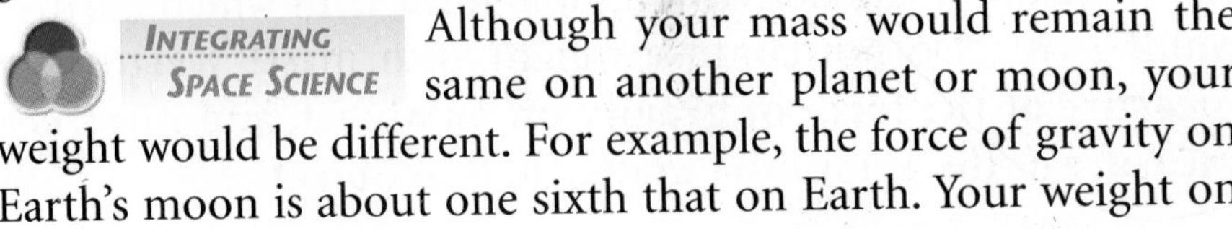

INTEGRATING SPACE SCIENCE Although your mass would remain the same on another planet or moon, your weight would be different. For example, the force of gravity on Earth's moon is about one sixth that on Earth. Your weight on

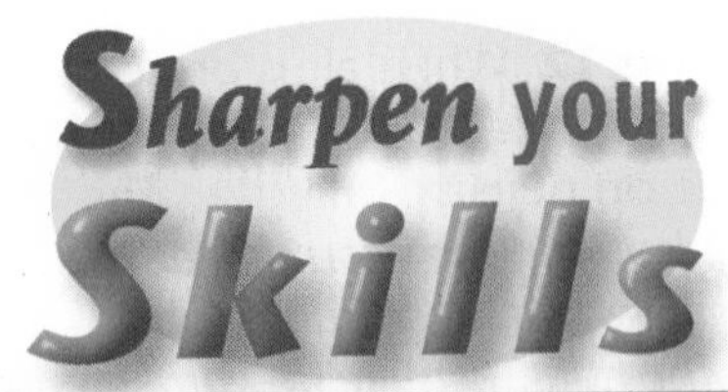

Calculating ACTIVITY

You can determine the weight of an object if you measure its mass.

1. Estimate the weight of four objects. (*Hint:* An apple weighs about 1 N.)
2. Find the mass of each object. If the measurements are not in kilograms, convert them to kilograms.
3. Multiply each mass by 9.8 m/s^2 to find the weight in newtons.

How close to actual values were your estimates?

Figure 14 This astronaut jumps easily on the moon. *Comparing and Contrasting How do his mass and weight on the moon compare to his mass and weight on Earth?*

the moon, then, would be about a sixth of what it is on Earth. That is why the astronaut in Figure 14 can leap so easily.

If the gravitational force depends on mass, you might then expect to notice a force of attraction from a massive object, such as the moon or the sun. But you do not. The reason is that the gravitational force also depends on the distance between the objects. The farther apart the objects are, the weaker the force.

Astronauts travel great distances from Earth. As they travel from Earth toward the moon, Earth's gravitational pull becomes weaker. At the same time, the moon's gravitational pull becomes stronger. At the surface of the moon an astronaut feels the pull of the moon's gravity, but no longer notices the pull of Earth's gravity.

Section 3 Review

1. What factors determine the strength of the friction force when two surfaces slide against each other?
2. What is the difference between weight and mass?
3. State the law of universal gravitation in your own words.
4. **Thinking Critically** **Problem Solving** A squirrel drops a nut over a cliff. What is the velocity of the nut after 3 seconds? After 5 seconds? After 10 seconds? (Ignore air resistance. Remember that the acceleration due to gravity is 9.8 m/s^2.)

CHAPTER PROJECT 2

Check Your Progress

Draw a diagram of your vehicle. Use labeled arrows to show each place that a force is acting on it. Be sure to include friction forces in your diagram. Brainstorm ways to reduce forces that slow down your vehicle.

Real-World Lab

You, the Consumer

Sticky Sneakers

The appropriate sneaker for an activity should have a specific type of tread to grip the floor or the ground. In this lab you will test different sneakers by measuring the amount of friction between the sneakers and a table.

Problem

How does the amount of friction between a sneaker and a surface compare for different types of sneakers?

Skills Focus

forming operational definitions, measuring, controlling variables

Materials 

three or more different types of sneakers
2 spring scales, 5 N and 20 N, or force sensors
mass set(s)
tape
3 large paper clips
balance

Procedure 

1. Sneakers are designed to deal with various friction forces, including these:
   - starting friction, which is involved when you start from a stopped position
   - forward-stopping friction, which is involved when you come to a forward stop
   - sideways-stopping friction, which is involved when you come to a sideways stop
2. Prepare a data table in which you can record each type of friction for each sneaker.
3. Place each sneaker on a balance. Then put masses in each sneaker so that the total mass of the sneaker plus the masses is 1,000 g. Spread the masses out evenly inside the sneaker.
4. You will need to tape a paper clip to each sneaker and then attach a spring scale to the paper clip. (If you are using force sensors, see your teacher for instructions.) To measure
   - starting friction, attach the paper clip to the back of the sneaker.
   - forward-stopping friction, attach the paper clip to the front of the sneaker.
   - sideways-stopping friction, attach the paper clip to the side of the sneaker.

DATA TABLE

Sneaker	Starting friction (N)	Sideways-stopping friction (N)	Forward-stopping friction (N)
A			
B			

5. To measure starting friction, pull the sneaker backward until it starts to move. Use the 20-N spring scale first. If the reading is less than 5 N, use a 5-N scale. The force necessary to make the sneaker start moving is equal to the friction force. Record the starting friction force in your data table.
6. To measure either type of stopping friction, use the spring scale to pull each sneaker at a slow, constant speed. Record the stopping friction force in your data table.
7. Repeat Steps 4–6 for the remaining sneakers.

Analyze and Conclude

1. What are the manipulated and responding variables in this experiment? Explain. (See the Skills Handbook for a discussion of experimental variables.)
2. Why is the reading on the spring scale equal to the friction force in each case?
3. Do you think that using a sneaker with a small amount of mass in it is a fair test of the friction of the sneakers? (Consider the fact that sneakers are used with people's feet inside them.) Explain your answer.
4. Draw a diagram that shows the forces acting on the sneaker for each type of motion.
5. Why did you pull the sneaker at a slow speed to test for stopping friction? For starting friction, why did you pull a sneaker that wasn't moving?
6. Which sneaker had the most starting friction? Which had the most forward stopping friction? Which had the most sideways stopping friction?
7. Can you identify a relationship between the type of sneaker and the type of friction you observed? What do you observe about the sneakers that would cause one to have better traction than another?
8. **Apply** Wear a pair of your own sneakers. Start running and notice how you press against the floor with your sneaker. How do you think this affects the friction between the sneaker and the floor? How can you test for this variable?

Getting Involved

Go to a store that sells sneakers. If possible take a spring scale and, with the clerk's permission, do a quick friction test on sneakers designed for different activities. Also, note the materials they are made of, the support they provide for your feet, and other features. Then decide whether it is necessary to buy specific sneakers for different activities.

Action and Reaction

DISCOVER — ACTIVITY

How Pushy Is a Straw?

1. Stretch a rubber band around the middle of the front cover of a small or medium-size hardcover book.
2. Place four marbles in a small square on a table. Carefully place the book on the marbles so that the cover with the rubber band is on top.
3. Hold the book steady by placing one index finger on the center of the binding. Then, as shown in the illustration, push a straw against the rubber band with your other index finger.

4. Push the straw so that the rubber band stretches about ten centimeters. Then let go of both the book and the straw at the same time.

Think It Over

Developing Hypotheses What did you observe about the motion of the book and the straw? Write a hypothesis to explain what happened in terms of the forces on the book and the straw.

GUIDE FOR READING

- **What is Newton's third law of motion?**
- **What is the law of conservation of momentum?**

Reading Tip **Before you read, preview the illustrations and predict what *action* and *reaction* mean.**

Imagine that you are an astronaut making a space walk outside your space station. In your excitement about your walk, you lose track of time and use up all the fuel in your jet pack. How do you get back to the station? Your jet pack is empty, but it can still get you back to the station if you throw it away. To understand how, you need to know Newton's third law of motion.

Newton's Third Law of Motion

Newton realized that forces are not "one-sided." Whenever one object exerts a force on a second object, the second object exerts a force back on the first object. The force exerted by the second object is equal in strength and opposite in direction to the first force. The first force is called the "action" and the other force the "reaction." **Newton's third law of motion states that if one object exerts a force on another object, then the second object exerts a force of equal strength in the opposite direction on the first object.**

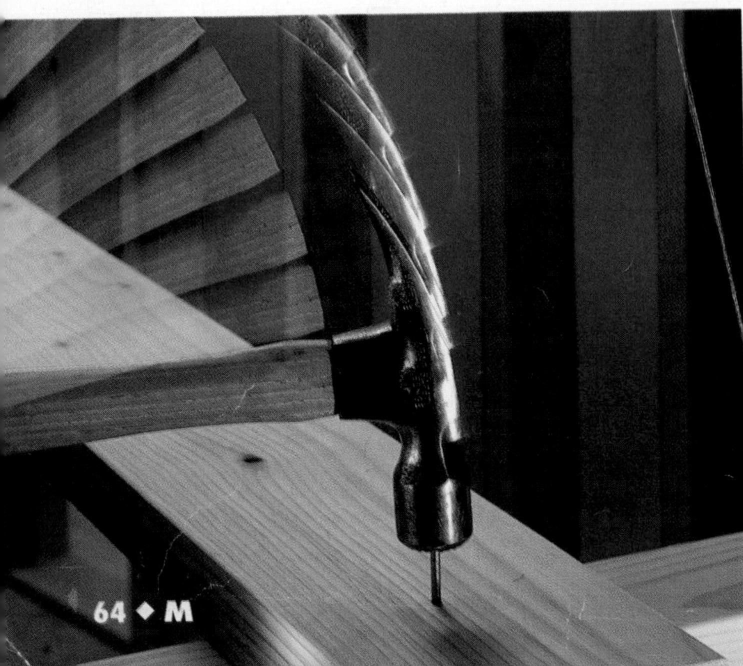

Figure 15 A hammer exerts a force on a nail, pushing it into a piece of wood. At the same time, the nail exerts a force back on the hammer, causing its motion to come to a sudden stop.

Equal but Opposite You may already be familiar with examples of Newton's third law of motion. Perhaps you have watched figure skaters and have seen one skater push on the other. As a result, both skaters move—not only the skater who was pushed. The skater who pushed is pushed back with an equal force, but in the opposite direction.

The speeds with which the two skaters move depend on their masses. If they have the same mass, they will move at the same speed. But if one skater has a greater mass than the other, she will move backward more slowly. Although the action and reaction forces will be equal and opposite, the same force acting on a greater mass results in a smaller acceleration. Recall that this is Newton's second law of motion.

Now can you figure out how to return from your space walk? In order to get a push back to the space station, you need to push on some object. You can remove your empty jet pack and push it away from you. In return, the jet pack will exert an equal force on you, sending you back to the safety of the space station.

Figure 16 One skater pushes gently on the other. The result is that the other skater pushes back with an equal force—even if she isn't trying. *Applying Concepts Which of Newton's laws describes this phenomenon?*

Action-Reaction in Action Newton's third law is in action all around you. When you walk, you push the ground with your feet. The ground pushes back on your feet with an equal and opposite force. You go forward when you walk because the ground is pushing you! A bird flies forward by exerting a force on the air with its wings. The air pushes back on those wings with an equal force that propels the bird forward.

INTEGRATING LIFE SCIENCE A squid applies Newton's third law of motion to move itself through the water. The squid exerts a force on the water that it expels from its body cavity. At the same time, the water exerts an equal and opposite force on the squid, causing it to move.

Figure 17 When a squid pushes water out, the expelled water pushes back and forces the squid to move ahead (to the right). The force the squid exerts on the water is the action force.

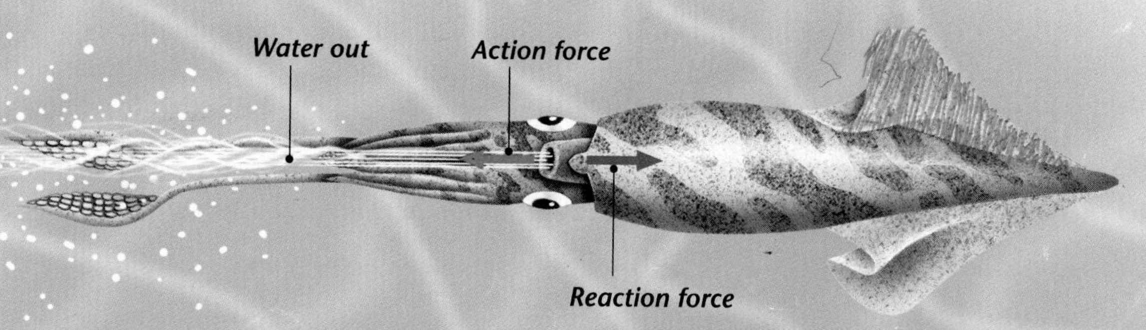

Figure 18 In these photographs, red arrows show action forces and blue arrows show reaction forces. **A.** The player's wrists exert the action force. **B.** As two players jump for the ball, the ball exerts reaction forces on both of them.

Do Action-Reaction Forces Cancel? In Section 1 you learned that balanced forces, which are equal and opposite, add up to zero. In other words, balanced forces cancel out. They produce no change in motion. Why then don't the action and reaction forces in Newton's third law of motion cancel out as well? After all, they are equal and opposite.

To answer this question, you have to consider the object on which the forces are acting. Look, for example, at the two volleyball players in Figure 18B. When they hit the ball from opposite directions, each of their hands exerts a force on the ball. If the forces are equal in strength, but opposite in direction, the forces cancel out. The ball does not move either to the left or to the right.

Newton's third law, however, refers to forces on two different objects. If only one player hits the ball, as shown in Figure 18A, the player exerts an upward action force on the ball. In return, the ball exerts an equal but opposite downward reaction force back on her wrists. One force is on the ball, and the other is on the player. The action and reaction forces cannot be added together because they are acting on different objects. Forces can be added together only if they are acting on the same object.

☑ *Checkpoint* ***Why don't action and reaction forces cancel each other?***

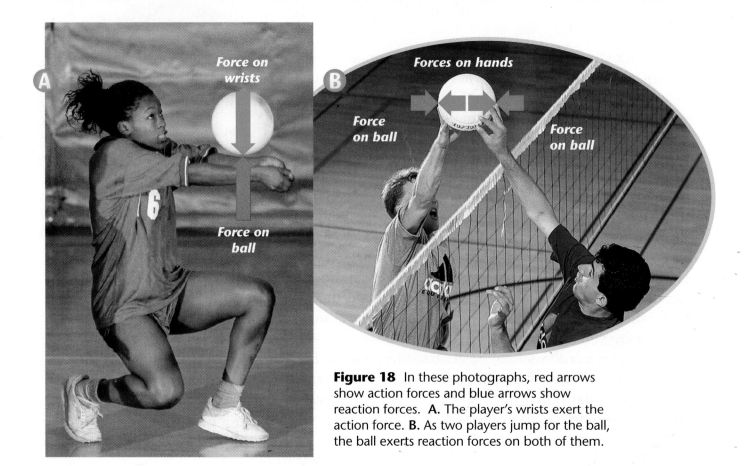

Momentum

When Newton presented his three laws of motion, he used two different words to describe moving objects. He used the word velocity, but he also wrote about something that he called the "quantity of motion." What is this quantity of motion? Today we call it momentum. The **momentum** (moh MEN tum) of an object is the product of its mass and its velocity.

Momentum = Mass × Velocity

What is the unit of measurement for momentum? Since mass is measured in kilograms and velocity is measured in meters per second, the unit for momentum is kilogram-meters per second (kg·m/s). Like velocity and acceleration, momentum is described by its direction as well as its quantity. The momentum of an object is in the same direction as its velocity.

The more momentum an object has, the harder it is to stop. You can catch a baseball moving at 20 m/s, for example, but you cannot stop a car moving at the same speed. Why does the car have more momentum than the ball? The car has more momentum because it has a greater mass.

A high velocity also can produce a large momentum, even when mass is small. A bullet shot from a rifle, for example, has a large momentum. Even though it has a small mass, it travels at a high speed.

Sample Problem

Which has more momentum: a 3-kg sledgehammer swung at 1.5 m/s or an 4-kg sledgehammer swung at 0.9 m/s?

Analyze. You know the mass and velocity of two different objects. You need to determine the momentum of each.

Write the formula. *Momentum = Mass × Velocity*

Substitute and solve. *(a) 3 kg × 1.5 m/s = 4.5 kg·m/s*

(b) 4 kg × 0.9 m/s = 3.6 kg·m/s

Think about it. The lighter hammer has more momentum than the heavier one, because it is swung at a greater velocity—almost twice as fast.

Practice Problems

1. A golf ball travels at 16 m/s, while a baseball moves at 7 m/s. The mass of the golf ball is 0.045 kg and the mass of the baseball is 0.14 kg. Which has greater momentum?
2. What is the momentum of a bird with a mass of 0.018 kg flying at 15 m/s?

Figure 19 In the absence of friction, momentum is conserved when two train cars collide. This is true regardless of whether the train cars bounce off each other or couple together during the collision. *Interpreting Diagrams In which diagram is all of the momentum transferred from car X to car Y?*

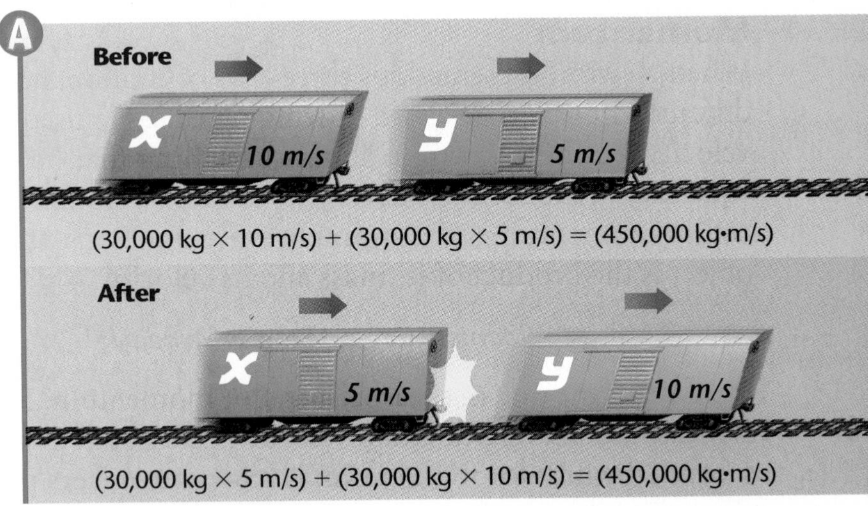

Colliding Cars

ACTIVITY

Momentum is always conserved—even by toys!

1. Find two nearly identical toy cars that roll easily.
2. Make two loops out of masking tape (sticky side out). Put one loop on the front of one of the cars and the other loop on the back of the other car.
3. Place the car that has tape on the back on the floor. Then gently roll the other car into the back of the stationary car. Was momentum conserved? How do you know?

Predicting What will happen if you put masking tape on the fronts of both cars and roll them at each other with equal speeds? Will momentum be conserved in this case? Test your prediction.

Conservation of Momentum

You know that if someone bumps into you from behind, you gain momentum in the forward direction. Momentum is useful for understanding what happens when an object collides with another object. When two objects collide in the absence of friction, momentum is not lost. This fact is called the law of conservation of momentum. The **law of conservation of momentum** states that the total momentum of the objects that interact does not change. The quantity of momentum is the same before and after they interact. **The total momentum of any group of objects remains the same unless outside forces act on the objects.** Friction is an example of an outside force.

Before you hear the details of this law, you should know that the word *conservation* means something different in physical science than in everyday usage. In everyday usage, conservation means saving resources. You might conserve water or fossil fuels, for example. In physical science, the word conservation refers to conditions before and after some event. A quantity that is conserved is the same after an event as it was before the event.

Two Moving Objects Look at the two train cars traveling in the same direction on a track shown in Figure 19A. Car X is traveling at 10 m/s and car Y is traveling at 5 m/s. Eventually, car X will catch up with car Y and bump into it. During this collision, the speed of each car changes. Car X slows down to 5 m/s, and car Y speeds up to 10 m/s. Momentum is conserved—the momentum of one train car decreases while the momentum of the other increases.

One Moving Object Suppose that car X moves down the track at 10 m/s and hits car Y, which is not moving. Figure 19B shows that after the collision, car X is no longer moving, but car Y is moving.

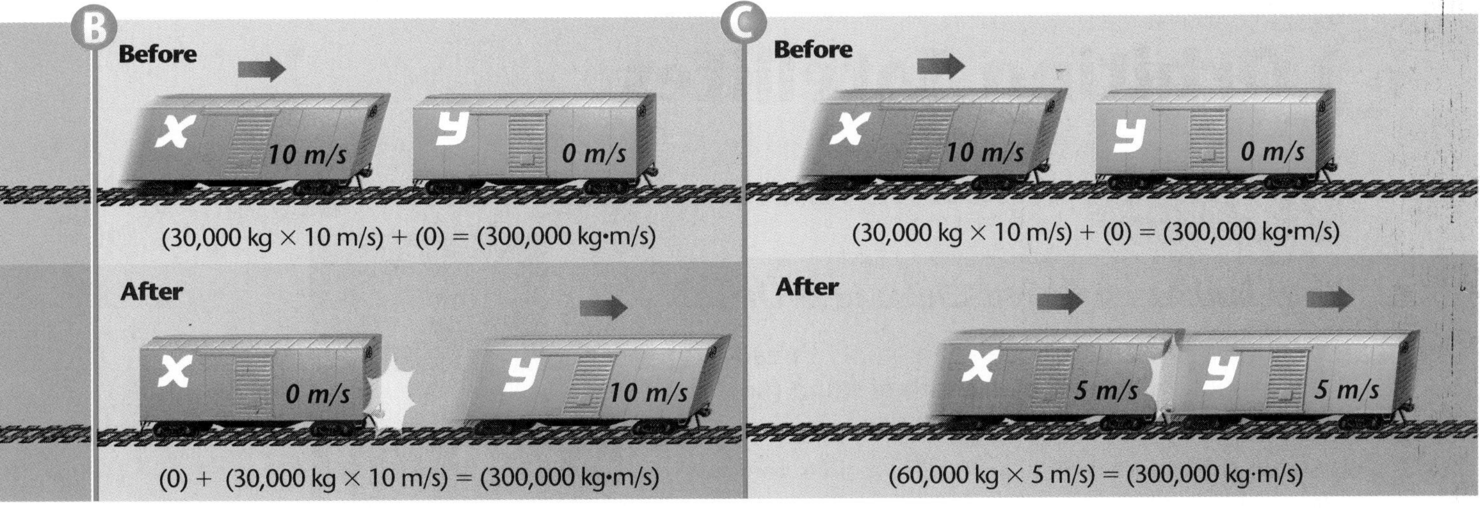

Even though the situation has changed, momentum is still conserved. The total momentum is the same before and after the collision. This time, all of the momentum has been transferred from car X to car Y.

Two Connected Objects Now suppose that, instead of bouncing off each other, the two train cars couple together when they hit. Is momentum still conserved? The answer is yes. You can see in Figure 19C that the total momentum before the collision is again 300,000 kg·m/s. But after the collision, the coupled train cars make one object with a total mass of 60,000 kilograms (30,000 kilograms + 30,000 kilograms). The velocity of the coupled trains is 5 m/s—half the velocity of car X before the collision. Since the mass is doubled, the velocity must be divided in half in order for momentum to be conserved.

Section 4 Review

1. According to Newton's third law of motion, how are action and reaction forces related?
2. What is meant by "conservation of momentum"?
3. Suppose you and a friend, who has exactly twice your mass, are on skates. You push away from your friend. How does the force with which you push your friend compare to the force with which your friend pushes you? How do your accelerations compare?
4. **Thinking Critically Comparing and Contrasting** Which has more momentum, a 250-kg dolphin swimming at 6 m/s, or a 450-kg manatee swimming at 2 m/s?

CHAPTER PROJECT 2

Check Your Progress

Construct your vehicle. Is your vehicle powered according to Newton's third law of motion? Add to your diagram so that it shows the force exerted by your vehicle and the force exerted on your vehicle to make it move. What exerts the force that moves your vehicle? Be ready to explain the diagram to other students.

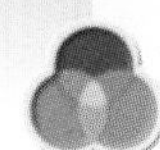

SECTION 5

Orbiting Satellites

DISCOVER

ACTIVITY

What Makes an Object Move in a Circle?

1. Tie a small mass, such as an empty thread spool, to the end of a length of string (no more than one meter long).
2. Swing the object rapidly around in a circle that is perpendicular to the floor. Make sure no one is near the swinging object, and don't let it go!
3. Predict what will happen if you decrease the speed of the object. Test your prediction.
4. Predict how the length of the string affects the motion of the object. Test your prediction.

Think It Over

Forming Operational Definitions Describe the motion of the object. How do you know that the string exerts a force?

GUIDE FOR READING

- **How does a rocket lift off the ground?**
- **What keeps a satellite in orbit?**

Reading Tip **As you read, make a list of main ideas and supporting details about rockets and satellites.**

What would it be like to be at Cape Canaveral in Florida for a space shuttle launch? The countdown is broadcast over a loudspeaker—ten—nine—eight—seven—six—five—four. White steam comes out of the base of the rocket—three—two—one. The rocket rises into space and begins to turn slightly and roll. The noise hits you, and the ground shakes. With an astonishingly loud rumble, the rocket rises in the distance. Everyone cheers. You watch the rocket until it is too far away to see.

How Do Rockets Lift Off?

The awesome achievement of lifting a rocket into space against the force of gravity can be explained using Newton's third law of motion. As a rocket burns fuel, it expels exhaust gases. When the gases are forced out of the rocket, they exert an equal and opposite force back on

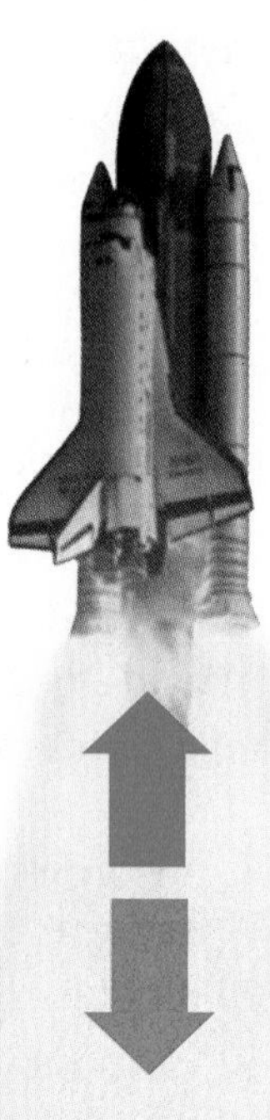

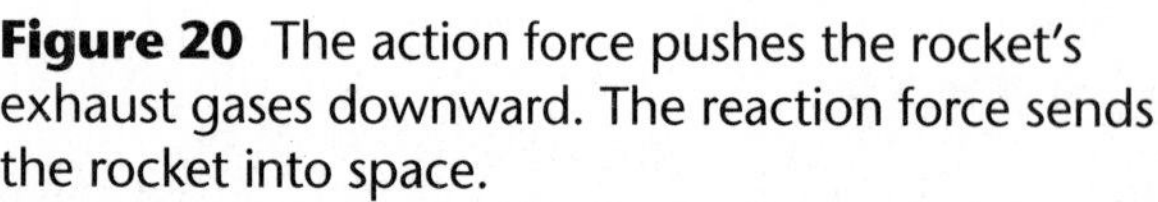

Figure 20 The action force pushes the rocket's exhaust gases downward. The reaction force sends the rocket into space.

the rocket. **A rocket can rise into the air because the gases it expels with a downward force exert an equal but opposite force on the rocket.** As long as this upward pushing force, called thrust, is greater than the downward pull of gravity, there is a net force in the upward direction. As a result, the rocket accelerates upward.

Checkpoint *When a rocket is launched, what is the direction of the reaction force?*

Figure 21 As this rocket moves higher, its path tilts more and more. Eventually its path is parallel to Earth's surface. *Predicting How will the direction of the accelerating force change?*

What Is a Satellite?

Rockets are often used to carry satellites into space. A **satellite** is any object that travels around another object in space. An artificial satellite is a device that is launched into orbit around Earth. Artificial satellites are designed for many purposes. They are used in space research, communications, military intelligence, weather analysis, and geographical surveys.

Circular Motion Artificial satellites travel around Earth in an almost circular path. Recall that an object traveling in a circle is accelerating because it is constantly changing direction. If an object is accelerating, there must be a force acting on it to change its motion. Any force that causes an object to move in a circle is called a **centripetal force** (sen TRIP ih tul). The word *centripetal* means "center-seeking." For a satellite, the centripetal force is the gravitational force that pulls the satellite toward the center of Earth.

Satellite Motion If gravity pulls satellites toward Earth, why doesn't a satellite fall, as a ball thrown into the air would? The answer is that satellites do not travel straight up into the air. Instead, they move around Earth. If you throw a ball horizontally, for example, it will move out in front of you at the same time that it is pulled to the ground. If you throw the ball faster, it will land even farther in front of you. The faster you throw a projectile, the farther it travels before it lands.

Figure 22 The faster a projectile like this ball is thrown, the farther it travels before it hits the ground.

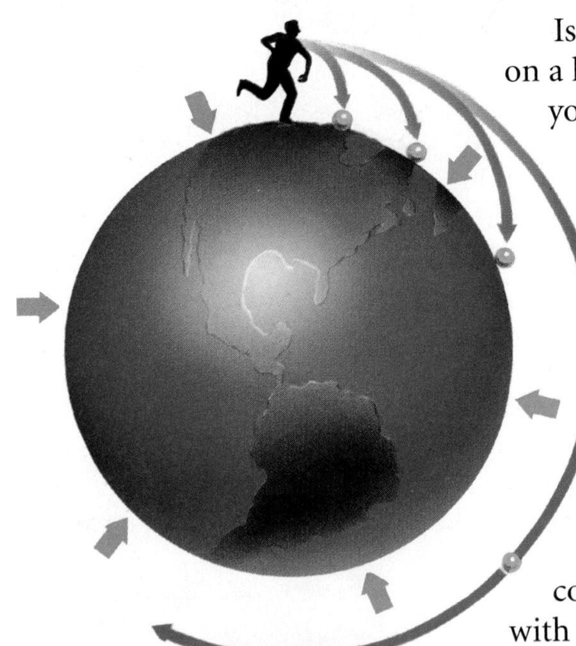

Figure 23 A projectile with enough velocity will move in a circular orbit around Earth. *Interpreting Diagrams The force of gravity is always toward the center of Earth. How does the direction of gravity compare to the direction of the projectile's motion at any point?*

Isaac Newton wondered what would happen if you were on a high mountain and were able to throw a stone as fast as you wanted. The faster you threw it, the farther away it would land. At a certain speed, the path of the object would match the curve of Earth. Although the stone would keep falling due to gravity, Earth's surface would curve away from the stone at the same rate. Thus the object would circle Earth, as in Figure 23.

Satellites in orbit around Earth continually fall toward Earth, but because Earth is curved they travel around it. In other words, a satellite is a projectile that falls around Earth rather than into it. A satellite does not need fuel because it continues to move ahead due to its inertia. At the same time, gravity continuously changes the satellite's direction. The speed with which an object must be thrown in order to orbit Earth turns out to be about 7,900 m/s! This speed is almost 200 times as fast as a pitcher can throw a baseball.

Satellite Location Some satellites, such as the space shuttle, are put into low orbits. The time to complete a trip around Earth in a low orbit is about 90 minutes. Other satellites are sent into higher orbits. At these distances, the satellite travels more slowly and takes longer to circle Earth. For example, communications satellites travel about 36,000 kilometers above the surface. At this height they circle Earth once every 24 hours. Since Earth rotates once every 24 hours, a satellite above the equator always stays above the same point on Earth as it orbits.

Section 5 Review

1. Use action-reaction forces to explain why a rocket can lift off the ground.
2. Why doesn't an orbiting satellite fall back to Earth?
3. Is it correct to say that satellites stay in orbit rather than falling to Earth because they are beyond the pull of Earth's gravity? Explain.
4. **Thinking Critically Applying Concepts** When a rocket travels higher, air resistance decreases as the air becomes less dense. The force of gravity also decreases because the rocket is farther from Earth, and the rocket's mass decreases as its fuel is used up. Explain how acceleration is affected.

Science at Home

Fill a small plastic bucket halfway with water and take it outdoors. Challenge a family member to swing the bucket in a vertical circle. Explain that the water won't fall out at the top if the bucket is moving fast enough. Tell your family member that if the bucket falls as fast as the water, the water will stay in the bucket. Relate this activity to a satellite that also falls due to gravity, yet remains in orbit.

CHAPTER 2 STUDY GUIDE

The Nature of Force

Key Ideas

- ◆ The sum of all the forces acting on an object is the net force.
- ◆ Unbalanced forces change the motion of an object, whereas balanced forces do not.
- ◆ According to Newton's first law of motion, an object at rest will remain at rest and an object in motion will continue in motion at constant speed unless the object is acted upon by an unbalanced force.

Key Terms

force
net force
unbalanced forces
balanced forces
inertia
mass

Force, Mass, and Acceleration

Key Idea

- ◆ Newton's second law of motion states that the net force on an object is the product of its acceleration and its mass.

Key Term

newton

Friction and Gravity

Key Ideas

- ◆ Friction is a force that one surface exerts on another when they rub against each other.
- ◆ Weight is a measure of the force of gravity on an object, and mass is a measure of the amount of matter that an object contains.
- ◆ The force of gravity acts between all objects in the universe.

Key Terms

friction
sliding friction
rolling friction
fluid friction
gravity
free fall
projectile
air resistance
terminal velocity
weight

Action and Reaction

Key Ideas

- ◆ Newton's third law of motion states that every time there is an action force on an object, the object will exert an equal and opposite reaction force.
- ◆ The momentum of an object is the product of its mass and its velocity.
- ◆ The law of conservation of momentum states that the total momentum is the same before and after an event, as long as there are no outside forces.

Key Terms

momentum
law of conservation of momentum

Orbiting Satellites

INTEGRATING SPACE SCIENCE 

Key Ideas

- ◆ A rocket burns fuel and produces gases. The rocket pushes these gases downward. At the same time, the gases apply an equal force to the rocket, pushing it upward.
- ◆ Even though a satellite is pulled downward by gravity, it stays in orbit because it is moving so quickly. Earth's surface curves away from the satellite as the satellite falls.

Key Terms

satellite
centripetal force

Organizing Information

Compare/Contrast Table Copy the compare/contrast table below on a separate sheet of paper. Complete the table to compare and contrast friction and gravity. (For more information on compare/contrast tables see the Skills Handbook.)

Force	Direction of Force	Force Depends Upon
Friction	a. ?	b. ?
Gravity	c. ?	d. ?

Reviewing Content

For more review of key concepts, see the Interactive Student Tutorial CD-ROM.

Multiple Choice

Choose the letter of the best answer.

1. When an unbalanced force acts on an object, the force
   a. changes the motion of the object.
   b. is canceled by another force.
   c. does not change the motion of the object.
   d. is equal to the weight of the object.
2. When two equal forces act in opposite directions on an object, they are called
   a. friction forces. b. balanced forces.
   c. centripetal forces. d. gravitational forces.
3. The resistance of an object to any change in its motion is called
   a. inertia. b. friction.
   c. gravity. d. weight.
4. According to Newton's second law of motion, force is equal to mass times
   a. inertia. b. weight.
   c. direction. d. acceleration.
5. The product of an object's mass and its velocity is called the object's
   a. net force. b. weight.
   c. momentum. d. gravitation.

True or False

If the statement is true, write true. If it is false, change the underlined word or words to make the statement true.

6. According to Newton's third law of motion, whenever you exert a force on an object, the object exerts a force back on you that is <u>greater than</u> your force.
7. Mass is a measure of the amount of <u>force</u> that an object has.
8. <u>Weight</u> is the measure of the force of gravity exerted on an object.
9. <u>Conservation</u> in science refers to the amount of some quantity staying the same before and after an event.
10. The force that causes a satellite to orbit Earth is <u>gravity</u>.

Checking Concepts

11. Explain how force, mass, and acceleration are related.
12. Why do slippery fluids such as oil reduce sliding friction?
13. One student tosses a chalkboard eraser horizontally so that the eraser hits the ground 5 meters away. At exactly the same time, another student drops an eraser. Which eraser hits the ground first? Explain.
14. Explain why a flat sheet of paper dropped from a height of 2 meters will not accelerate at the same rate as a sheet of paper crumpled into a ball.
15. Why do athletes' shoes often have cleats?
16. Compare your mass and weight on Earth with your mass and weight on an asteroid, which is much smaller than Earth.
17. When you drop a golf ball to the pavement, it bounces up. Is a force needed to make it bounce up? If so, what exerts the force?
18. Draw a diagram showing the motion of a satellite around Earth. Is the satellite accelerating?
19. **Writing to Learn** You are a reporter for a local television station, and you like to give your stories a physical-science twist. Write a story for the evening news in which you describe an event in terms of the forces involved. Use a catchy title.

Thinking Critically

20. **Comparing and Contrasting** If you stand up in a rowboat and take a step toward the dock, you may fall in the water. Explain what happens in this situation. How is it similar to what happens when you take a step on land? How is it different?
21. **Problem Solving** If a toy train has a mass of 1.5 kg and accelerates at a rate of 20 m/s^2, calculate the force acting on it.
22. **Applying Concepts** You are riding fast on a skateboard when your wheel suddenly gets stuck in a crack on the sidewalk. Using the term *inertia*, explain what happens.

Applying Skills

Use the illustration showing a collision between two balls to answer Questions 23–25.

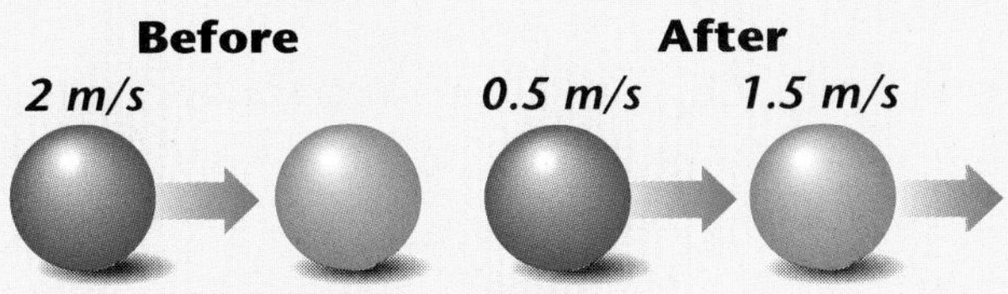

23. **Calculating** Use the formula for momentum to find the momentum of each ball before and after the collision. Assume the mass of each ball is 0.4 kg.
24. **Inferring** Find the total momentum before and after collision. Is the law of conservation of momentum satisfied in this collision? Explain.
25. **Designing Experiments** Design an experiment in which you could show that momentum is not conserved between the balls when friction is strong.

Performance Assessment

CHAPTER PROJECT 2

Project Wrap Up Test your vehicle to make sure it will work on the type of floor in your classroom. Will the vehicle stay within the bounds set by your teacher? Identify all the forces acting on the vehicle. List at least three features you included in the design of the vehicle that led to an improvement in its performance. For example, did you give it a smooth shape for low air resistance?

Reflect and Record What was the most significant source of friction for your vehicle? What was the most successful way to overcome the friction? In your journal, describe the features of your vehicle that led to its success or that kept it from succeeding.

Test Preparation

Use these questions to prepare for standardized tests.

Read the information. Then answer Questions 26–30.

Two students are pulling the volleyball equipment with the forces indicated. The friction force between the bag and the floor is 15 N.

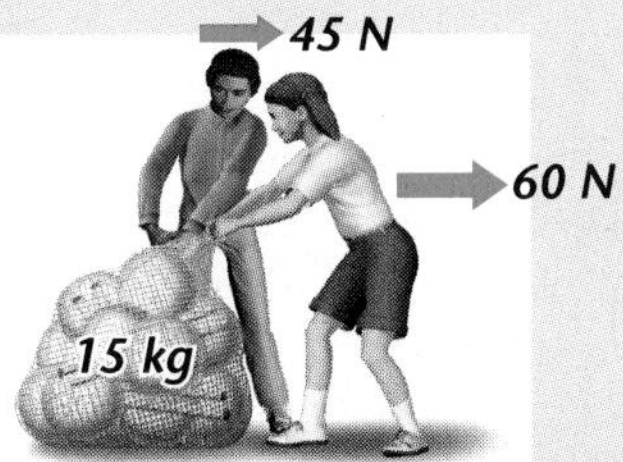

26. What law can you use to calculate the acceleration of the bag?
    a. Newton's first law of motion
    b. Newton's second law of motion
    c. Newton's third law of motion
    d. the law of universal gravitation

27. What is the net force on the bag?
    a. 90 N **b.** 105 N
    c. 120 N **d.** 15 N

28. What is the acceleration of the bag?
    a. 6.0 m/s **b.** 6.0 m/s^2
    c. 6.5 m/s^2 **d.** 7.0 m/s

29. How could they make the bag accelerate more?
    a. They could move it a shorter distance.
    b. They could add mass to it.
    c. They could exert a smaller force.
    d. They could exert a greater force.

30. What would happen to the motion if a third student pulled the bag in the opposite direction with a force of 40 N?
    a. The bag will move in the opposite direction.
    b. The bag will stop moving.
    c. The bag will continue to move in the same direction, but it will accelerate more slowly.
    d. The bag will continue to move in the same direction, but it will accelerate more quickly.

Forces in Fluids

www.phschool.com

Pressure

Discover **Can You Blow Up a Balloon in a Bottle?**
Sharpen Your Skills **Developing Hypotheses**
Real-World Lab **Spinning Sprinklers**

Transmitting Pressure in a Fluid

Discover **How Does Pressure Change?**

Floating and Sinking

Discover **What Can You Measure With a Straw?**
Sharpen Your Skills **Measuring**
Skills Lab **Sink and Spill**
Try This **Dive!**

PROJECT 3

Staying Afloat

With its powerful hind legs, a frog can jump several times its own length—if it is on land. The frog shown here isn't exerting itself. Instead, it's swimming slowly and letting the water carry its weight. Whether an object sinks or floats depends on more than just its weight. In this chapter, you will learn about forces that act in water and other fluids. You will find out how these forces make an object sink or float. You will also learn how these forces make common devices work.

Your Goal To construct a boat that can carry a cargo and float in water. You should compare different materials and designs in order to build the most efficient boat you can.

Your boat should
- be made of metal only
- support a cargo of 50 pennies without allowing any water to enter for at least 10 seconds
- be built following the safety guidelines in Appendix A

Get Started Begin by thinking about the shape of real ships. Then look for common objects made from metal that you can form into a boat. You might want to look ahead at Section 3 to learn more about what makes an object float.

Check Your Progress You'll be working on this project as you study this chapter. To keep your project on track, look for Check Your Progress boxes at the following points.

Section 2 Review, page 89: Experiment with materials and shapes.

Section 3 Review, page 96: Measure the weight of your boat, and modify your design.

Wrap Up At the end of the chapter (page 103), launch your boat to see if it will float and to show that it can carry its cargo of pennies.

A frog barely shows its head above the water as it waits for its breakfast to fly by.

Integrating Technology

SECTION 4 **Applying Bernoulli's Principle**

Discover **Does Water Push or Pull?**

SECTION 1 Pressure

DISCOVER ACTIVITY

Can You Blow Up a Balloon in a Bottle?

1. Holding the neck, insert a balloon into an empty bottle. Try to blow up the balloon.
2. Now insert a straw into the bottle, next to the balloon. Keep one end of the straw sticking out of the container as shown in the photo. Try again to blow up the balloon.

Think It Over

Developing Hypotheses Did holding the straw next to the balloon make a difference? If it did, develop a hypothesis to explain why.

GUIDE FOR READING

- **What causes pressure in fluids?**
- **How does pressure change with altitude and depth?**

Reading Tip **Before you read, write down what you know about pressure. Then check how your understanding of pressure changes as you read.**

Think of the last time you heard a friend say "I'm under a lot of pressure!" Maybe she was talking about having two tests on the same day. That sort of pressure is over in a day or two. But everyone is under another kind of pressure that never lets up. This pressure, as you will learn, is due to the air that surrounds you!

What Is Pressure?

The word *pressure* is related to the word *press*. It refers to a force pushing on a surface. For example, when you lean against a wall, you push against the wall and so exert pressure on it. When you stand on the ground, the force of gravity pulls you downward. So the soles of your shoes push down on the ground and exert pressure on it.

Figure 1 Snowshoes make it easier to travel in deep snow. The woman on the right wishes she had a pair.

Force and Pressure Suppose you try to walk on top of deep snow. Most likely you will sink into the snow, much as the woman on the right in Figure 1. But if you walk with snowshoes, you will be able to walk without sinking. The downward force you exert on the snow—your weight—doesn't change. Your weight is the same whether you wear boots or snowshoes. So what's the difference?

The difference is the size of the area over which your weight is distributed. When your weight is distributed over the smaller area of the soles of your boots, you sink. When your weight is distributed over the much larger area of the snowshoes, you don't sink. The larger area results in less downward pressure on the snow under the snowshoes. So force and pressure are closely related, but they are not the same thing.

Calculating Pressure The relationship of force, area, and pressure is summarized by this formula.

$$\text{Pressure} = \frac{\text{Force}}{\text{Area}}$$

Pressure is equal to the force exerted on a surface divided by the total area over which the force is exerted. Force is measured in newtons (N). When area is measured in square meters (m^2), the SI unit of pressure is the newton per square meter (N/m^2). This unit of pressure is also called the **pascal** (Pa): $1\ N/m^2 = 1$ Pa.

A smaller unit of measure for area is often more practical to use, such as a square centimeter instead of a square meter. When square centimeters are used, the unit of pressure is N/cm^2.

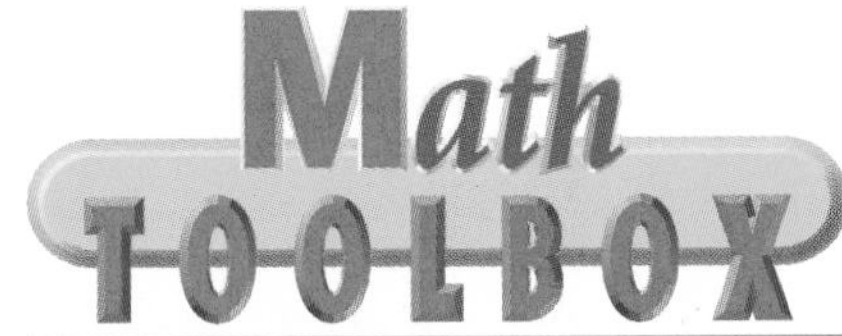

Area

Area is a measure of a surface. The area of a rectangle is found by multiplying the length by the width. The area of the rectangle below is $2\text{ cm} \times 3\text{ cm}$, or 6 cm^2.

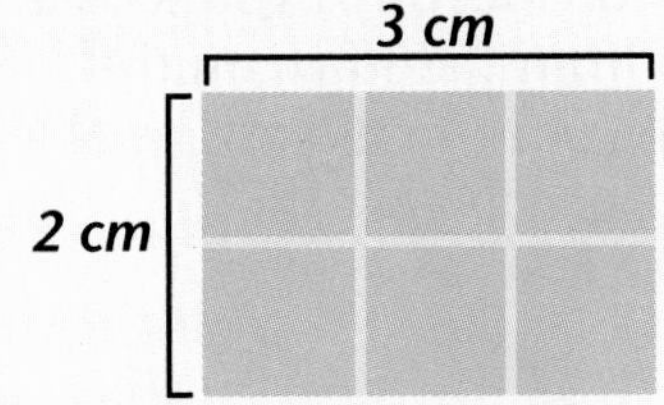

Notice that area is written as cm^2. This is read as "square centimeter."

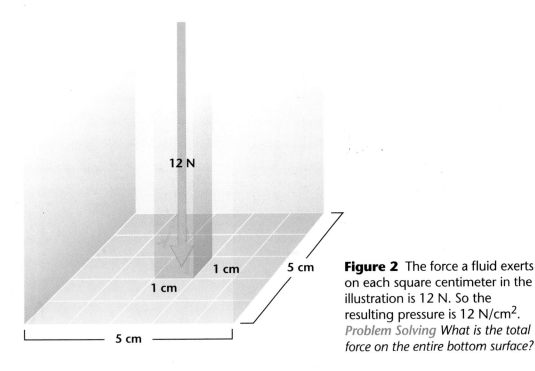

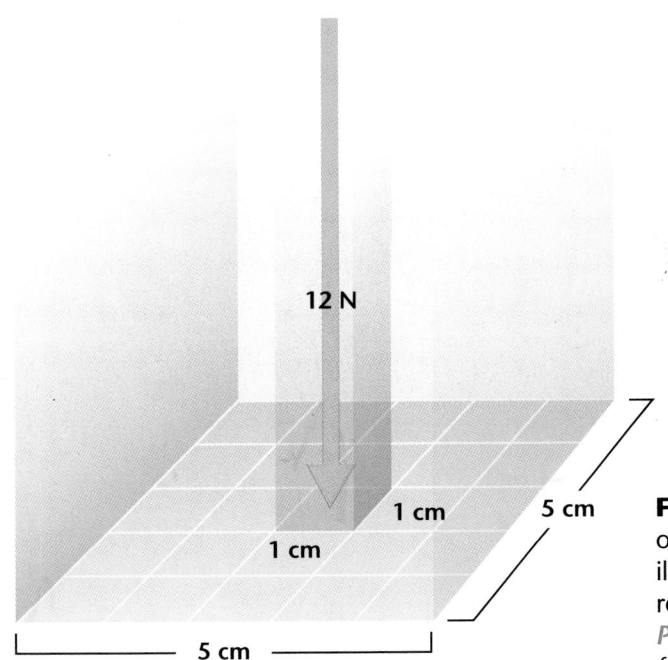

Figure 2 The force a fluid exerts on each square centimeter in the illustration is 12 N. So the resulting pressure is $12\ N/cm^2$. *Problem Solving What is the total force on the entire bottom surface?*

Sharpen your Skills

Developing Hypotheses

ACTIVITY

If you took a sip from the straw on the left, you would be able to drink the lemonade. But if you took a sip from the straw on the right, you would not be able to quench your thirst.

What is the difference between the two illustrations? What can you conclude about how you drink through a straw? Write a hypothesis that explains why you can drink through one straw and not the other.

You can produce a lower pressure by increasing the area a force acts on. Or you can work the other way around. You can produce a much higher pressure by decreasing the area a force acts on. For instance, the blades of ice skates have a very small surface area. They exert a much higher pressure on the ice than ordinary shoes would.

Fluid Pressure

In this chapter, you will learn about the pressure exerted by fluids. A **fluid** is a substance that can easily flow. As a result, a fluid is able to change shape. Both liquids and gases have this property. Air, helium, water, and oil are all fluids.

Fluids exert pressure against the surfaces they touch. To understand how fluids exert forces on surfaces, you must think about the particles that make up the fluid. Fluids, like all matter, are made up of molecules. These molecules are tiny particles that are much too small to be seen using your eyes or even a good microscope. One liter of water contains about 33 trillion trillion molecules (that's 33 followed by 24 zeros)!

In fluids, molecules are constantly moving in all directions. In air, for example, molecules are moving around at high speeds. They are constantly colliding with each other and with any surface that they meet.

As each molecule collides with a surface, it exerts a force on the surface. **All of the forces exerted by the individual molecules in a fluid add together to make up the pressure exerted by the fluid.** The number of particles is so large that you can consider the fluid as if it were not made up of individual particles. Thus fluid pressure is the total force exerted by the fluid divided by the area over which the force is exerted.

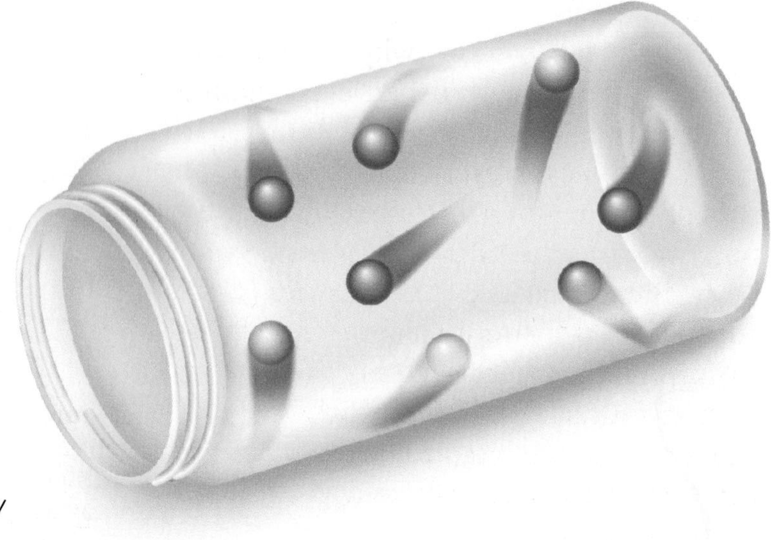

Figure 3 In a gas, molecules move at different speeds in all directions. As they hit surfaces, the molecules exert forces on those surfaces. The total force divided by the area of the surface gives the pressure of the gas. *Inferring Do you think that the pressure inside the jar is the same as the pressure outside the jar? How can you tell?*

Fluid Pressure All Around

Hold your hand out in front of you, palm up. You are holding up a weight equivalent to that of a washing machine. How can this be? You are surrounded by a fluid that presses down on you all the time. This fluid is the mixture of gases that makes up Earth's atmosphere. The pressure exerted by the air is usually referred to as air pressure, or atmospheric pressure.

Air exerts pressure because it has mass. You may forget that air has mass, but each cubic meter of air around you has a mass of about 1 kilogram. The force of gravity on this mass produces air pressure. The pressure from the weight of air in the atmosphere is great because the atmosphere is over 100 kilometers high.

Average air pressure at sea level is 10.13 N/cm^2. Think about a square measuring one centimeter by one centimeter on the palm of your hand. Air is pushing against that small square with a force of 10.13 newtons. The total surface area of your hand is probably about 100 square centimeters. So the total force due to the air pressure on your hand is about 1,000 newtons.

☑ *Checkpoint* ***Why does the atmosphere exert pressure on you?***

Balanced Pressures

How could your hand possibly support the weight of the atmosphere when you don't feel a thing? In a fluid that is not moving, pressure at a given point is exerted equally in all directions. Air is pushing down on the palm of your hand with 10.13 N/cm^2 of pressure. It is also pushing up on the back of your hand with the same 10.13 N/cm^2 of pressure. These two pressures balance each other exactly.

INTEGRATING LIFE SCIENCE So why aren't you crushed even though the air pressure outside your body is so great? The reason again has to do with a balance of pressures. Pressure inside your body balances the air pressure outside your body. But where does the pressure inside your body come from? It comes from fluids within your body. Some parts of your body, such as your lungs, sinus cavities, and your inner ear, contain air. Other parts of your body, such as your cells and your blood vessels, contain liquids.

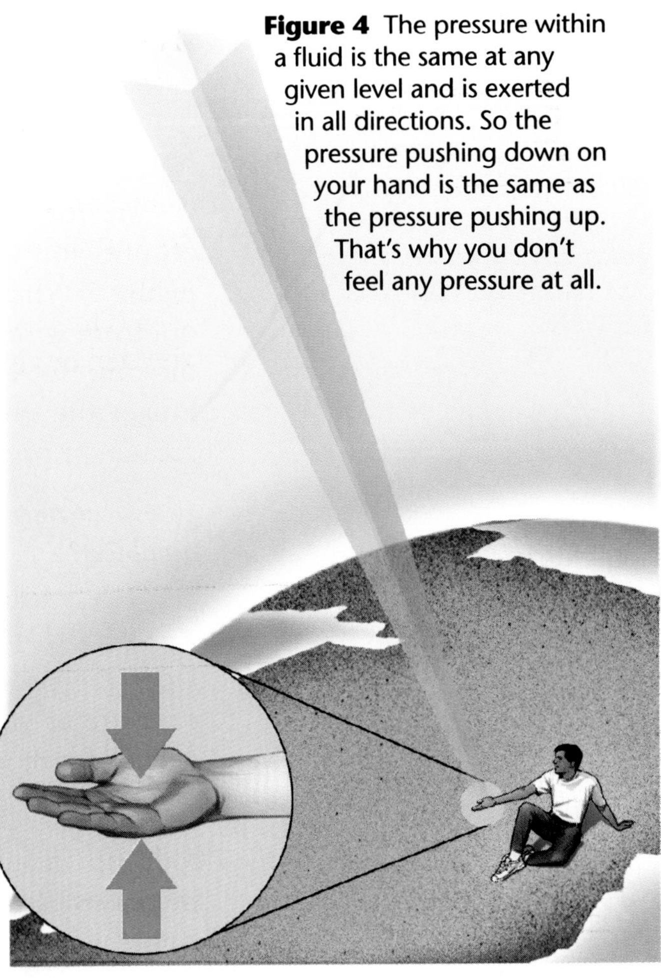

Figure 4 The pressure within a fluid is the same at any given level and is exerted in all directions. So the pressure pushing down on your hand is the same as the pressure pushing up. That's why you don't feel any pressure at all.

Figure 5 A vacuum pump removes the air from a metal can. The pump produces dramatic results in a few moments. *Inferring Can you think of a way to crush the can without pumping out the air inside it? Explain why your idea works.*

Are you still having trouble believing that the air pressure around you is so high? Take a look at the metal container in Figure 5. When the can is filled with air, the air pressure pushing out from within the can balances the air pressure pushing in on the can. But when the air is removed from the can, there is no longer the same pressure pushing from within the can. The greater air pressure outside the can crushes it.

☑ *Checkpoint* ***What is the effect of balanced pressures acting on an object?***

Variations in Fluid Pressure

Does the pressure of a fluid ever change? What happens to pressure as you move up to a higher elevation or down to a deeper depth within a fluid?

Pressure and Elevation Have your ears ever "popped" as you rode up in an elevator? **Air pressure decreases as elevation increases.** Remember that air pressure at a given point results from the weight of air above that point. At higher elevations, there is less air above and therefore less weight of air to support.

The fact that air pressure decreases as you move up in elevation explains why your ears pop. When the air pressure outside your body changes, the air pressure inside will adjust too, but more slowly. For a moment, the air pressure behind your eardrums is greater than it is outside. Your body releases this pressure with a "pop" so that the pressures are once again balanced.

Pressure and Depth Fluid pressure depends on depth. The pressure at one meter below the surface of a swimming pool is the same as the pressure one meter below the surface of a lake. But if you dive deeper into the water in either case, pressure becomes greater as you descend. The deeper you swim, the greater the pressure you feel. **Water pressure increases as depth increases.**

As with air, you can think of water pressure as being due to the weight of the water above a particular point. At greater depths, there is more water above that point and therefore more weight to support. In addition, air in the atmosphere pushes down on the water. Therefore, the total pressure at a given point beneath the water results from the weight of the water plus the weight of the air above it. In the deepest parts of the ocean, the pressure is more than 1,000 times the air pressure you experience every day.

Figure 6 The strength of the stream of water coming out of the holes in the jug depends on the water pressure at each level. *Interpreting Photos At which hole is the pressure greatest?*

Section 1 Review

1. Explain how fluids exert pressure.
2. How does air pressure change as you move farther away from the surface of Earth? Explain why it changes.
3. Why aren't deep-sea fish crushed by the tremendous pressure of the water above them?
4. **Thinking Critically Applying Concepts** Why do you think an astronaut must wear a pressurized suit in space?
5. **Thinking Critically Comparing and Contrasting** Suppose two women each have a mass of 50 kg. If one woman is wearing shoes with spiked heels and the other is wearing work boots, which one exerts more pressure on the floor with each step? Explain.

Science at Home

Fill a small plastic container—a bottle or a cup—to the brim with water. Place an index card over the entire opening of the container. Ask your family to predict what would happen if the container were turned upside down. Test the predictions by slowly turning the container upside down while holding the card in place. Let go of the card and see what happens. Without touching the card, turn the container on its side. Use air pressure to explain why the card stays in place and why the water stays in the container.

Real-World Lab

How It Works

Spinning Sprinklers

There's nothing like running through a lawn sprinkler on a hot summer day. One type of sprinkler uses the pressure of the escaping water to cause it to spin. Its operation is similar to an ancient device known as Hero's engine. Hero's engine used the pressure of escaping steam to cause a sphere to spin.

Problem

What factors affect the speed of rotation of a lawn sprinkler?

Skills Focus

making models, designing experiments, controlling variables

Materials

3 empty soda cans with tabs attached
fishing line, 30 cm
waterproof marker
wide-mouth jar or beaker
stopwatch or clock with second hand
small nail
medium nail
large nail
large basin to catch water

Procedure 

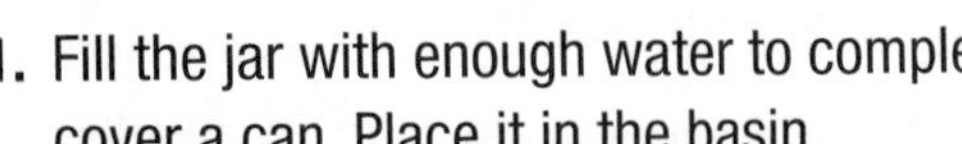

1. Fill the jar with enough water to completely cover a can. Place it in the basin.
2. Bend up the tab of a can and tie the end of a length of fishing line to it. **CAUTION:** *Be careful not to cut yourself on the edge of the can opening.*
3. Place a mark on the can to help you keep track of how many times the can spins. Copy the data table into your notebook.
4. Using the small nail, make a hole in the side of the can about 1 cm up from the bottom. Poke the nail straight in. Then twist the nail until it makes a right angle with the radius of the can. See the diagram below. **CAUTION:** *Nails are sharp and should be used only to puncture the cans.*

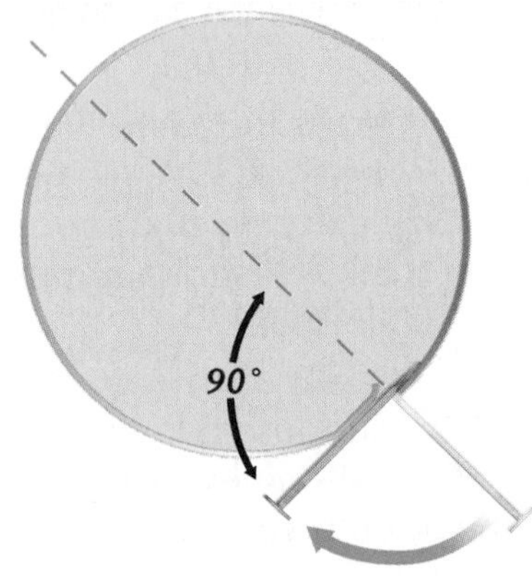

DATA TABLE

Nail Size	# of Holes	# of spins in 15 seconds
small	1	
small	2	
medium	1	
medium	2	
large	1	
large	2	

5. Submerge the can in the jar and fill the can to the top with water.
6. Quickly lift the can with the fishing line so that it is 1–2 cm above the water level in the jar. Count how many spins the can completes in 15 seconds. Record the result.
7. Design a way to investigate how the size of the hole affects the number of spins made by the can. Propose a hypothesis and then test the relationship. Record your results.
8. Design a way to investigate how the number of holes affects the number of spins made by the can. Propose a hypothesis and then test the relationship. Record your results.

Analyze and Conclude

1. How does the size of the hole affect the rate of spin of the can?
2. How does the number of holes affect the rate of spin of the can?
3. Explain the motion of the can in terms of water pressure.
4. Explain the motion of the can in terms of Newton's third law of motion (Chapter 2).
5. How could you make the can spin in the opposite direction?
6. What will cause the can to stop spinning?
7. You made a hole in the can at about 1 cm above the bottom of the can. Predict what would happen if you made the hole at a higher point on the can. How could you test your prediction?
8. **Apply** Use your observations to explain why a spinning lawn sprinkler spins.

Getting Involved

Many sprinkler systems use water pressure to spin the sprinklers. Examine one of these sprinklers to see the size, direction, and number of holes. What would happen if you put a second sprinkler in line with the first? If possible, try it.

Transmitting Pressure in a Fluid

DISCOVER — ACTIVITY

How Does Pressure Change?

1. Fill an empty two-liter plastic bottle to the top with water. Then screw on the cap tightly. There should be no bubbles in the bottle (or only very small bubbles).
2. Lay the bottle on its side. Pick a spot on the bottle, and push in with your left thumb.
3. With your right thumb, push in fairly hard on a spot at the other end of the bottle, as shown in the diagram. What does your left thumb feel?
4. Pick another spot on the bottle for your left thumb and repeat Step 3.

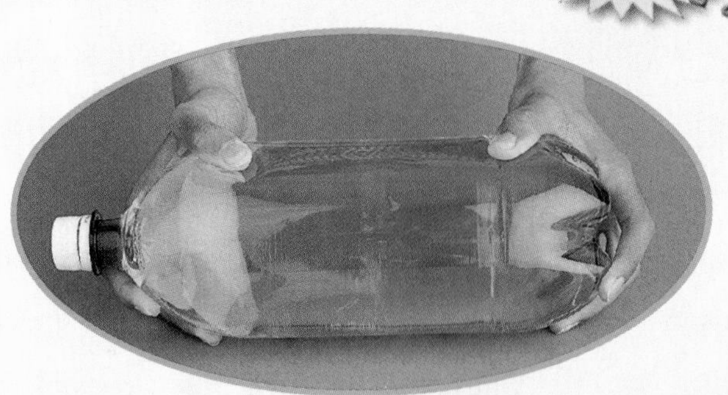

Think It Over

Observing When you push in with your right thumb, does the water pressure in the bottle increase, decrease, or remain the same? How do you know?

GUIDE FOR READING

- **What does Pascal's principle say about an increase in fluid pressure?**
- **How does a hydraulic device work?**

Reading Tip **As you read, make a list of devices that apply Pascal's principle. Write one sentence describing each device.**

Piercing sirens shatter the morning quiet. Dark smoke rolls into the air. Bright flames shoot from a burning building. Firefighters arrive on the scene. Quickly, with the push of a button, a huge ladder is raised to the top floor. The firefighters climb up the ladder and soon have the blaze under control.

Thanks to equipment on the firetruck, this story has a happy ending. You might be surprised to discover that the truck is capable of using fluids to lift the ladder and its equipment to great heights. As you read on, you'll find out how.

Figure 7 A fire truck uses fluids under high pressure both to lift its ladder and to put out a fire.

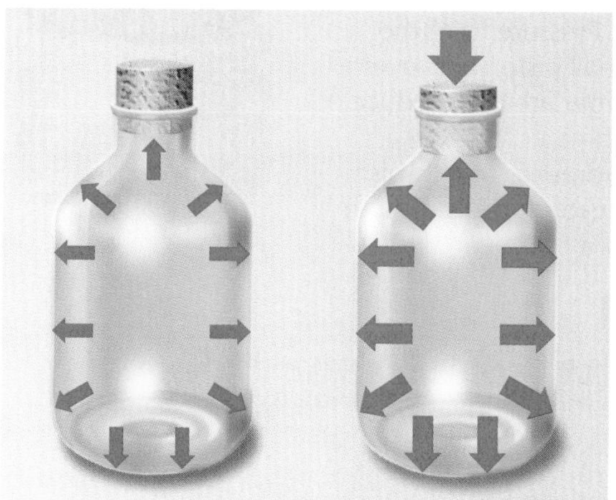

Figure 8 A liquid completely filling a bottle exerts pressure in all directions. When the stopper is pushed farther into the bottle, the pressure increases. *Predicting Suppose you poked a hole in the side of the bottle. What would happen when you pushed down on the stopper? Explain why.*

Pascal's Principle

As you learned in the last section, a fluid exerts pressure on any surface in contact with it. For example, the water in each bottle in Figure 8 exerts pressure on the entire inside surface of the bottle—up, down, and sideways.

What happens if you push the stopper down even farther? The water has nowhere to go, so it presses harder on the inside surface of the bottle. The pressure in the water increases everywhere in the bottle. This is shown by the increased width of the arrows on the right in Figure 8.

Pressure increases by the same amount throughout an enclosed, or confined, fluid. This fact was discovered in the 1600s by a French mathematician named Blaise Pascal. (Pascal's name is used for the unit of pressure.) **When force is applied to a confined fluid, an increase in pressure is transmitted equally to all parts of the fluid.** This relationship is known as **Pascal's principle.**

Force Pumps

What would happen if you increased the pressure at one end of a fluid in a container with a hole at the other end? If you have ever used a squeeze bottle or a medicine dropper, you already know what happens. Because it is not confined by the container, the fluid is pushed out of the opening. This simple example shows you how a force pump works. A force pump causes a fluid to move from one place to another by increasing the pressure in the fluid.

Your heart consists of two force pumps. One of them pumps blood to the lungs, where it can pick up oxygen from the air you breathe. This blood, now carrying oxygen, returns to your heart. It is then pumped to the rest of the body by the second pump.

☑ *Checkpoint* ***What is the effect on fluid pressure if you press down on the stopper of a bottle full of water?***

Social Studies CONNECTION

The French mathematician and philosopher Blaise Pascal lived from 1623 until 1662. He first became famous for a mechanical calculator he designed before he was 21. He later explored the behavior of fluids, and was a pioneer in the mathematics of probability. Near the end of his life, he wrote about philosophical and religious subjects.

In Your Journal

Create a time line showing when the following people lived and worked: Galileo, Archimedes, Newton, Pascal, and Bernoulli. On your time line, write a brief description of each one's work.

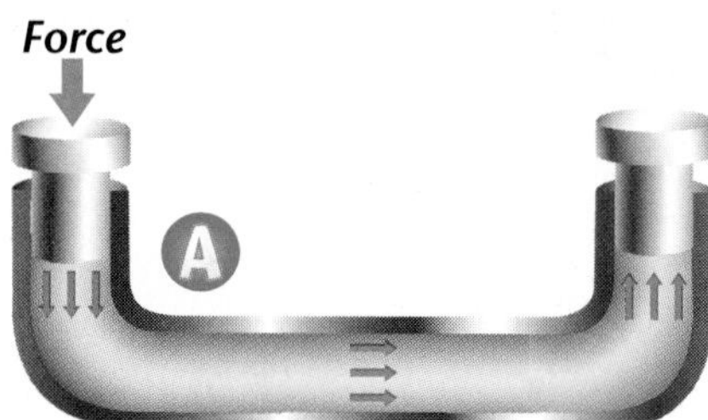

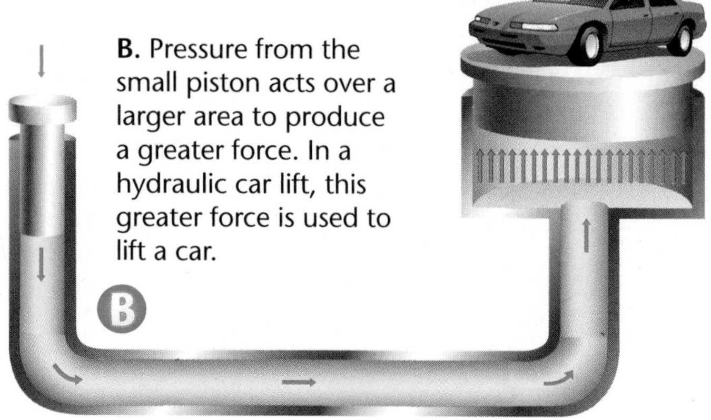

Figure 9 **A.** In a hydraulic device, a force applied to one piston increases the pressure in the fluid. **B.** Pressure from the small piston acts over a larger area to produce a greater force. In a hydraulic car lift, this greater force is used to lift a car.

Using Pascal's Principle

Suppose you fill the small U-shaped tube shown in Figure 9A with water and push down on the piston on the left side. (A piston is similar to a stopper that can slide up and down inside the tube.) The increase in pressure will be transmitted to the piston on the right.

What can you determine about the force exerted on the right piston? According to Pascal's principle, both pistons will experience the same fluid pressure. If both pistons have the same area, then they will also experience the same force.

Now suppose that the right piston has a greater area than the left piston. For example, the small piston in the U-shaped tube in Figure 9B has an area of 1 square meter. The large piston has an area of 20 square meters. If you push down on the left piston with a force of 500 newtons, the increase in pressure on the fluid is 500 N/m^2. A pressure increase of 500 N/m^2 means that the force on every square meter of the piston's surface increases by 500 newtons. Since the surface area of the right piston is 20 square meters, the total increase in force on the right piston is 10,000 newtons. The push exerted on the left piston is multiplied twenty times on the right piston! By changing the size of the pistons, you can multiply force by almost any amount you wish.

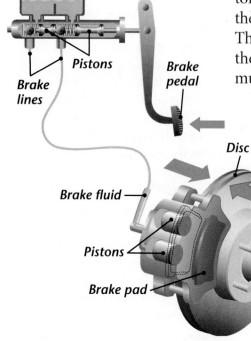

Figure 10 The hydraulic brake system of a car multiplies the force exerted on the brake pedal.

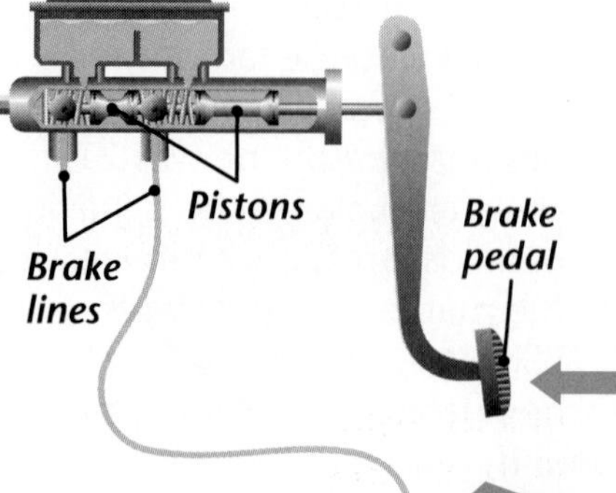

Hydraulic Systems **Hydraulic systems** are designed to take advantage of Pascal's principle. **A hydraulic system multiplies a force by applying the force to a small surface area. The increase in pressure is then transmitted to another part of a confined fluid, which pushes on a larger surface area.** In this way, the force is multiplied. A common hydraulic system is used to lift the heavy ladder on a fire truck.

You also rely on Pascal's principle every time you ride in a car. The brake system of a car is a hydraulic system. A brake system with disc brakes is shown in simplified form in Figure 10. When a driver pushes down on

Figure 11 A sea star exerts pressure on fluids in its cavities in order to move around. *Classifying* *Why are the tube feet considered part of a hydraulic device?*

the brake pedal, he or she pushes a piston. The piston exerts pressure on the brake fluid. The increased pressure is transmitted through the brake lines to pistons within the wheels of the car. Each of these pistons pushes on a brake pad. The brake pad then rubs against the brake disc, and the wheel's motion is slowed down by the force of friction. Because the brake system multiplies force, a person can stop a very large car with only a light push on the brake pedal.

Pascal's Principle in Nature The sea stars shown in Figure 11

INTEGRATING LIFE SCIENCE

use a natural hydraulic system called the water vascular system in order to move. Sea stars have rows of small suckers at the ends of their hollow tube feet. Each tube foot is filled with fluid. A valve is located at each foot. When the valve closes, the foot becomes a hydraulic container. As the sea star contracts different muscles, it changes the pressure in the fluid. The change in pressure causes the tube foot to either push down or pull up on the sucker. By the coordinated action of all of its tube feet, a sea star is able to move—even to climb straight up rock surfaces!

Section 2 Review

1. Explain Pascal's principle in your own words.
2. How does a hydraulic device multiply force?
3. What fluid is pumped by your heart?
4. **Thinking Critically** **Applying Concepts** How can you increase the force a hydraulic device produces without increasing the size of the force you apply to the small piston?
5. **Thinking Critically** **Comparing and Contrasting** How is the braking system of a car similar to the water vascular system of a sea star?

Check Your Progress

CHAPTER PROJECT 3

Experiment with various metal items in your home to see how they work as boats. Keep in mind that your designs don't have to look like real boats. Experiment with various shapes. Determine how the material and the shape relate to whether or not the boat floats or sinks. What works better: a wide but shallow boat or a narrow but deep boat? Keep a log that describes the material, the shape, and your results.

SECTION 3 Floating and Sinking

DISCOVER ACTIVITY

What Can You Measure With a Straw?

1. Cut a plastic straw to a 10-centimeter length.
2. Use a waterproof marker to make marks on the straw that are 1 centimeter apart.
3. Roll a ball of modeling clay about 1.5 centimeters in diameter. Stick one end of the straw in the clay. You have constructed a hydrometer.
4. Place the hydrometer in a glass of water. About half of the straw should remain above water. If it sinks, remove some clay. Make sure no water gets into the straw.

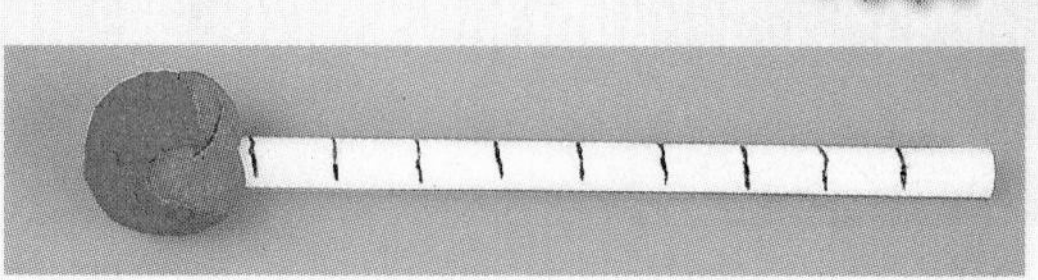

5. Dissolve 10 spoonfuls of sugar in a glass of water. Try out your hydrometer in this liquid.

Think It Over

Predicting Compare your observations in Steps 4 and 5. Then predict what will happen if you use 20 spoonfuls of sugar in a glass of water. Test your prediction.

GUIDE FOR READING

- **What is the efffect of the buoyant force?**
- **What is Archimedes' principle?**
- **How does the density of an object determine whether it floats or sinks?**

Reading Tip **As you read, write a paragraph explaining how buoyancy and Archimedes' principle are related.**

In April of 1912, the *Titanic* departed from England on its first and only voyage. It was as long as three football fields and as tall as a twelve-story building. It was the largest ship that had been built as of that time, and its furnishings were the finest and most luxurious. The *Titanic* was also the most technologically advanced ship afloat. Its hull was divided into compartments, and it was considered to be unsinkable.

Yet a few days into the voyage, the *Titanic* struck an iceberg. Two hours and forty minutes later, the bow of the great ship slipped underwater. As the stern rose high into the air, the ship broke in two. Both pieces sank to the bottom of the Atlantic Ocean. More than a thousand people died.

Figure 12 This painting shows the bow section of the *Titanic* resting on the sea floor.

How is it possible that a huge ship can float easily in water under certain conditions, and then in a few hours become a sunken wreck? And why does most of an iceberg lie hidden beneath the surface of the water? To answer these questions, you need to find out what makes an object float and what makes an object sink.

Buoyancy

If you have ever picked up an object under water, you know that it seems lighter in water than in air. Water exerts a force called the **buoyant force** that acts on a submerged object. **The buoyant force acts in the upward direction, against the force of gravity, so it makes an object feel lighter.**

As you can see in Figure 13, a fluid exerts pressure on all surfaces of a submerged object. Since the pressure in a fluid increases with depth, the upward pressure on the bottom of the object is greater than the downward pressure on the top. The result is a net force acting upward on the submerged object. This is the buoyant force.

A submerged object displaces, or takes the place of, a volume of fluid equal to its own volume. You can see this by looking at Figure 14. An object that floats on the surface of a fluid, however, displaces a smaller volume. It displaces a volume of fluid equal to the portion of the object that is submerged.

Archimedes' principle relates the amount of fluid a submerged object displaces to the buoyant force on the object. This relationship is named for its discoverer, the ancient Greek mathematician Archimedes. **Archimedes' principle states that the buoyant force on an object is equal to the weight of the fluid displaced by the object.**

☑ *Checkpoint Compare the direction of the buoyant force to the direction of the force of gravity.*

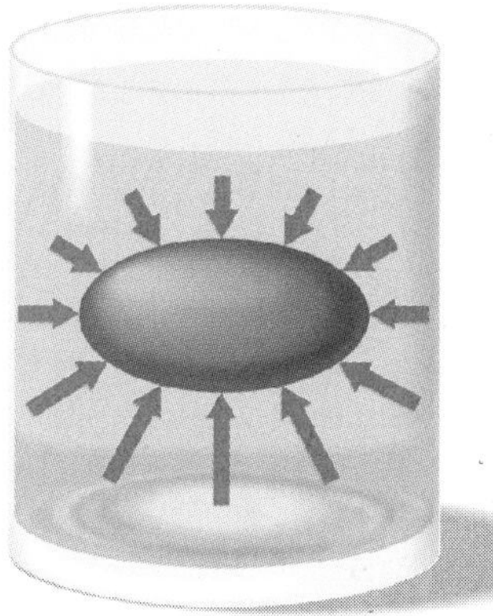

Figure 13 The pressure at the bottom of a submerged object is greater than the pressure at the top. The result is a net force in the upward direction. *Applying Concepts What is this upward force called?*

Figure 14 The volume of water displaced by an object is equal to the volume of the object. If the object floats, the volume of displaced water is equal to the volume of the portion of the object that is under water.

Measuring ACTIVITY

How can you measure an object's volume?

Measure in centimeters (cm) the length, width, and height of a wooden block. Then multiply length times width times height. The product is the volume. Volume has units of cubic centimeters (cm^3).

Skills Lab

Drawing Conclusions

Sink and Spill

In this lab, you will use data on floating objects to practice the skill of drawing conclusions.

Problem

How is the buoyant force on a floating object related to the weight of the water it displaces?

Materials

paper towels
pie pan
triple-beam balance
beaker, 600 mL
table salt
jar with watertight lid, about 30 mL
water

Procedure  

1. Preview the procedure and copy the data table into your notebook.
2. Find the mass, in grams, of a dry paper towel and the pie pan together. Multiply the mass by 0.01. This gives you the weight in newtons. Record it in your data table.
3. Place the 600-mL beaker, with the dry paper towel under it, in the middle of the pie pan. Fill the beaker to the very top with water.
4. Fill the jar about halfway with salt. (The jar and salt must be able to float in water.) Then find the mass of the dry jar (with its cover on) in grams. Multiply the mass by 0.01. Record this weight in your data table.
5. Gently lower the jar into the 600-mL beaker. (If the jar sinks, take it out and remove some salt. Repeat Steps 2, 3, and 4.) Estimate the fraction of the jar that is underwater, and record it.
6. Once all of the displaced water has been spilled, find the total mass of the paper towel and pie pan containing the water. Multiply the mass by 0.01 and record the result in your data table.
7. Empty the pie pan. Dry off the pan and the jar.
8. Repeat Steps 2 through 7 several more times. Each time fill the jar with a different amount of salt, but make sure the jar still floats.

DATA TABLE

Jar	Weight of Empty Pie Pan and Dry Paper Towel (N)	Weight of Jar, Salt, and Cover (N)	Weight of Pie Pan with Displaced Water and Paper Towel (N)	Fraction of Jar Submerged in Water	Buoyant Force (N)	Weight of Displaced Water (N)
1						
2						
3						

9. Calculate the buoyant force for each trial and record it in your data table. (*Hint:* When an object floats, the buoyant force is equal to the weight of the object.)
10. Calculate the weight of the displaced water in each case. Record it in your data table.

Analyze and Conclude

1. In each trial, the jar had a different weight. How did this affect the way that the jar floated?
2. The jar had the same volume in every trial. Why did the volume of displaced water vary?
3. What can you conclude about the relationship between the buoyant force and the weight of the displaced water?
4. Can you suggest places where errors may have been introduced?
5. **Think About It** If you put too much salt in the jar, it will sink. What can you conclude about the buoyant force in this case? How can you determine the buoyant force for an object that sinks?

Design an Experiment

How do you think your results would change if you used a different liquid that is more dense or less dense than water? Design an experiment to test your hypothesis. What liquid or liquids will you use? Will you need equipment other than what you have used for this experiment? If so, what will you need? If you carry out your new experiment, be sure to have your teacher check your design before you begin.

Figure 15 The illustration shows the forces on three different cubes. All three cubes have the same volume. *Comparing and Contrasting* *Why don't all three cubes float?*

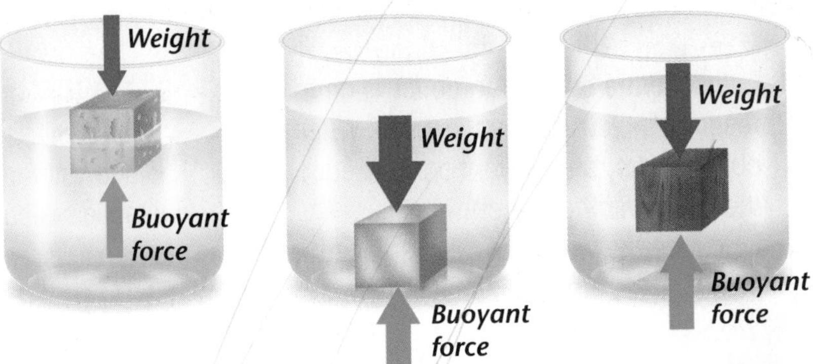

Dive! ACTIVITY

In this activity you will construct a device called a Cartesian diver.

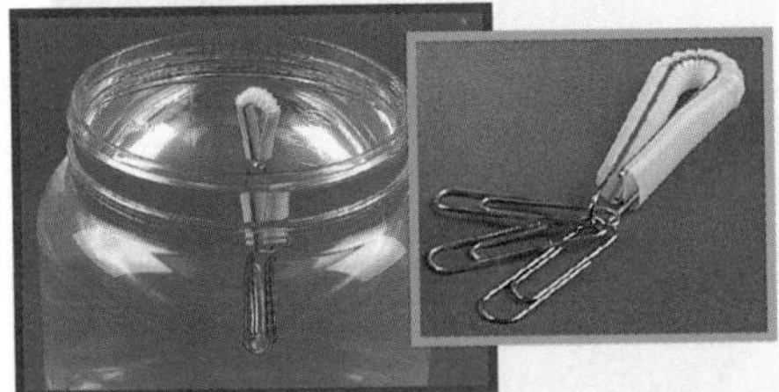

1. Bend a plastic straw into a U shape and cut the ends so that each side is about 4 cm long. Attach the ends with a paper clip.
2. Attach additional paper clips to the first paper clip. The straw should float with its top about half a centimeter above the surface. This is the diver.
3. Fill a plastic jar or bottle almost completely with water. Drop the diver in, paper clips first. Then put the lid on the jar.
4. Slowly squeeze and release the jar several times.

Drawing Conclusions Explain the behavior of the diver.

Floating and Sinking

Remember that there is always a downward force on a submerged object. That force is the weight of the object. If the weight of the object is greater than the buoyant force, the net force on a submerged object will be downward. The object will sink. If the weight of the object is less than the buoyant force, the object will begin to sink. It will only sink deep enough to displace a volume of fluid with a weight equal to its own. At that level, it will stop sinking deeper, and will float. If the weight of the object is exactly equal to the buoyant force, the two forces are balanced.

Density

Exactly why do some objects float and others sink? By comparing the density of an object to the density of a fluid, you can decide if it will float. But what is density?

The **density** of a substance is its mass per unit volume.

$$\text{Density} = \frac{\text{Mass}}{\text{Volume}}$$

For example, one cubic centimeter (cm^3) of lead has a mass of 11.3 grams, so its density is 11.3 g/cm^3.

$$\text{Density of lead} = \frac{11.3\ g}{1\ cm^3} = 11.3\ g/cm^3$$

In contrast, one cubic centimeter of cork has a mass of only about 0.25 gram. So its density is about 0.25 g/cm^3. You would say that lead is more dense than cork. The density of water is 1.0 g/cm^3, so it is less dense than lead but more dense than cork.

By comparing densities, you can explain the behavior of the objects shown in Figure 15. **An object that is more dense than the fluid in which it is immersed sinks. An object that is less dense than the fluid in which it is immersed floats to the surface.** And if the density of an object is equal to the density of the fluid in which it is immersed, the object neither rises nor sinks in the fluid. Instead it floats at a constant level.

Now you know why lead sinks: It is several times denser than water. Cork, which is less dense than water, floats. An ice cube floats in water because the density of ice is less than the density of water. But it's just a little less! So most of a floating ice cube is below the surface. Since an iceberg is really a very large ice cube, the part that you see above water is only a small fraction of the entire iceberg. This is one reason why icebergs are so dangerous to ships.

☑ *Checkpoint* ***To calculate the density of a substance, what two properties of the substance do you need to know?***

Densities of Substances Figure 16 shows several substances and their densities. Notice that liquids can float on top of other liquids. (You may have seen that salad oil floats on top of vinegar.) Notice also that the substances with the greatest densities are near the bottom of the cylinder.

Don't forget that air is also a fluid. Objects float in air if their densities are less than the density of air. A helium balloon rises because helium is less dense than air. An ordinary balloon filled with air, however, is more dense than the surrounding air because it is under pressure. So the balloon falls to the ground once you let go of it.

Changing the density of an object can make it float or sink in a given fluid. The density of a submarine, for example, is decreased when water is pumped out of its flotation tanks. The overall mass of the submarine decreases. Since its volume remains the same, its density decreases when its mass decreases. So the submarine will float to the surface. To dive, the submarine takes in water. In this way, it increases its mass (and thus its density), and sinks.

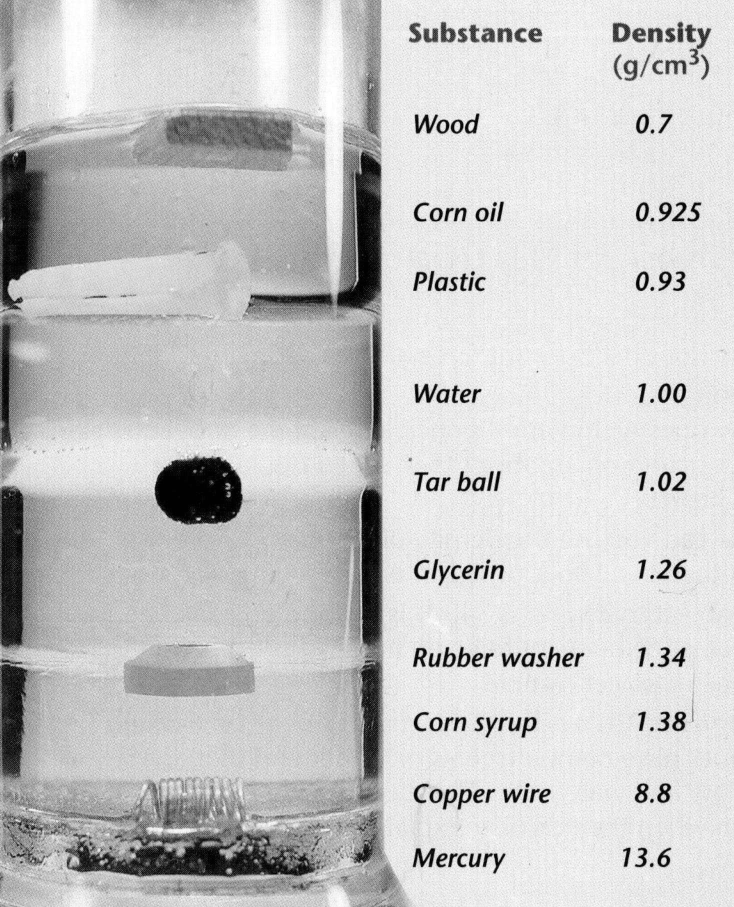

Substance	Density (g/cm^3)
Wood	*0.7*
Corn oil	*0.925*
Plastic	*0.93*
Water	*1.00*
Tar ball	*1.02*
Glycerin	*1.26*
Rubber washer	*1.34*
Corn syrup	*1.38*
Copper wire	*8.8*
Mercury	*13.6*

Figure 16 You can use density to predict whether an object will sink or float when placed in a liquid. *Interpreting Data Will a rubber washer sink or float in corn oil?*

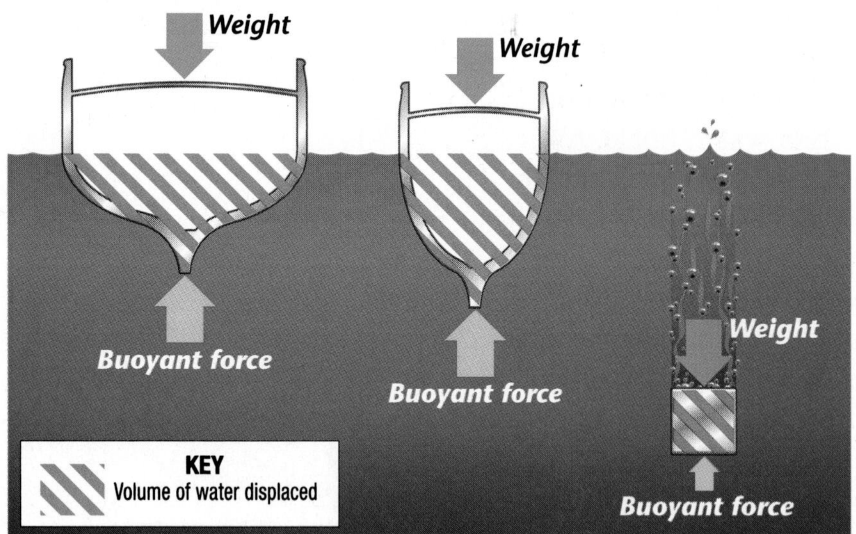

Figure 17 A solid cube of steel sinks when placed in water. A steel ship with the same weight floats.

Buoyancy and Density Another way of changing density is to change volume. In Figure 17, the amount of steel present in the three objects is the same. Yet two of the figures float, and one sinks. Solid steel sinks rapidly in water, and so will the hull of a ship that is full of water. Usually, however, the hull of a ship contains a large volume of air. This air reduces the ship's overall density, and so allows it to float.

You can explain why a ship floats not just in terms of density, but also by means of the force of buoyancy. Since the buoyant force is equal to the weight of the displaced fluid, the buoyant force will increase if more fluid is displaced. The amount of fluid displaced depends on the volume of a submerged object. A large object displaces more fluid than a small object. Therefore, the object with greater volume has a greater buoyant force acting on it—even if the objects have the same weight.

The shape of a ship causes it to displace a greater volume of water than a solid piece of steel of the same mass. The greater the volume of water displaced, the greater the buoyant force. A ship stays afloat as long as the buoyant force is greater than its weight.

Section 3 Review

1. How does the buoyant force affect a submerged object?
2. How does Archimedes' principle relate the buoyant force acting on an object to the fluid displaced by the object?
3. How can you use the density of an object to predict whether it will float or sink in water?
4. An object that weighs 340 N is floating on a lake. What is the buoyant force on it? What is the weight of the displaced water?
5. **Thinking Critically Applying Concepts** Some canoes have compartments on either end that are hollow and watertight. These canoes won't sink, even when they capsize. Explain why.

CHAPTER PROJECT 3

Check Your Progress

Don't be content with the first design that floats. Try several more, considering the characteristics that make your boat useful. How much space does your boat have for cargo? How does the weight of your boat affect the amount of cargo it can carry? (*Hint:* To measure the weight of each boat, see how many pennies will balance it on a double-pan balance.) Select your best boat and determine the number of pennies it can carry as it floats.

Applying Bernoulli's Principle

DISCOVER — ACTIVITY

Does Water Push or Pull?

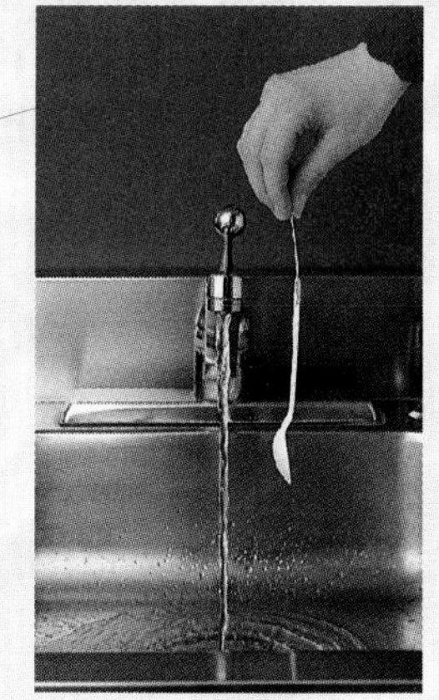

1. Hold a plastic spoon loosely by the edges of its handle so it is swinging freely between your fingers.
2. Turn on a faucet to produce a steady stream of water. Predict what will happen if you bring the curved back of the spoon into contact with the stream of water.
3. Test your prediction. Repeat the test several times.
4. Predict how your observations might change if you were to use a plastic fork instead of a spoon.
5. Test your prediction.

Think It Over

Inferring On what side of the spoon is the pressure lower? How do you know? Does the fork behave any differently from the spoon? If so, develop a hypothesis to explain why.

GUIDE FOR READING

- **How is fluid pressure related to the motion of a fluid?**

Reading Tip **Before you read, preview *Exploring Wings* and predict how you can explain flight in terms of fluid pressure.**

In December of 1903, Wilbur and Orville Wright brought an odd-looking vehicle to a deserted beach in Kitty Hawk, North Carolina. People had flown in balloons for more than a hundred years, but the Wright brothers' goal was something no one had ever done before. They flew a plane that was heavier (denser) than air! They had spent years experimenting with different wing shapes and surfaces, and they had carefully studied the flight of birds. Their first flight at Kitty Hawk lasted just 12 seconds. The plane flew 36 meters and made history.

What did the Wright brothers know about flying that allowed them to construct the first airplane? And how can the principles they used explain how a jumbo jet can fly across the country? The answer has to do with fluid pressure and what happens when a fluid moves.

Figure 18 On December 17, 1903, Wilbur Wright watched his brother Orville take off in *Flyer I*, the first successful airplane.

Bernoulli's Principle

So far in this chapter you have learned about fluids that are not moving. But what happens when a fluid, such as air or water, moves? Consider what happens if you hold a plastic spoon in a stream of running water. You might predict that the spoon would be pushed away by the water. But it is not. Surprisingly, the spoon is pushed toward the stream of water.

The behavior of the spoon demonstrates **Bernoulli's principle.** The Swiss scientist Daniel Bernoulli (bur NOO lee) found that the faster a fluid moves, the less pressure the fluid exerts. **Bernoulli's principle states that the pressure exerted by a moving stream of fluid is less than the pressure of the surrounding fluid.** The water running along the spoon is moving but the air on the other side of the spoon is not. The moving water exerts less pressure than the still air. The result is that the greater pressure of the still air on one side of the spoon pushes the spoon into the stream of water.

Similarly, if you blow above a sheet of tissue paper, the paper will rise. Moving air blown over the tissue paper exerts less pressure than the still air below the paper. The greater pressure below the paper pushes it upward.

☑ *Checkpoint* ***How is the pressure exerted by a fluid related to how fast the fluid moves?***

Objects in Flight

Bernoulli's principle is one factor that can help explain flight—from a small bird to a huge airplane. Objects can be designed so that their shapes cause air to move at different speeds above and below them. If the air moves faster above the object, pressure pushes the object upward. But if the air moves faster below the object, pressure pushes it downward. The shape of the sail of a ship is somewhat like an airplane wing. The difference in the pressure on the two sides of the sail moves the ship forward. Look through *Exploring Wings* to see how Bernoulli's principle can be applied to airplanes, birds, and race cars.

Bernoulli's Principle at Home

Bernoulli's principle can help you understand many common occurrences. For example, you can sit next to a fireplace enjoying a cozy fire thanks in part to Bernoulli's principle. Smoke rises up the chimney partly because hot air rises, and partly because it is pushed. Wind blowing across the top of a chimney lowers the air pressure there. The higher pressure at the bottom then pushes air and smoke up the chimney.

Figure 19 Thanks to Bernoulli's principle, you can enjoy an evening by a warm fireplace without having the room fill up with smoke. *Making Generalizations Why does the smoke rise up the chimney?*

EXPLORING *Wings*

Bernoulli's principle helps explain how air moving around a wing produces a force.

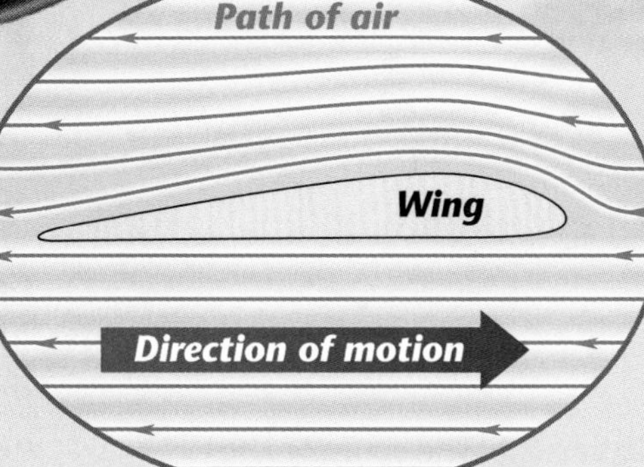

Airplane Wings

The top of this airplane wing is curved. Air that moves over the top of the wing must travel farther than air that moves along the bottom of the wing. Also, the air moving over the top moves faster and exerts less pressure than the air on the bottom. This difference in pressure creates an upward force on the wing, called lift.

Bird Wings

Like the airplane wing above, a bird's wing is curved on the top. A bird's wing is flexible, allowing it to propel the bird as well as producing lift.

Direction of motion
Spoiler
Path of air

Spoilers

The spoiler on the back of a racing car is curved on the lower side, so a spoiler is an upside-down version of the airplane wing above. The greater pressure pushing downward on a spoiler gives the car better traction from its rear wheels.

Figure 20 The spray of perfume from an atomizer is an application of Bernoulli's principle. *Applying Concepts* *Why is the perfume pushed up and out of the flask?*

Bernoulli's principle can help you understand the operation of other familiar devices. In the atomizer shown in Figure 20, you squeeze a rubber bulb. Squeezing the bulb causes air to move quickly past the top of the tube. The bottom of the tube is in the liquid in the flask. The moving air lowers the pressure at the top of the tube. The greater pressure in the flask pushes the liquid up into the tube. When the liquid reaches the air stream, the action of the air stream breaks it into small drops. The liquid comes out as a fine mist.

Section 4 Review

1. What does Bernoulli's principle say about the pressure exerted by a moving fluid?
2. Why does the air pressure above an airplane wing differ from the pressure below it? How is this pressure difference involved in flight?
3. **Thinking Critically Relating Cause and Effect** A roof is lifted off a building during a severe windstorm. Explain this in terms of Bernoulli's principle.
4. **Thinking Critically Applying Concepts** You are riding in a car on a highway when a large truck speeds by you. Explain why your car is forced toward the truck.

Science at Home

You can make your own atomizer using a straw. Cut a plastic straw part-way through. Hold one end of the straw in a glass of water and bend the other half of the straw at a right angle at the cut, as shown. Blow hard through the straw, making sure that no one is in the way! Show your device to your family. See if they know what it is and why it works. Explain the device to them in terms of Bernoulli's principle.

CHAPTER 3 STUDY GUIDE

Section 1 Pressure

Key Ideas

- Pressure is the force per unit area on a surface.
- Fluid pressure results from the motion of the atoms or molecules that make up the fluid.
- Pressure at a given level in a fluid is the same in all directions. Pressure decreases with altitude and increases with depth.

Key Terms

pressure
pascal
fluid

Section 2 Transmitting Pressure in a Fluid

Key Ideas

- According to Pascal's principle, an increase in pressure on a confined fluid is transmitted equally to all parts of the fluid.
- A hydraulic device works by transmitting an increase in pressure from one part of a confined fluid to the other. A small force exerted over a small area at one place results in a large force exerted by a larger area at another place.

Key Terms

Pascal's principle   hydraulic system

Section 3 Floating and Sinking

Key Ideas

- The upward force on an object submerged in a fluid is called the buoyant force.
- The buoyant force on an object is equal to the weight of the fluid displaced by the object. This is Archimedes' principle.
- An object will sink, rise to the surface, or stay where it is in a fluid depending on whether its density is less than, greater than, or equal to the density of the fluid.

Key Terms

buoyant force   density
Archimedes' principle

Section 4 Applying Bernoulli's Principle

INTEGRATING TECHNOLOGY

Key Idea

- The pressure in a fluid decreases as the speed of the fluid increases. This is Bernoulli's principle.

Key Term

Bernoulli's principle

Organizing Information

Flowchart Create a flowchart that shows how a hydraulic device multiplies force. (For more on flowcharts, see the Skills Handbook.)

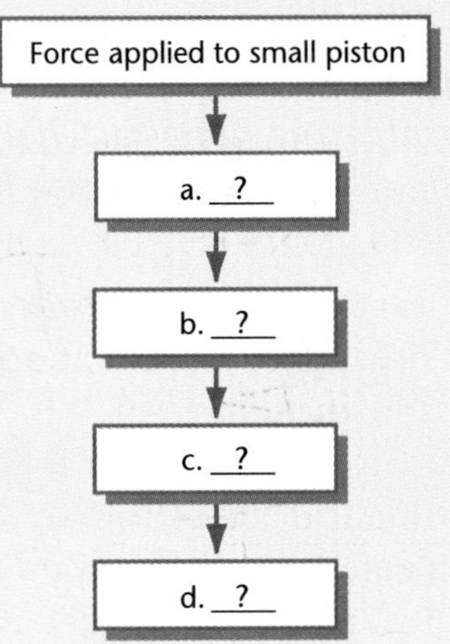

Reviewing Content

For more review of key concepts, see the Interactive Student Tutorial CD-ROM.

Multiple Choice

Choose the letter of the answer that best completes each statement.

1. Pressure can be measured in units of
   a. N. **b.** N/cm^2.
   c. N/cm. **d.** N/cm^3.
2. The operation of a hydraulic device can be explained in terms of
   a. Pascal's principle.
   b. Bernoulli's principle.
   c. Archimedes' principle.
   d. Newton's third law.
3. If the buoyant force on an object in water is greater than the object's weight, the object will
   a. sink.
   b. hover beneath the surface of the water.
   c. rise to the surface and float.
   d. be crushed by the water pressure.
4. A stone will sink in water because
   a. it is very heavy.
   b. its density is less than that of water.
   c. it has a small buoyant force on it.
   d. its density is greater than that of water.
5. Much of the lift that enables an airplane to fly can be explained using
   a. Pascal's principle.
   b. Bernoulli's principle.
   c. Archimedes' principle.
   d. Newton's first law.

True or False

If the statement is true, write true. If it is false, change the underlined word or words to make the statement true.

6. Pressure is force per unit of <u>mass</u>.
7. As you rise higher into the atmosphere, the air pressure <u>increases</u>.
8. The braking system of a car is an example of a <u>hydraulic device</u>.
9. You can determine the buoyant force on an object if you know the weight of the <u>object</u>.
10. The pressure exerted by a moving stream of fluid is <u>less than</u> the pressure exerted by the same fluid when it is not moving.

Checking Concepts

11. How does the amount of pressure you exert on the floor when you are lying down compare with the amount of pressure you exert when you are standing up?
12. You have a closed bottle of soda. The force on the bottle cap due to the carbonation of the soda is 14 N. If the area of the bottle cap is 7 cm^2, what is the pressure on the cap?
13. Name two hydraulic devices that an auto mechanic is familiar with.
14. Why do you seem to weigh more in air than you do in water?
15. Explain how Bernoulli's principle can keep a bird in the air.
16. **Writing to Learn** You have a job greeting vacationers who are learning to scuba dive. Prepare a brochure or handout explaining the pressure changes they should expect to experience as they dive. Be sure to describe the reasons for the changes.

Thinking Critically

17. **Developing Hypotheses** A sphere made of steel is put in water and, surprisingly, it floats. Develop a hypothesis to explain this observation.
18. **Applying Concepts** One method of raising a sunken ship to the surface is to inflate large bags or balloons inside its hull. Explain why this procedure could work.
19. **Designing Experiments** You have two fluids of unknown density. Suggest an experiment to determine which is denser without mixing the two fluids.
20. **Relating Cause and Effect** Your kite rises into the air as you run quickly on a windy day. Is the air pressure greater above the kite or below it? Explain your answer.

Applying Skills

Use the illustration to answer Questions 21–24. It shows an object being supported by a spring scale in and out of water.

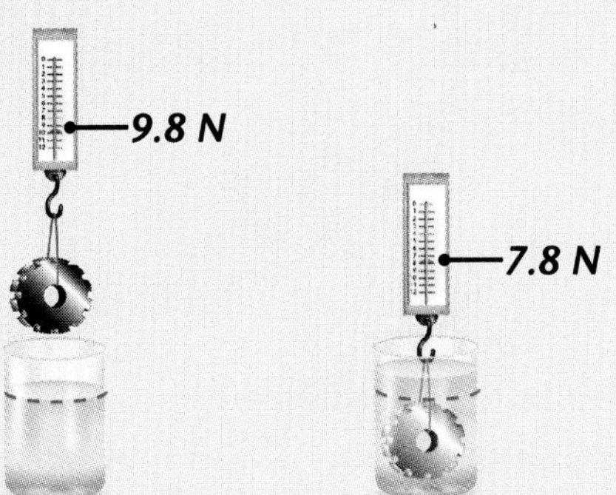

21. **Applying Concepts** Why is there a difference between the weight of the object in air and its weight in water?
22. **Calculating** What is the buoyant force on the object?
23. **Drawing Conclusions** What can you conclude about the water above the dotted line in the right half of the illustration?
24. **Predicting** If the spring scale were removed, would the object float or sink? How do you know?

Performance Assessment

Project Wrap Up Test your boat to make sure it does not leak. Then display it for the class and demonstrate how it floats. Be sure to include the diagrams you drew of the different designs you tried. Display the observations and data you recorded for each design. Point out to your classmates the features you incorporated into your final design.

Reflect and Record Suppose you had no limitations on what materials you could use for your boat. Also suppose you could form your material into any shape you choose. In your journal, sketch and describe the boat you would design.

Test Preparation

Use these questions to prepare for standardized tests.

Read the passage. Then answer Questions 25–28.

Luis has a small stone. He fills a large beaker to the top with water and places a small beaker below the spout of the large beaker. Luis drops the stone into the large beaker and it sinks to the bottom. He then notes the volume of water that spills into the small beaker.

25. What does Luis learn about the stone?
    a. its mass **b.** its volume
    c. its density **d.** its composition
26. Luis can find the buoyant force on the stone by finding the
    a. weight of the displaced water.
    b. weight of the small beaker and the displaced water.
    c. weight of the large beaker with the water and stone in it.
    d. increase in the weight of the large beaker after the stone is dropped into it.
27. What conclusion can Luis draw about the density of the stone?
    a. It is less than the density of the water.
    b. It is equal to the density of the water.
    c. It is greater than the density of the water.
    d. It depends on the initial volume of water in the large beaker.
28. Luis chips a piece off the stone and repeats his experiment. What does he notice?
    a. The density of the stone decreases.
    b. The volume of displaced water decreases.
    c. The density of the stone increases.
    d. The volume of displaced water increases.

4 Work and Machines

WEB ACTIVITY www.phschool.com

What Is Work?

Discover What Happens When You Pull at an Angle?
Sharpen Your Skills Inferring

Mechanical Advantage and Efficiency

Discover Is It a Machine?
Try This Going Up
Skills Lab Seesaw Science

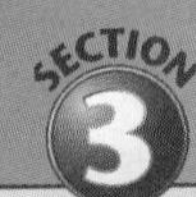

Simple Machines

Discover How Can You Increase Your Force?
Try This Modeling a Screw
Sharpen Your Skills Classifying
Real-World Lab Angling for Access

PROJECT 4

The Nifty Lifting Machine

For thousands of years, machines have helped people do work. Whether a person is using a diesel-powered crane to unload a lumber truck, or a shovel to dig in the garden, any task is made easier by using machines. Even complex machines such as automobiles accomplish a given task by combining the action of many simple machines.

In this chapter, you will learn about the different types of machines and how you use them in your daily life. As you work through this chapter, you will build your own lifting machine and demonstrate it at work.

Your Goal To use a combination of at least two simple machines to build a machine that can lift a 600-gram soup can 5 centimeters.

Your machine must

- consist of at least two simple machines working in combination
- use another soup can gradually filled with sand as the input force
- be built following the safety guidelines in Appendix A

Get Started Brainstorm with your classmates ideas for different designs of machines. Discuss possible materials that might be useful for constructing each machine.

Check Your Progress You'll be working on the project as you study this chapter. To keep your project on track, look for Check Your Progress boxes at the following points.

Section 1 Review, page 109: Determine the amount of work your machine must do.

Section 3 Review, page 128: Analyze factors affecting efficiency and mechanical advantage, and construct your machine.

Wrap Up At the end of the chapter (page 137), demonstrate your machine.

Horses or oxen would once have done the work of this machine.

Integrating Life Science

SECTION 4 **Machines in the Human Body**

Discover **Are You an Eating Machine?**

SECTION 1

What Is Work?

DISCOVER ACTIVITY

What Happens When You Pull at an Angle?

1. Fill a mug half full with water.
2. Cut a rubber band so that you have a medium-weight piece of elastic. Loop the elastic through the handle of the mug. You can pull on the elastic to move the mug at constant speed across a table.
3. You can hold the two halves of elastic parallel to each other or at an angle to each other as shown. Predict which way will be more effective in moving the mug.
4. Pull on the elastic both ways. Observe any differences.

Think It Over

Developing Hypotheses Which of the two pulls was more effective in moving the mug? Can you explain why? What do you think would happen if you increased the angle?

GUIDE FOR READING

- **When is work done on an object?**
- **How do you calculate the work done on an object?**

Reading Tip **Before you read, preview the headings and turn them into questions. As you read, write brief answers to the questions.**

After a heavy snowstorm, a neighbor's car gets stuck in a snowdrift. You shovel some snow away from the car, and then try to push it backward. The spinning tires whine as the driver attempts to move. Although you try as hard as you can, the car just won't budge. After 10 minutes of strenuous pushing, you are nearly exhausted. Unfortunately, the car is still lodged in the snow. That was sure hard work, wasn't it? You exerted a lot of force. You did some work shoveling the snow. But you might be surprised to discover that in scientific terms you didn't do any work at all on the car!

The Meaning of Work

In science you do **work** on an object when you exert a force on the object that causes the object to move some distance. If you push a child on a swing, for example, you are doing work on the child. If you pull your books out of your

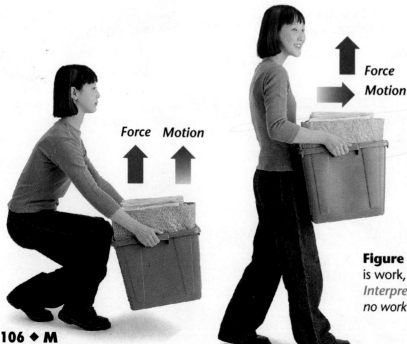

Figure 1 Lifting a bin full of newspapers is work, but carrying the bin is not. *Interpreting Photos Why does the girl do no work when she carries the bin?*

book bag, you do work on the books. If you lift a bag of groceries out of a shopping cart, you do work on the bag of groceries.

No Work Without Motion So why didn't you do work when trying to push the car out of the snow? The car didn't move. **In order for you to do work on an object, the object must move some distance as a result of your force.** If the object does not move, no work is done no matter how much force is exerted.

There are many situations in which you exert a force but don't do any work. Suppose, for example, you are asked to hold a piece of wood while you are helping on a construction project. You definitely exert a force to hold the wood in place, so it might seem as if you do work. But because the force you exert does not make the wood move, you are not doing any work on it.

Figure 2 You may be making a great effort, but if the car doesn't move, you do no work.

Only Force in the Same Direction How much work do you do when you carry your heavy books to school? You may think you do a lot of work, but actually you don't. **In order to do work on an object, the force you exert must be in the same direction as the object's motion.** When you carry an object at constant velocity, you exert an upward force to hold the object so that it doesn't fall to the ground. The motion of the object, however, is in the horizontal direction. Since the force is vertical and the motion is horizontal, you don't do any work on the object as you carry it.

How much work do you do when you pull a sled? When you pull a sled, you pull on the rope at an angle to the ground. Therefore your force has both a horizontal part (to the right in Figure 3) and a vertical part (upward). When you pull this way, only part of your force does work—the part in the same direction as the motion of the sled. The rest of your force does not help pull the sled forward.

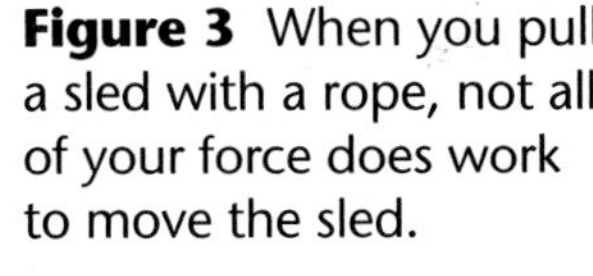

Figure 3 When you pull a sled with a rope, not all of your force does work to move the sled.

Inferring

ACTIVITY

You do work when you drag your family's trash cans out to the curb. You exert a force and the trash cans move. Does this mean that work is always done on an object if the object is moving? Recall how a satellite orbits Earth. Is work done on the satellite as it orbits? Draw a diagram to support your answer.

If you did the Discover activity, you know that your effort will be more effective when you reduce the angle at which you push or pull an object. That is, exert as much of your force as possible in the direction of the object's motion. Keep this in mind the next time you rake a pile of leaves or vacuum a floor.

Checkpoint ***How can you determine if work is done on an object?***

Calculating Work

Which do you think involves more work: exerting a force of 100 N to lift a potted tree a meter off the ground or exerting a force of 200 N to lift a heavier tree to the same height? Is it more work to lift a tree from the ground to a wheelbarrow or from the ground to the top story of a building? Your common sense may suggest that lifting a heavier object, which demands a greater force, requires more work than lifting a lighter object. Also, moving an object a greater distance requires more work than moving the object a shorter distance. Both of these are true.

The amount of work you do depends on both the amount of force you exert and the distance the object moves:

$$\text{Work} = \text{Force} \times \text{Distance}$$

The amount of work done on an object can be determined by multiplying force times distance.

Sample Problem

To help rearrange the furniture in your classroom, you exert a force of 20 N to push a desk 10 m. How much work do you do?

Analyze. You know the force exerted on the desk and the distance the desk moved. You want to find the amount of work done. Draw a diagram similar to the one shown to help you.

Write the formula. $\text{Work} = \text{Force} \times \text{Distance}$

Substitute and solve. $\text{Work} = 20\ \text{N} \times 10\ \text{m}$

$\text{Work} = 200\ \text{N}\cdot\text{m}$, which is 200 J

Think about it. The answer tells you that the work you do on the desk is 200 J.

Force = 20 N

Distance = 10 m

Practice Problems

1. A hydraulic lift exerts a force of 12,000 N to lift a car 2 m. How much work is done on the car?
2. You exert a force of 0.2 N to lift a pencil off the floor. How much work do you do if you lift it 1.5 m?

When force is measured in newtons and distance is measured in meters, the SI unit of work is the newton × meter (N•m). This unit is also called a joule (JOOL) in honor of James Prescott Joule, a physicist who studied work in the middle 1800s. One **joule** (J) is the amount of work you do when you exert a force of 1 newton to move an object a distance of 1 meter.

With the work formula, you can compare the amount of work you do to lift the trees. When you lift an object at constant speed, the upward force you exert must be equal to the object's weight. To lift the first tree, you would have to exert a force of 100 newtons. If you were to raise it 1 meter, you would do 100 newtons × 1 meter, or 100 joules of work. To lift the heavier tree, you would have to exert a force of 200 newtons. So the amount of work you do would be 200 newtons × 1 meter, or 200 joules. Thus you do more work to move the heavier object.

Now think about lifting the tree higher. You did 100 joules of work lifting it 1 meter. Suppose an elevator lifted the same tree to the top floor of a building 40 meters tall. The elevator would exert the same force on the tree for a greater distance. The work done would be 100 newtons × 40 meters, or 4,000 joules. The elevator would do 40 times as much work as you did.

Figure 4 These students are doing work as they transplant a tree. *Inferring How much work would they do if the tree weighed twice as much? If they had to lift it four times as far?*

Section 1 Review

1. If you exert a force, do you always do work? Explain your answer.
2. What is the formula for calculating work?
3. Compare the amount of work done when a force of 2 N moves an object 3 meters with the work done when a force of 3 N moves an object 2 meters.
4. **Thinking Critically Applying Concepts** You need to move five large cans of paint from the basement to the second floor of a house. Will you do more work on the cans of paint if you take them up all at once (if possible) or if you take them up individually? Explain.

CHAPTER PROJECT 4

Check Your Progress

Determine the amount of work that your machine must do to lift a 600-g soup can 5 cm. Draw a diagram showing the forces involved and the direction of those forces. Jot down some suggestions for accomplishing this work. Brainstorm with classmates about what materials you could use to build your machine.

Section 2 Mechanical Advantage and Efficiency

Discover Activity

Is It a Machine?

1. Your teacher will give you an assortment of objects. Examine each object closely.
2. Sort the objects into those that you think are machines and those you think are not machines.
3. Determine how each object that you have identified as a machine functions. Explain each object to another student.

Think It Over

Forming Operational Definitions Why did you decide certain objects were machines while other objects were not?

Guide for Reading

- **How do machines make work easier?**
- **What is the difference between actual and ideal mechanical advantage?**
- **How can you calculate the efficiency of a machine?**

Reading Tip **As you read, use the headings to make an outline showing what machines do.**

A truckload of mulch for your new garden has just arrived. The only problem is that the pile of mulch has been dumped 10 meters from where it belongs. What can you do? You could move the mulch by handfuls, but that would take a very long time. You could use a shovel and a wheelbarrow, which would make the job much easier. Or you could have a bulldozer move it. That would make the job easier still.

What Is a Machine?

Shovels and bulldozers are examples of machines. A **machine** is a device with which you can do work in a way that is easier or more effective. You may be used to thinking of machines as complex gadgets that run on electricity, but a machine can be as simple as a shovel or even a ramp.

Perhaps you think that a machine decreases the amount of work that is done. But it doesn't. Moving the pile of mulch, for example, will involve the same amount of work no matter how you do it. Similarly, you have to do the same amount of work to lift a piano whether you lift it by hand or push it up a ramp.

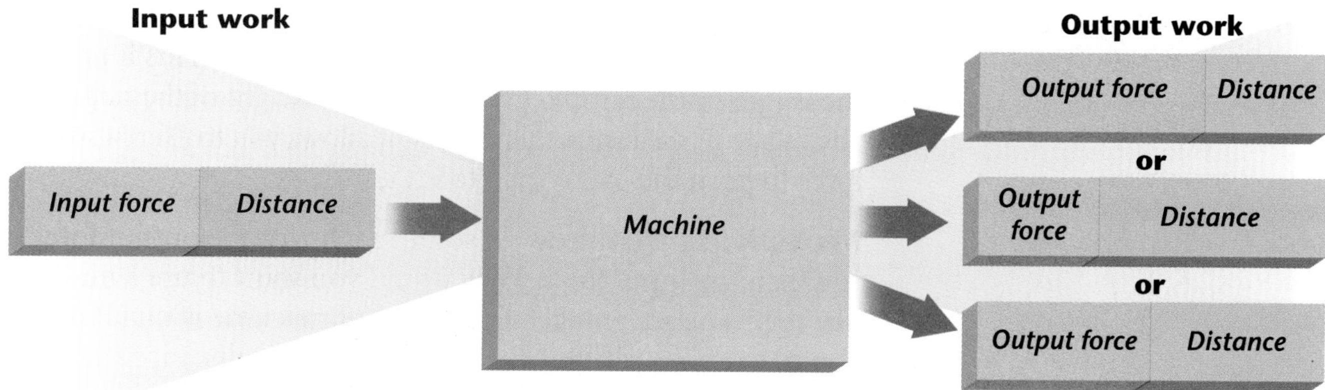

Figure 5 A machine can make a task easier in one of three ways. *Interpreting Diagrams How does the output force compare to the input force in each type of machine?*

What the shovel and the ramp do is to change the way in which you do the work. **A machine makes work easier by changing the amount of force you exert, the distance over which you exert your force, or the direction in which you exert your force.** You might say that a machine makes work easier by multiplying either force or distance, or by changing direction.

When you do work with a machine, you exert a force over some distance. For example, you exert a force on the handle when you use a shovel to lift mulch. The force you exert on the machine is called the **input force,** or sometimes the effort force. The machine then does work, by exerting a force over some distance. The shovel, in this case, exerts a force to lift the mulch. The force exerted by the machine is called the **output force.** Sometimes the term resistance force is used instead, because the machine must overcome some resistance.

Multiplying Force In some machines, the output force is greater than the input force. How can you exert a smaller force than is necessary for a job if the amount of work is the same? Remember the formula for work: Work = Force × Distance. If the amount of work stays the same, a decrease in force must mean an increase in distance. So if a machine allows you to use less force to do some amount of work, you must apply the input force over a greater distance. In the end, you do as much work with the machine as you would without the machine, but the work is easier to do.

What kind of device might allow you to exert a smaller force over a longer distance? Think about a ramp. Suppose you have to lift a piano onto the stage in your school auditorium. You could try to lift it vertically, or you could push it up a ramp.

Figure 6 The input force exerted on the shovel is greater than the output force exerted by the shovel.

If you use the ramp, the distance over which you must exert your force is greater than if you lift the piano directly. This is because the length of the ramp is greater than the height of the stage. The advantage of the ramp, then, is that it allows you to exert a smaller force to push the piano than to lift it.

Multiplying Distance In some machines, the output force is less than the input force. Why would you want to use a machine like this? The advantage of this kind of machine is that it allows you to exert your input force over a shorter distance than you would without the machine. For you to apply a force over a shorter distance, you need to apply a greater force.

When do you use this kind of machine? Think about taking a shot with a hockey stick. You move your hands a short distance, but the other end of the stick moves a greater distance to hit the puck. The hockey puck moves much faster than your hands. What happens when you fold up a sheet of paper and wave it back and forth to fan yourself? You move your hand a short distance, but the other end of the paper moves a longer distance to cool you off on a warm day. And when you ride a bicycle in high gear, you apply a large force to the pedals over a short distance. The bicycle, meanwhile, moves a much longer distance.

Changing Direction Some machines don't multiply either force or distance. What could be the advantage of these machines? Well, think about raising the sail in Figure 7. You could raise the sail by climbing the mast of the boat and pulling up on the sail with a rope. But it is much easier to stand on the deck and pull down than to lift up. By running a rope through the top of the mast as shown, you can raise the sail by pulling down on the rope. This rope system is a machine that makes your job easier by changing the direction in which you exert your force.

☑ *Checkpoint* ***What are three ways in which a machine can make work easier?***

Figure 7 One, two, three, pull! Up goes the sail. This sailor pulls down on the rope in order to hoist the sail into position. *Applying Concepts Why is the rope system considered a machine?*

Figure 8 Chop, chop, chop. A knife is a machine that makes your work easier when you prepare a tasty meal.

Mechanical Advantage

If you compare the input force to the output force, you can determine the advantage of using a machine. **A machine's mechanical advantage is the number of times a force exerted on a machine is multiplied by the machine.** Finding the ratio of output force to input force gives you the **mechanical advantage** of a machine.

$$\text{Mechanical advantage} = \frac{\text{Output force}}{\text{Input force}}$$

Mechanical Advantage of Multiplying Force For a machine that multiplies force, the mechanical advantage is greater than 1. That is because the output force is greater than the input force. For example, consider a manual can opener. If you exert a force of 20 newtons on the opener, and the opener exerts a force of 60 newtons on a can, the mechanical advantage of the can opener is 60 newtons ÷ 20 newtons, or 3. The can opener tripled your force! Or suppose you would have to exert 3,200 newtons to lift a piano. If you use a ramp, you might need to exert only 1,600 newtons. The mechanical advantage of this ramp is 3,200 newtons ÷ 1,600 newtons, or 2. The ramp doubles the force that you exert.

Mechanical Advantage of Multiplying Distance For a machine that multiplies distance, the output force is less than the input force. So in this case, the mechanical advantage is less than 1. If, for example, you exert an input force of 20 newtons and the machine produces an output force of 10 newtons, the mechanical advantage is 10 newtons ÷ 20 newtons, or 0.5. The output force of the machine is half your input force, but the machine exerts that force over a longer distance.

Mechanical Advantage of Changing Direction What can you predict about the mechanical advantage of a machine that changes the direction of the force? If only the direction changes, the input force will be the same as the output force. The mechanical advantage will be 1.

Going Up ACTIVITY

Does a rope simply turn your force upside down? Find out!

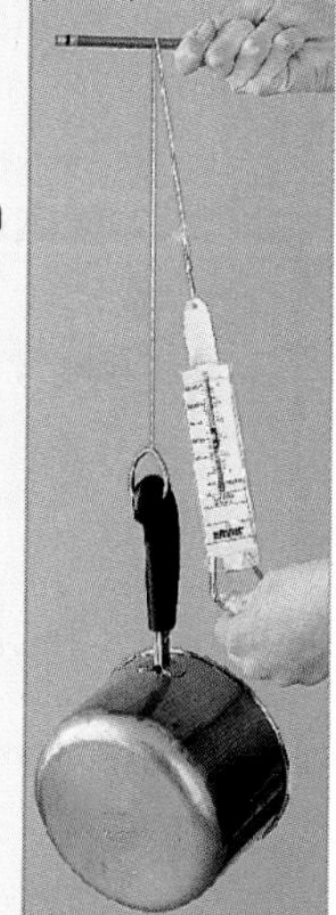

1. Tie a piece of string about 50 cm long to an object, such as an empty cooking pot. Make a small loop on the other end of the string.
2. Using a spring scale, slowly lift the pot 20 cm. Note the reading on the scale.
3. Now loop the string over a pencil and pull down on the spring scale to lift the pot 20 cm. Predict the reading on the scale. Were you correct?

Developing Hypotheses How did the readings on the spring scale compare? If the readings were different, suggest a reason why. What might be an advantage to using this system?

Efficiency of Machines

So far you have learned that the work you put into a machine (input work) is exactly equal to the work done by the machine (output work). In an ideal situation, this is true. In real situations, however, the output work is always less than the input work. If you have ever tried to cut something with scissors that barely open and close, you know that a large part of your work is wasted overcoming the tightness, or friction, between the parts of the scissors.

In any machine, some work is wasted overcoming friction. The less friction there is, the closer the output work is to the input work. The **efficiency** of a machine compares the output work to the input work. Efficiency is expressed as a percent. The higher the percent, the more efficient the machine is.

If the tight scissors described above have an efficiency of 60%, a little more than half of the work you do goes into cutting the paper. The rest is wasted overcoming the friction in the scissors. A machine that has an efficiency of 95% loses very little work. An ideal machine would have an efficiency of 100%.

You cut the lawn with a hand lawn mower. You do 250,000 J of work to move the mower. If the work done by the mower in cutting the lawn is 200,000 J, what is the efficiency of the lawn mower?

Analyze. You are given the input work and the output work. You are asked to find the efficiency.

Write the formula.

$$\text{Efficiency} = \frac{\text{Output work}}{\text{Input work}} \times 100\%$$

Substitute and solve.

$$\text{Efficiency} = \frac{200{,}000}{250{,}000} \times 100\%$$

$$\text{Efficiency} = 0.8 \times 100\% = 80\%$$

Think about it. An efficiency of 80% means that 80 out of every 100 joules of work went into cutting the lawn. This answer makes sense, because most of the input work is converted to output work.

Practice Problems

1. You do 1,500 J of work in using a hammer. The hammer does 825 J of work on a nail. What is the efficiency of the hammer?
2. Suppose you left your lawn mower outdoors all winter. It's now rusty. Of your 250,000 joules of work, only 100,000 go to cutting the lawn. What is the efficiency of the lawn mower now?

Calculating Efficiency If you know the input work and output work for a machine, you can calculate a machine's efficiency. **To calculate the efficiency of a machine, divide the output work by the input work and multiply the result by 100 percent.** This is summarized by the following formula.

INTEGRATING MATHEMATICS

$$\text{Efficiency} = \frac{\text{Output work}}{\text{Input work}} \times 100\%$$

Actual and Ideal Mechanical Advantage The mechanical advantage that a machine provides in a real situation is called the **actual mechanical advantage.** You can only determine the actual mechanical advantage by measuring the true input and output forces. It cannot be determined in advance because the actual values depend on the efficiency of the machine.

You cannot predict the actual mechanical advantage of a machine. But you can predict a quantity related to the actual mechanical advantage if you ignore losses due to friction. In other words, you can consider the machine under ideal conditions. **The mechanical advantage of a machine without friction is called the ideal mechanical advantage of the machine.** The more efficient a machine is, the closer the actual mechanical advantage is to the **ideal mechanical advantage.** By keeping a machine clean and well lubricated, you can make its operation closer to the ideal. In this way you can increase the machine's efficiency and make your own work easier.

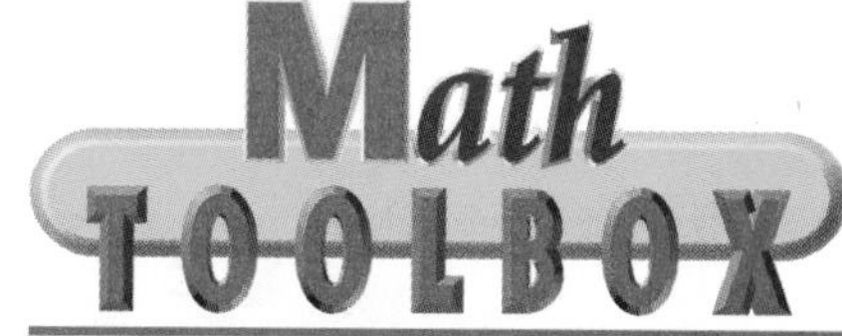

Percents

When you compare a number to 100, you are finding a percent. For example, 25 out of 100 can be written as 25 ÷ 100 or 25%.

Any ratio can be written as a percent by multiplying the fraction by 100 ÷ 1 and expressing the answer with a percent symbol. For example,

$$\frac{11}{20} \times \frac{100}{1} = 55\%$$

$$\frac{3}{4} \times \frac{100}{1} = 75\%$$

The efficiency of a machine is compared to an ideal machine, which would be 100% efficient.

Section 2 Review

1. Explain how machines make work easier if they do not decrease the amount of work you need to do.
2. Why is the actual mechanical advantage of a machine different from a machine's ideal mechanical advantage?
3. What do you need to know to calculate the efficiency of a machine?
4. Can a machine increase both force and distance? Explain why or why not.
5. **Thinking Critically Comparing and Contrasting** Make a comparison table for two machines: one that increases force and one that increases distance. For each machine, compare input and output force, input and output distance, and input and output work.

Science at Home

Have a family member examine a hand-powered device around your home. You might pick a hand tool such as a shovel, hammer, or screwdriver, or a kitchen utensil such as a knife or egg beater. Explain the idea of input and output forces. Then have him or her identify the input and output forces for the device you picked.

Skills Lab

Controlling Variables

Seesaw Science

In this lab, you will use the skill of controlling variables as you investigate the properties of seesaws.

Problem

What is the relationship between distance and weight for a balanced seesaw?

Materials

meter stick
masking tape
28 pennies, post-1982
small object, mass about 50 g
dowel or other cylindrical object for pivot point, about 10 cm long and 3 cm in diameter

Procedure

1. Begin by using the dowel and meter stick to build a seesaw. Tape the dowel firmly to the table so that it does not roll.
2. Choose the meter stick mark that will rest on the dowel from the following: 55 cm or 65 cm. Record your choice. Position your meter stick so that it is on your chosen pivot point with the 100-cm mark on your right.
3. Slide the 50-g mass along the shorter end of the meter stick until the meter stick is balanced, with both sides in the air. (This is called "zeroing" your meter stick.)
4. Copy the data table into your notebook.
5. Place a stack of 8 pennies exactly over the 80-cm mark. Determine the distance, in centimeters, from the pivot point to the pennies. Record this distance in the "Distance to Pivot" column for the right side of the seesaw.
6. Predict where you must place a stack of 5 pennies in order to balance the meter stick. Test your prediction and record the actual position in the "Position of Pennies" column for the left side of the seesaw.

DATA TABLE

Your group's pivot point position: _____ cm

Trial #	Side of Seesaw	# of Pennies or Weight of Pennies (pw)	Position of Pennies (cm)	Distance to Pivot (cm)	Weight of Pennies × Distance
1	right				
	left				
2	right				
	left				
3	right				

7. Determine the distance, in centimeters, from the pivot point to the left stack of pennies. Record this distance in the "Distance to Pivot" column for the left side of the seesaw.
8. If you use an imaginary unit of weight, the pennyweight (pw), then one penny weighs 1 pw. Multiply the weight of each stack of pennies by the distance to the pivot point. Record the result in the last column of the data table.
9. Predict how the position of the pennies in Step 6 would change if you used 7, 12, 16, and 20 pennies instead of 5 pennies. Test your predictions.

Analyze and Conclude

1. In this experiment, what is the manipulated variable? The responding variable? How do you know which is which?
2. As you increase the number of pennies on the right, what happens to the distance at which you must place the stack in order to balance the meter stick?

3. What conclusion can you draw about the relationship between distances and weights needed to balance a seesaw?
4. Why was it important to zero the meter stick with the 50-g mass?
5. Compare your results with the other groups. How do different positions of the pivot point affect the results?
6. **Think About It** Name two other variables that could be manipulated in this experiment.

Design an Experiment

Suppose you have a seesaw with a movable pivot. You want to use it with a friend who weighs half what you weigh. You and your friend want to sit on the two ends of the seesaw. Make a hypothesis about where you should position the pivot point. Explain how you could modify the pennies experiment to see if you are right.

SECTION 3 Simple Machines

DISCOVER ACTIVITY

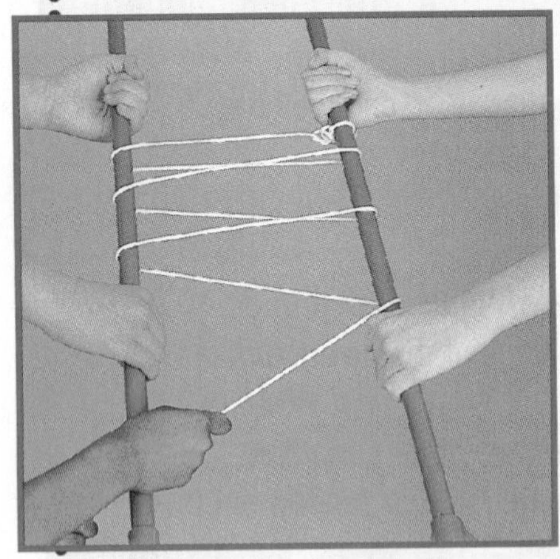

How Can You Increase Your Force?

1. Working with two partners, wrap a rope around two broomsticks as shown.
2. Your two partners should try to hold the brooms apart with the same amount of force throughout the activity. For safety, they should hold firmly, but not with all their strength.
3. Try to pull the two students together by pulling on the broomsticks. Can you do it?
4. Can you pull them together by pulling on the rope?

Think It Over

Predicting What do you think will be the effect of wrapping the rope around the broomstick several more times?

GUIDE FOR READING

- What are the six kinds of simple machines?
- How can you calculate the mechanical advantage of simple machines?

Reading Tip As you read, make a list of the six kinds of simple machines. Describe each one in your own words.

Look at the objects shown on these pages. Which of them would you call machines? Would it surprise you to find out that each is an example of a simple machine? As you learned in the last section, a machine helps you do work by changing the amount or direction of the force you need to apply.

There are six basic kinds of simple machines: the inclined plane, the wedge, the screw, the lever, the wheel and axle, and the pulley. In this section you will learn how the different types of simple machines help you.

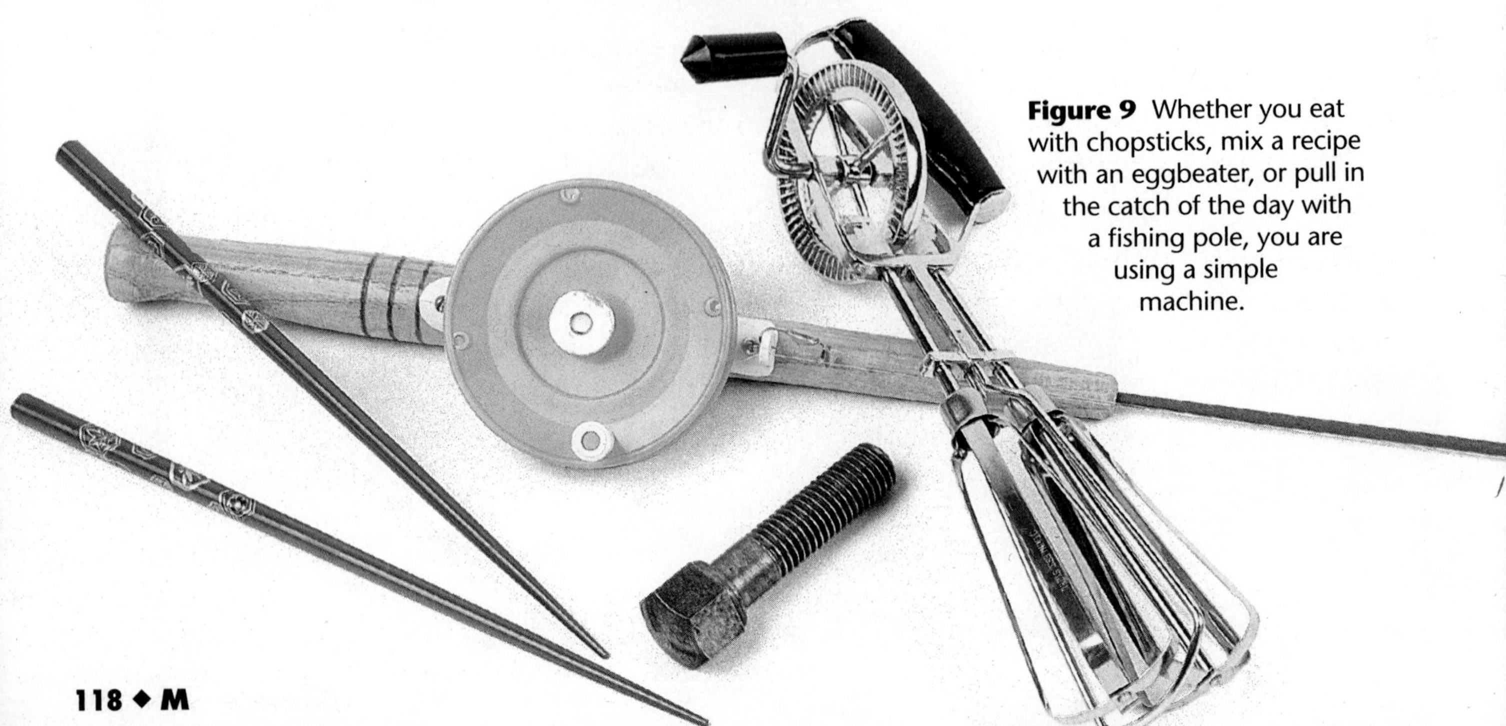

Figure 9 Whether you eat with chopsticks, mix a recipe with an eggbeater, or pull in the catch of the day with a fishing pole, you are using a simple machine.

Inclined Plane

Figure 10 Although the amount of work is the same whether you lift the loaded cart or push it up the ramp to the truck, you need less force when you use an inclined plane.
Relating Cause and Effect What happens to the distance over which you exert your force?

Have you ever faced the task of lifting something from a lower level to a higher level? You probably know that the job is much easier if you have a ramp. For example, a ramp makes it much easier to push a grocery cart over a curb or a cart into a truck. A ramp is an example of a simple machine called an inclined plane. An **inclined plane** is a flat, slanted surface.

An inclined plane allows you to exert your input force over a longer distance. The input force necessary will then be less than the output force. The input force that you use on an inclined plane is the force with which you push or pull an object. The output force is the force that you would need to lift the object without the inclined plane. This force is equal to the weight of the object.

Advantage of an Inclined Plane **You can determine the ideal mechanical advantage of an inclined plane by dividing the length of the incline by its height.**

$$\text{Ideal mechanical advantage} = \frac{\text{Length of incline}}{\text{Height of incline}}$$

Suppose you are loading a truck that is 1 meter high and you set up a ramp 3.0 meters long, as shown in Figure 11. The ideal mechanical advantage of this inclined plane is 3.0 meters ÷ 1 meter, or 3.0. This inclined plane multiplies your input force three times.

What can you conclude about how the length of the inclined plane affects the ideal mechanical advantage? If the height of the incline does not change, increasing the length of the incline causes the ideal mechanical advantage to increase. So the longer the incline (the less steep the incline), the less input force you need to push or pull an object.

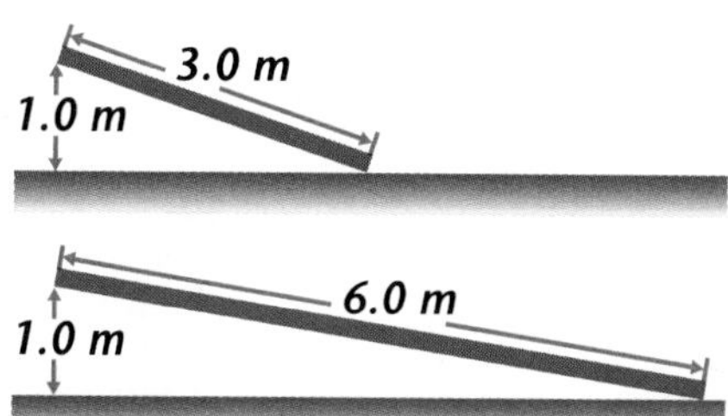

Figure 11 If you double the length of a ramp and leave its height unchanged, you double the mechanical advantage.

Efficiency of an Inclined Plane Even though an inclined plane has no moving parts, work is lost due to friction just as it is in any machine. The friction in this case is between the object and the inclined plane. For example, if you pull a crate up an

Figure 12 A large force is required to split a log in two. But with the use of a wedge, a small force is multiplied to do the job.

incline, friction acts between the bottom of the crate and the surface of the incline. You can increase the efficiency of an inclined plane by decreasing this friction. There would be less friction, for example, if you put the crate on a dolly with wheels and rolled it up the inclined plane instead of sliding it.

Wedge

If you've ever sliced an apple with a knife or seen someone chop wood with an ax, you are familiar with another simple machine known as a wedge. A **wedge** is a device that is thick at one end and tapers to a thin edge at the other end. It might be helpful to think of a wedge as an inclined plane (or two inclined planes back to back) that can move. As in the case of the inclined plane, the longer and thinner a wedge is, the less input force is required to do the same work.

In a wedge, instead of an object moving along the inclined plane, the inclined plane itself moves. For example, when someone uses an ax to split wood, the person applies an input force to the ax handle. The ax handle exerts a force on the thicker end of the wedge. That force pushes the wedge down into the wood. The wedge in turn exerts an output force that pushes through the wood, splitting it in two.

A zipper is another device that depends on the wedge. Have you ever tried to interlock the two sides of a zipper with your hands? It is almost impossible to create enough force with your fingers to join the two rows of teeth. But when you close a zipper, the part that you pull contains small wedges that multiply your input force. The result is a strong output force that either closes or separates the two sides of the zipper.

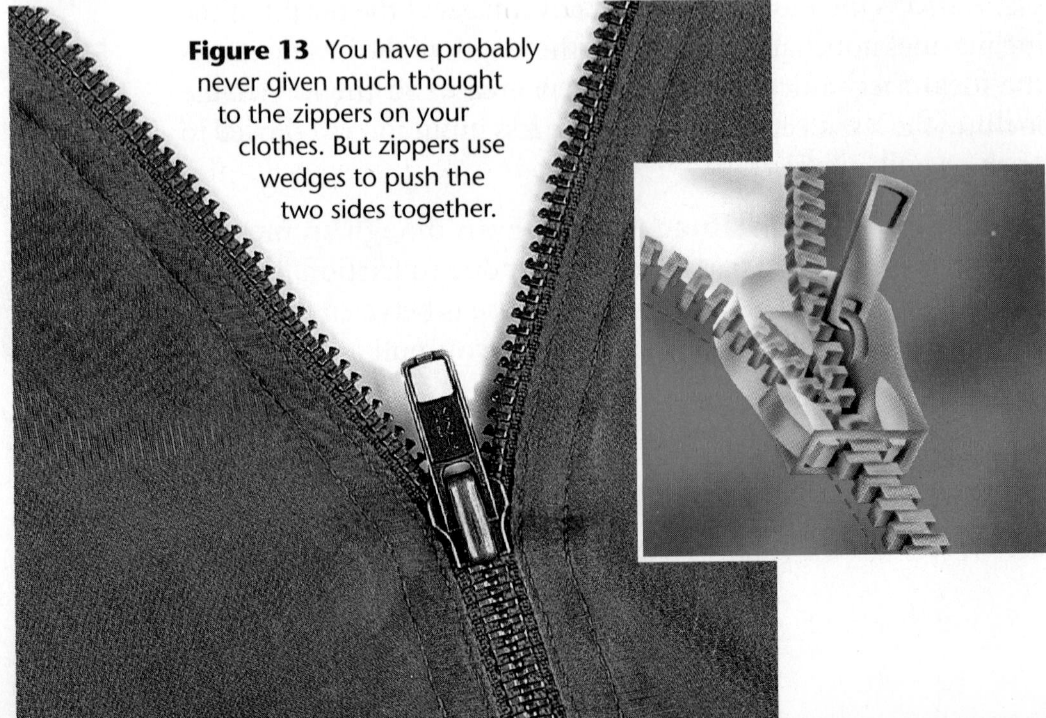
Figure 13 You have probably never given much thought to the zippers on your clothes. But zippers use wedges to push the two sides together.

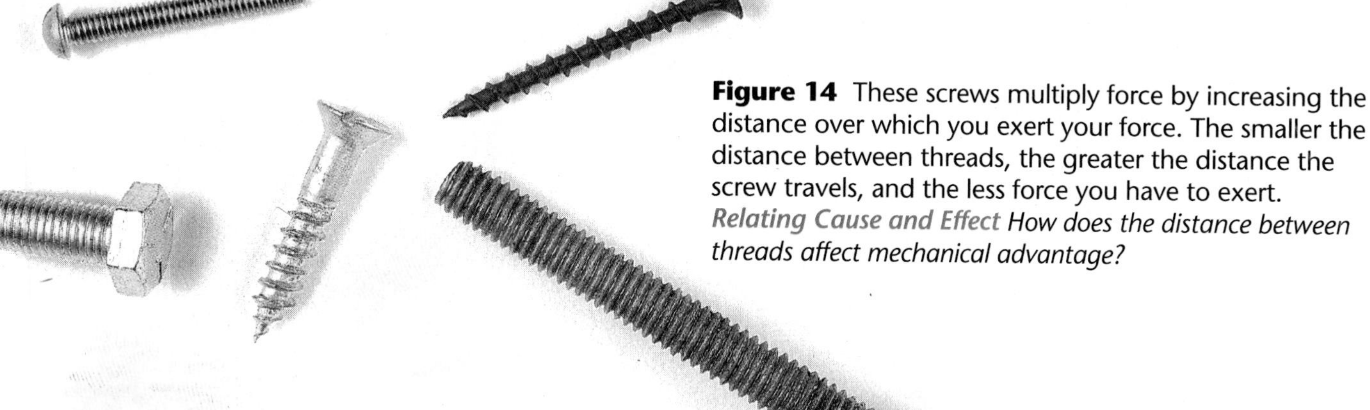

Figure 14 These screws multiply force by increasing the distance over which you exert your force. The smaller the distance between threads, the greater the distance the screw travels, and the less force you have to exert. *Relating Cause and Effect How does the distance between threads affect mechanical advantage?*

Screws

Like a wedge, a screw is a simple machine that is related to the inclined plane. A **screw** can be thought of as an inclined plane wrapped around a cylinder. This spiral inclined plane forms the threads of the screw.

When you use a screwdriver to twist a screw into a piece of wood, you exert an input force on the screw. As the threads of the screw turn, they exert an output force on the wood. If the threads of a screw are close together, you need to turn the screw many times in order to screw it into something. In other words, you apply your input force over a long distance. As with all machines, this increased distance results in an increased output force. The closer together the threads are, the greater is the mechanical advantage.

There are many other devices besides ordinary screws that take advantage of this principle. Examples include bolts, faucets, and jar lids. Think about a jar lid for a moment. You exert a relatively small input force when you turn the lid, but this force is greatly increased because of the screw threads on the lid (which fit into matching threads on the jar). The result is that the lid is pulled against the top of the jar with a strong enough output force to make a tight seal.

☑ *Checkpoint How are wedges and screws related?*

Levers

Have you ever ridden on a seesaw or pried open a paint can with an opener? If so, then you are already familiar with another simple machine called a lever. A **lever** is a rigid bar that is free to pivot, or rotate, about a fixed point. The fixed point that a lever pivots around is called the **fulcrum.**

TRY THIS

Modeling a Screw

ACTIVITY

Here's how to make a paper model of a screw.

1. Cut out a triangle from a piece of paper.
2. Tape the wide end of the triangle to a pencil. Then wind the paper around the pencil.

Making Models How does this model represent a real screw? Can you think of a way to calculate the ideal mechanical advantage of your model screw?

Visual Arts CONNECTION

Imagine creating a new form of art. Alexander Calder (1898–1976) did just that! Calder developed the art of mobiles. "A mobile is a piece of poetry that dances with the joy of life," he once said.

Calder combined his artistic flair with his knowledge of levers to express beauty through mobiles. You can, too.

In Your Journal

Make a mobile using construction paper, string, and a wire hanger. Write a description of your mobile and explain how you balanced it. Point out any adjustments you made to your design to balance the mobile.

Figure 15 This Calder mobile, entitled "Lobster Trap and Fish Tail," is in the Museum of Modern Art in New York City.

To understand how levers work, think about using a paint can opener. The opener acts as a lever. The opener rests against the edge of the can, which acts as the fulcrum. The tip of the opener is under the lid of the can. When you push down, you exert an input force on the handle and the opener pivots about the fulcrum. As a result, the tip of the opener pushes up, thereby exerting an output force on the lid.

The lever helps you in two ways. First, it increases the effect of your input force. Second, the lever changes the direction of your input force. You push down and the lid is pried up.

Different Types of Levers When a paint can opener is used as a lever, the fulcrum is located between the input and output forces. But this is not always the case. There are three different types of levers, classified according to the location of the fulcrum relative to the input and output forces. Examples are described in *Exploring the Three Classes of Levers.*

Advantage of a Lever When you used the paint can opener, you had to push the handle for a long distance in order to move the lid a short distance. However, you were able to apply a smaller force than you would have without the opener.

You can calculate the ideal mechanical advantage of a lever using the distances between the forces and the fulcrum.

$$\text{Ideal mechanical advantage} = \frac{\text{Distance from fulcrum to input force}}{\text{Distance from fulcrum to output force}}$$

Remember the case of the paint can opener. The distance from the fulcrum to the input force was greater than the distance from the fulcrum to the output force. This means that the ideal mechanical advantage was greater than 1. A typical ideal mechanical advantage for a paint can opener is 16 centimeters ÷ 0.8 centimeter = 20. That's a big advantage!

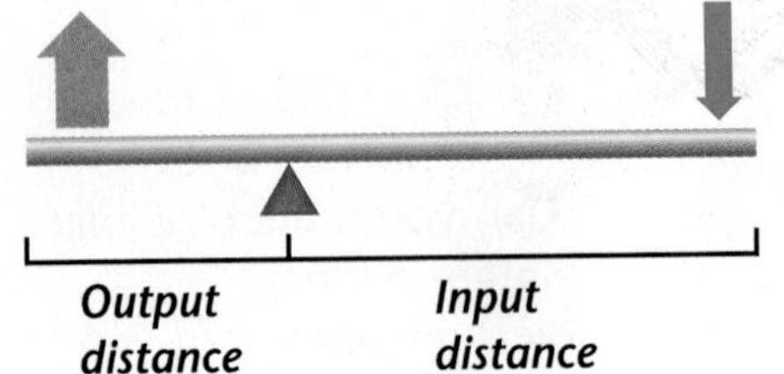

Figure 16 The mechanical advantage of this lever is greater than 1.

☑ *Checkpoint* ***What point on a lever does not move?***

EXPLORING the Three Classes of Levers

The three classes of levers differ in the positions of the fulcrum, input force, and output force. Note the locations of the labels in each example.

FIRST-CLASS LEVERS

If the distance from the fulcrum to the input force is greater than the distance from the fulcrum to the output force, these levers multiply force. Otherwise, they multiply distance. Note that this kind of lever also changes the direction of the input force. Other examples include scissors, pliers, and seesaws.

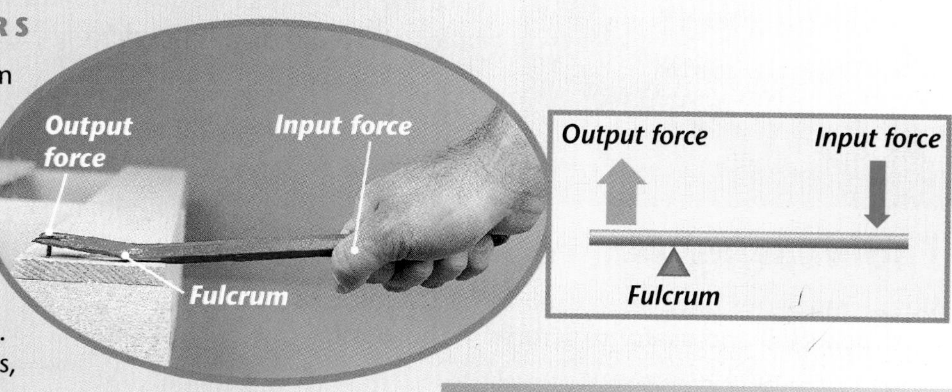

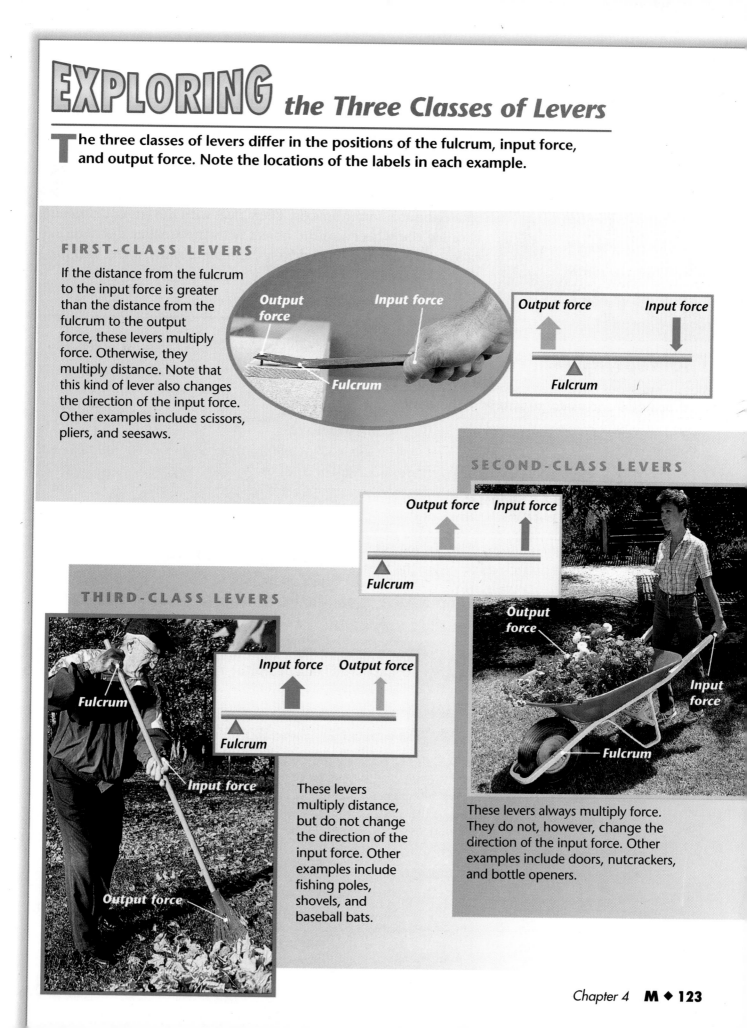

SECOND-CLASS LEVERS

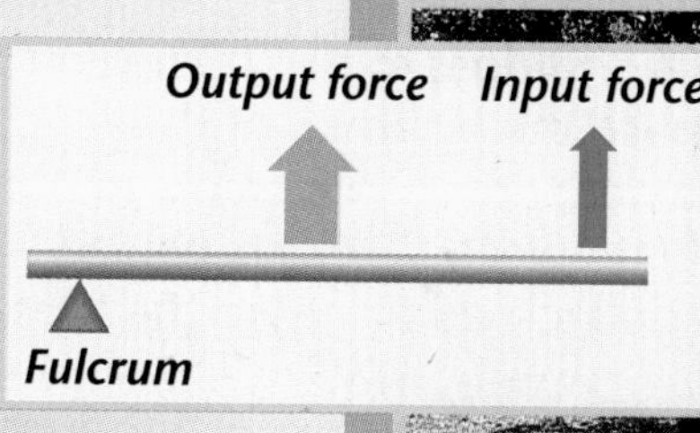

These levers always multiply force. They do not, however, change the direction of the input force. Other examples include doors, nutcrackers, and bottle openers.

THIRD-CLASS LEVERS

These levers multiply distance, but do not change the direction of the input force. Other examples include fishing poles, shovels, and baseball bats.

Wheel and Axle

Could you insert a screw into a piece of wood using nothing more than your fingers? You would find it almost impossible. But with a screwdriver, you can turn the screw with ease.

A screwdriver makes use of a simple machine known as the wheel and axle. A **wheel and axle** is a simple machine made of two circular or cylindrical objects that are fastened together and that rotate about a common axis. The object with the larger diameter is called the wheel and the object with the smaller diameter is called the axle. In a screwdriver, the handle is the wheel and the shaft is the axle.

Engineering Marvels

Simple machines have been used to create some of the most beautiful and useful structures in the world.

2550 B.C. Great Pyramid, Giza, Egypt

Workers used wooden wedges to cut 2.3 million blocks of stone to build the pyramid. At the quarry, the wedges were driven into cracks in the rock. The rock split into pieces. Workers hauled the massive blocks up inclined planes to the tops of pyramid walls.

2000 B.C. **1000 B.C.** **A.D. 1**

500 B.C.
Theater at Epidaurus, Greece

Instead of ramps, the Greeks relied on a crane powered by pulleys to lift the stone blocks to build this theater. The crane was also used to lower actors to the stage during performances.

Every time you turn a doorknob, you are using a wheel and axle. The knob is the wheel and the shaft is the axle. The water wheel of a mill, the steering wheel of a car, and the handle of an eggbeater are also examples of a wheel and axle.

Advantage of a Wheel and Axle How does a wheel and axle make work easier? You apply an input force to turn the wheel, which is larger than the axle. As a result, the axle rotates and exerts an output force to turn something such as a screw. The wheel and axle multiplies your force, but you must exert your force over a longer distance—in this case a circular distance.

Imagine that you are the person who first thought of using a simple machine at one of the construction sites in the time line. Write out your proposal. You'll need to research the time and place. Explain to the people in charge why the simple machine you suggest will give workers a mechanical advantage.

A.D. 1056

Yingxian Pagoda, China

Slanted wooden beams called *ang* act as first-class levers to hold up the roof of this pagoda. The weight of the center of the roof presses down on one end of the beam. The other end of the beam swings up to support the outer edge of the roof.

A.D. 1000 **A.D. 2000**

A.D. 1000

Brihadeshrava Temple, India

The temple's tower at Thanjavur rises to a height of more than 60 meters. Workers dragged the dome-shaped capstone, a mass of over 70,000 kilograms, to the top of the structure along an inclined plane several kilometers long.

A.D. 1994

The Chunnel, United Kingdom to France

Special drilling equipment was built to tunnel under the English Channel. Opened in May of 1994, the tunnel is 50 kilometers long. It carries only railway traffic.

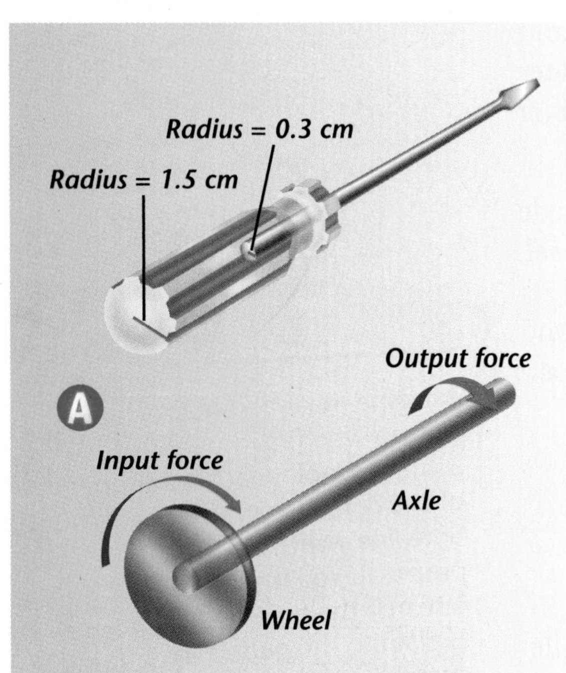

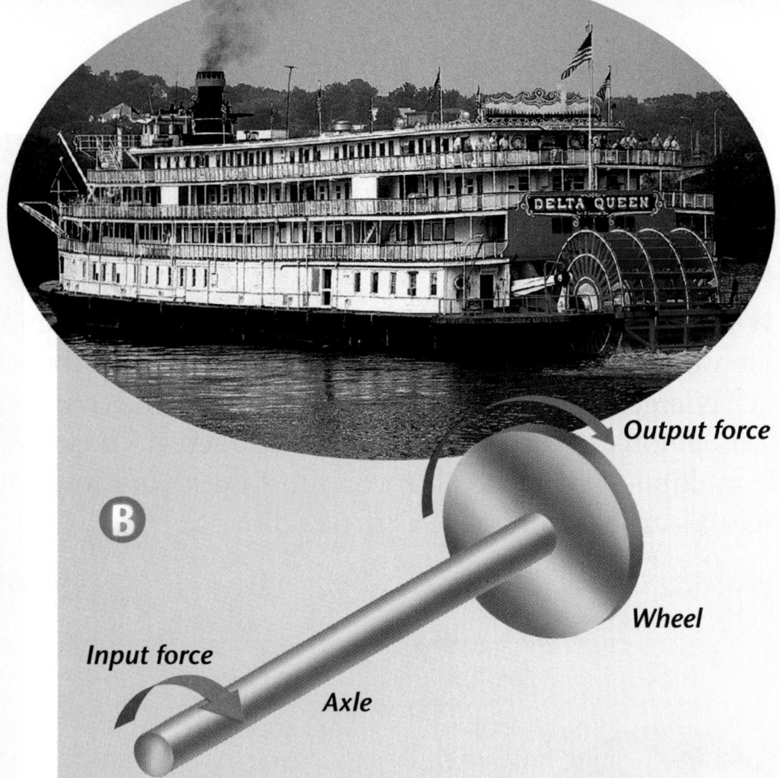

Figure 17 A. In some devices, such as a screwdriver, the wheel turns an axle. **B.** In the case of the riverboat paddle wheel, the axle turns the wheel. *Interpreting Photos How is work made easier by the wheel and axle on the riverboat?*

You can calculate the ideal mechanical advantage of a wheel and axle using the radius of the wheel and the radius of the axle. (Each radius is the distance from the outside to the common center of the wheel and axle.)

$$\text{Ideal mechanical advantage} = \frac{\text{Radius of wheel}}{\text{Radius of axle}}$$

For a screwdriver, a typical ideal mechanical advantage would be 1.5 centimeters ÷ 0.3 centimeter, or 5.

A Variation on the Wheel and Axle What would happen if the input force were applied to the axle rather than the wheel? For the riverboat in Figure 17, the force of the engine is applied to the axle of the large paddle wheel. The large paddle wheel in turn pushes against the water. In this case, the input force is exerted over a short distance while the output force is exerted over a long distance. So when the input force is applied to the axle, a wheel and axle multiplies distance. This means that the ideal mechanical advantage of the paddle wheel is less than 1.

☑ *Checkpoint How does a doorknob work?*

Pulley

When you raise or lower a flag on a flagpole or open and close window blinds, you are using a simple machine known as a pulley. A **pulley** is a grooved wheel with a rope (or a chain, or even a steel cable) wrapped around it. You use a pulley by pulling on the rope. As a result, you can change the amount and direction of your input force.

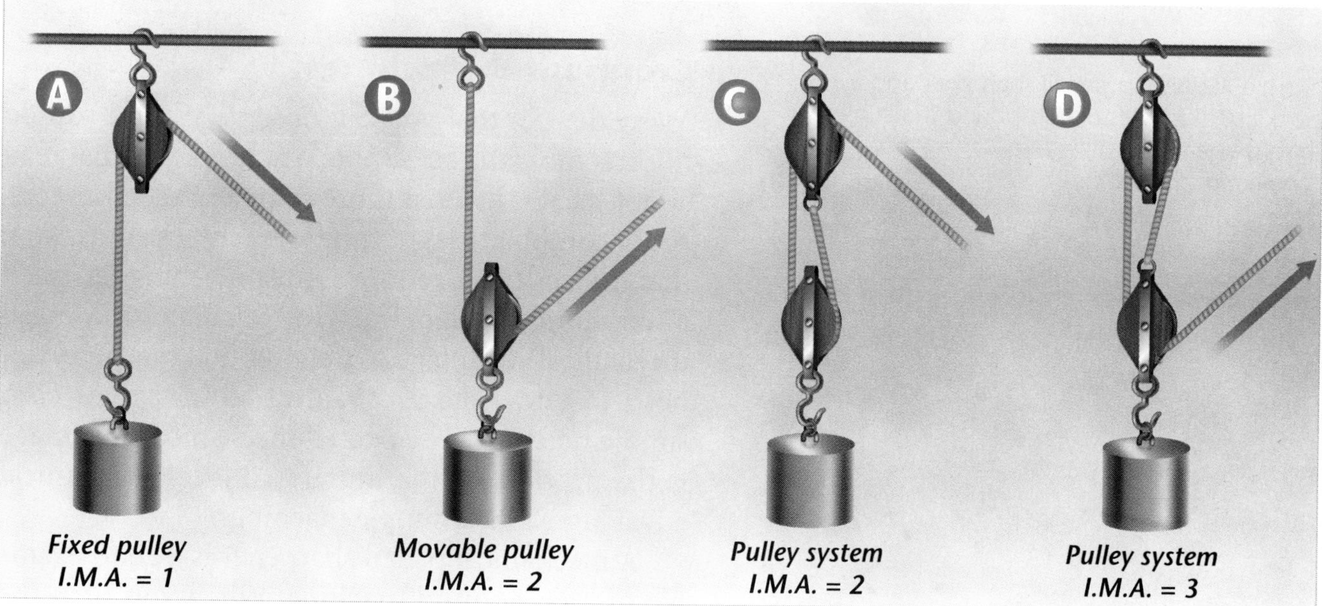

Figure 18 **A.** A fixed pulley changes the direction of your force. **B.** A movable pulley multiplies your force. **C, D.** You can combine fixed and movable pulleys to increase the mechanical advantage.

Fixed Pulleys A pulley that you attach to a structure is called a fixed pulley. A single fixed pulley, as shown in Figure 18A, does not change the amount of force you apply. Instead it changes the direction of the input force. The ideal mechanical advantage of a single fixed pulley is 1. A single fixed pulley can be used to raise a sail, as you read in the previous section.

Movable Pulleys If you attach a pulley to the object you wish to move, then you are using a movable pulley. As you see in Figure 18B, the object is then supported by each side of the rope that is looped around the pulley. As a result, the ideal mechanical advantage of a movable pulley is 2. The output force on the object is twice the input force that you exert on the rope. You can also see that you must exert your force over a greater distance. For every meter you lift the object with a movable pulley, you need to pull the rope two meters.

Notice that with the movable pulley, your input force is in the same direction as the output force. A movable pulley is especially useful when you are lifting an object from above. Large construction cranes often work with a movable pulley. A hook fastened to the pulley carries the building materials.

Pulley Systems If you combine fixed and movable pulleys, you can make a pulley system. Such a pulley system is also called a "block and tackle." The pulley system pictured in Figure 18C has an ideal mechanical advantage of 2. The pulley system in Figure 18D has an ideal mechanical advantage of 3. **The ideal mechanical advantage of a pulley system is equal to the number of sections of the rope that support the object.** (Don't include the rope on which you pull downward, because it does not support the object.)

Classifying ACTIVITY

Even though levers and pulleys may seem very different, pulleys can be classified as levers.

When you pull down on a fixed pulley, the object rises. In other words, the pulley changes the direction of your input force. This is what happens with a first-class lever. Instead of a bar, you apply your force to a rope. The center of the pulley acts like the fulcrum of the lever.

Draw a diagram showing how a single fixed pulley is like a first-class lever. Why is the mechanical advantage 1?

Figure 19 Both a pencil sharpener and a clock are examples of compound machines that use gears. *Applying Concepts What is a compound machine?*

Compound Machines

Many devices that you can observe around you do not resemble the six simple machines you just read about. That is because more complex machines consist of combinations of simple machines. A machine that utilizes two or more simple machines is called a **compound machine.** To calculate the ideal mechanical advantage of a compound machine, you need to know the mechanical advantage of each simple machine. The overall mechanical advantage is the product of the individual ideal mechanical advantages of the simple machines.

A mechanical pencil sharpener is a good example of a compound machine. When you turn the handle, you are using a wheel and axle to turn the mechanism inside the sharpener. The two cutting wheels inside are screws that whittle away at the end of the pencil until it is sharp.

Inside the pencil sharpener in Figure 19 is an axle that turns **gears.** The gears then turn the cutting wheels. A system of gears is a device with toothed wheels that fit into one another. Turning one wheel causes another to turn. Gears form a compound machine with one wheel and axle linked to another wheel and axle. Sometimes this link is direct, as in the gears shown in Figure 19. In other devices, such as a bicycle, this link is through a chain.

Section 3 Review

1. List and give an example of each of the six kinds of simple machines.
2. Explain how to find the ideal mechanical advantage of four types of simple machines.
3. What kind of lever is the flip-top opener on a soda can? Explain your answer with the help of a diagram.
4. **Thinking Critically Making Generalizations** Some machines give a mechanical advantage less than 1. Explain why you might want to use such a machine.

CHAPTER PROJECT 4

Check Your Progress

Think about whether force or distance is multiplied by each simple machine in your design. Consider how making levers longer, adding pulleys, or changing the angle of your inclined planes will affect the mechanical advantage. What measurements will you need to know to calculate the ideal mechanical advantage of your lifting machine? Finalize your design, and build your machine. As you build, consider how you can use lubrication or polishing to improve its efficiency.

SCIENCE AND SOCIETY

Automation in the Workplace — Lost Jobs or New Jobs?

Workers 150 years ago spent long days stitching clothes by hand. In a modern American factory, a worker makes a shirt with a sewing machine and much less effort. Since ancient times, people have invented machines to help with work. Today, factories can use automated machines to perform jobs that are difficult, dangerous, or even just boring. Like science-fiction robots, these machines can do a whole series of different tasks.

But if a machine does work instead of a person, then someone loses a job. How can society use machines to make work easier and more productive without having some people lose their chance to work?

The Issues

What Are the Effects of Automation? New machines replace some jobs, but they also can create jobs. Suppose an automobile factory starts using machines instead of people to paint cars. At first, some workers may lose their jobs. But the factory may be able to produce more cars. Then it may need to hire more workers—to handle old tasks as well as some new ones. New jobs are created for people who are educated and skilled in operating and taking care of the new machines.

Still, some workers whose skills are no longer needed lose their jobs. Some are forced to work in different jobs for less money. Others may be unable to find new jobs. The challenge to society is to provide workers who have lost jobs with the skills needed for good new jobs.

What Can People Do? Education programs can train young people for new jobs and give older workers new skills. Those who learn how to use computers and other new machines can take on new jobs. Learning how to sell or design a product can also prepare workers for new jobs. Workers who have lost jobs can train for very different types of work—work that cannot be done by machines. A machine, for example, cannot replace human skill in day care or medical care.

Who Should Pay? Teaching young people how to work in new kinds of jobs costs money. So do training programs for adult workers who have lost jobs. What is the fairest way to pay these costs? Businesses might share some of the costs. Some businesses give workers full pay until they are retrained or find new work. The government might provide unemployment pay or training for the unemployed. Then all taxpayers would share the costs.

You Decide

1. **Identify the Problem**
   Describe in your own words the benefits and drawbacks of workplace automation.
2. **Analyze the Options**
   List ways society could deal with the effects of automation. For each plan, give the benefits and drawbacks and tell how it would be paid for.
3. **Find a Solution**
   The owner of the pizza shop in your neighborhood has bought an automated pizza-making system. Make a plan for the shop to use the system without having to fire workers.

You and Your Community

Angling for Access

You and your friends have volunteered to help build a wheelchair-access ramp for the local public library. The design of the ramp has not been decided upon yet, so you need to build a model inclined plane. The model will help you determine what the steepness of the ramp should be.

Problem

How does the steepness of a wheelchair-access ramp affect its usefulness?

Skills Focus

making models, measuring, calculating

Materials 

4 books, about 2 cm thick
metric ruler
wooden block with eye-hook
marker
board, at least 10 cm wide and 50 cm long
spring scale, 0–10 N, or force sensor

Procedure

1. Preview the following steps that describe how you can construct and use a ramp. Then copy the data table into your notebook.
2. The output force with an inclined plane is equal to the weight of the object. Lift the block with the spring scale to measure its weight. Record this value in the data table. If you are using a force sensor, see your teacher for instructions.
3. Make a mark on the side of the board about 3 cm from one end. Measure the length from the other end of the board to the mark and record it in the data table.
4. Place one end of the board on top of a book. The mark you made on the board should be even with the edge of the book.

DATA TABLE

Number of Books	Output Force (N)	Length of Incline (cm)	Height of Incline (cm)	Input Force (N)	Ideal Mechanical Advantage	Actual Mechanical Advantage
1						
2						
3						
4						

5. Measure the vertical distance in centimeters from the top of the table to where the underside of the incline touches the book. Record this value in the data table as "Height of Incline."
6. Lay the block on its largest side and use the spring scale to pull the block straight up the incline at a slow, steady speed. Be sure to hold the spring scale parallel to the incline, as shown in the photograph. Measure the force needed and record it in the data table.
7. Predict how your results will change if you repeat the investigation using two, three, and four books. Test your predictions.
8. For each trial, calculate the ideal mechanical advantage and the actual mechanical advantage. Record the calculations in your data table.

Analyze and Conclude

1. How did the ideal mechanical advantage and the actual mechanical advantage compare each time you repeated the experiment? Explain your answer.
2. Why do you write ideal and actual mechanical advantage without units?
3. What happens to the mechanical advantage as the inclined plane gets steeper? On the basis of this fact alone, which of the four inclined planes models the best steepness for a wheelchair-access ramp?
4. What other factors, besides mechanical advantage, should you consider when deciding on the steepness of the ramp?
5. **Apply** Suppose the door of the local public library is 2 m above the ground and the distance from the door to the parking lot is 15 m. How would these conditions affect your decision about how steep to make the ramp?

Getting Involved

Find actual ramps that provide access for people with disabilities. Measure the heights and lengths of these ramps and calculate their ideal mechanical advantages. Find out what the requirements are for access ramps in your area. Should your ramp be made of a particular material? Should it level off before it reaches the door? How wide should it be? How does it provide water drainage?

Machines in the Human Body

DISCOVER ACTIVITY

Are You an Eating Machine?

1. Using your front teeth, bite off a piece of a cracker. As you bite, observe how your teeth are breaking the cracker. Also think about the shape of your front teeth.

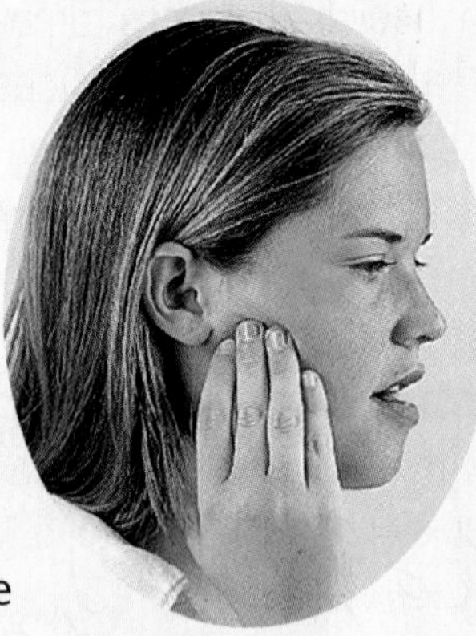

2. Now chew the cracker. Pay attention to how your lower jaw moves. Touch your jaw below your ear, as shown in the photo. As you chew, push in slightly there so that you can feel how your jaw moves. If the structure is still not clear, try opening your mouth wide while you feel the back of the jaw.

Think It Over

Observing When you bite and chew, your teeth and jaws serve as two kinds of machines. What are they?

GUIDE FOR READING

- **How does the body use levers and wedges?**

Reading Tip **Before you read, preview the illustrations and predict how simple machines are related to the human body.**

It's Saturday night, and you and your friends are taking a well-deserved break from your school work. You're watching a great movie, happily eating popcorn from a big bowl. Are you doing any work? Surprisingly, you are!

Every time you reach for the popcorn, your muscles exert a force that causes your arm to move. And when you chew on the popcorn, breaking it into bits that you can easily swallow, you are again doing work.

How are you able to do all this work without even noticing? The answer is machines! You probably don't think of the human body as being made of machines. But believe it or not, machines are involved in much of the work that your body does.

Living Levers

Most of the machines in your body are levers that consist of bones and muscles. Every time you move, you use a muscle. Your muscles are attached to your bones by tough connective tissue called **tendons.** Tendons and muscles pull on bones, making them work as levers. The joint, near where the tendon is attached to the bone, acts as the fulcrum of the lever. The muscles produce the input force. The output force is used for everything from lifting your hand to swinging a hammer.

A muscle by itself cannot push; it can only pull. When a muscle contracts, or becomes shorter, it pulls the bone to which it is attached. So how can you bend your arm as shown in *Exploring Levers in the Body?* The answer is that most muscles work in pairs. For example, when your biceps muscle (on the front of the upper arm) contracts, it exerts a force on the bone in your forearm. The result is that your arm bends at the elbow joint, which in this case is the fulcrum of the lever. When the triceps muscle (on the back of the upper arm) contracts, it opens the elbow joint.

EXPLORING Levers in the Body

You don't need to look any farther than your own body to find simple machines. Three different types of levers are responsible for many of your movements.

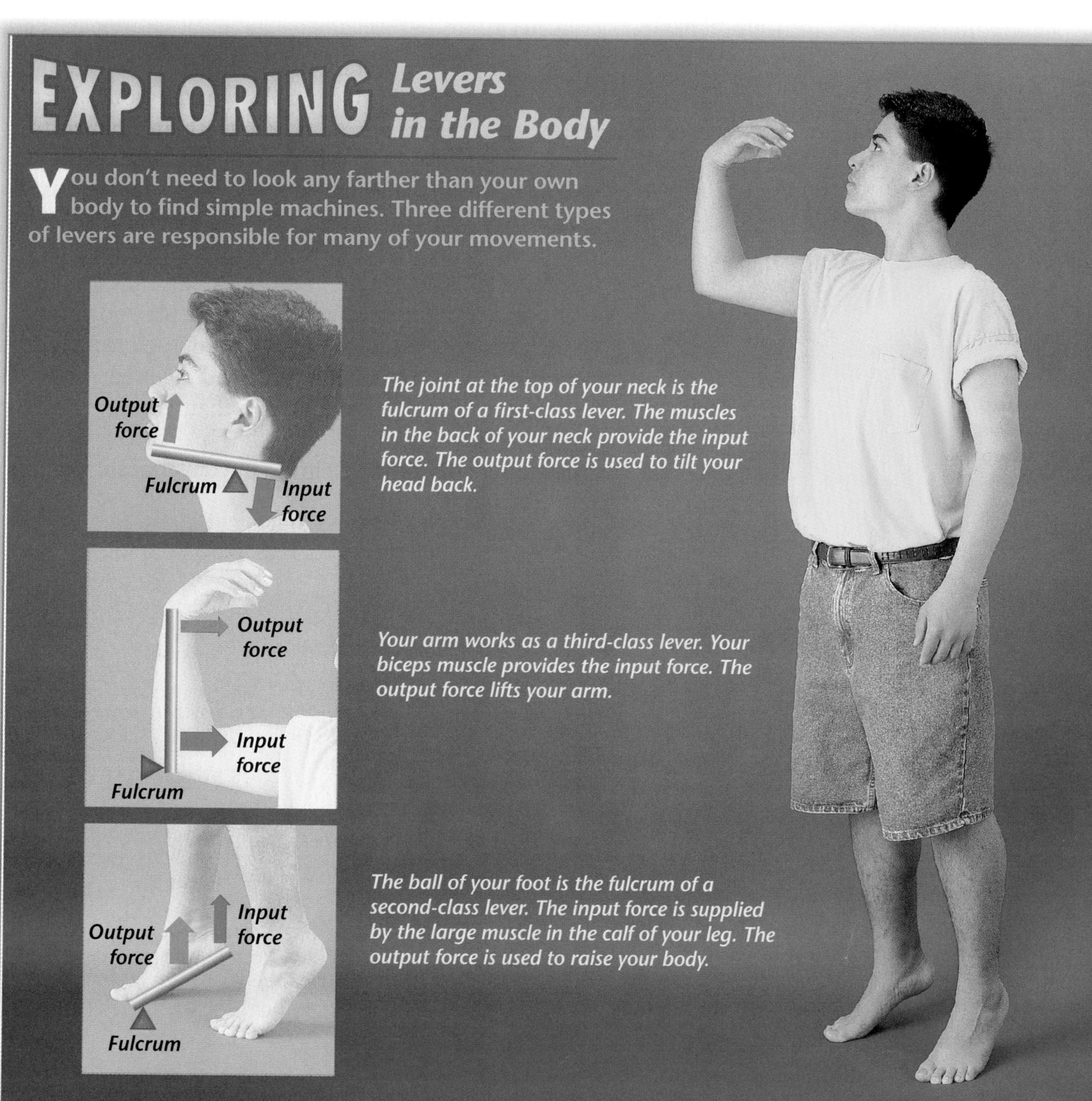

The joint at the top of your neck is the fulcrum of a first-class lever. The muscles in the back of your neck provide the input force. The output force is used to tilt your head back.

Your arm works as a third-class lever. Your biceps muscle provides the input force. The output force lifts your arm.

The ball of your foot is the fulcrum of a second-class lever. The input force is supplied by the large muscle in the calf of your leg. The output force is used to raise your body.

Figure 20 Your front teeth are shaped like wedges. These wedges allow you to cut through food, such as an apple.

Look again at the different levers in *Exploring Levers in the Body*. You will see that you can find a lever in your neck and another lever in your leg and foot. Just as you found with shovels, wheelbarrows, and fishing poles, the type of lever you find in the human body depends on the locations of the fulcrum, input force, and output force.

Working Wedges

Have you ever paid attention to the shape of your teeth? Some of your teeth are wedge-shaped, others are pointed, and still others are relatively flat. This is because they have different uses.

When you bite into an apple, you use your sharp front teeth, called incisors. These teeth are shaped to enable you to bite off pieces of food. What simple machine do these teeth resemble? **Your incisors are shaped like wedges.** When you bite down on something, the wedge shape of your front teeth produces enough force to break it in half, just as an ax is used to split a log. Your rear teeth, or molars, are more flat. These teeth are used to grind your food into pieces that are small enough to be swallowed and digested.

There's a lot more to chewing than you may have realized. The next time you take a bite of a crunchy apple, think about the machines in your mouth!

Section 4 Review

1. In what way do your bones and muscles operate as levers?
2. Where in your body can you identify wedges? What role do they play in your daily life?
3. Point your left index finger (your pointing finger) in front of you. Then move it to the right. Where is the fulcrum? Where is the input force? What kind of lever is your finger?
4. **Thinking Critically** **Inferring** Make a motion as if you were going to throw a ball. What muscle do you think you use to straighten out your arm when you throw? What kind of lever are you using?

Science at Home

Have a family member place a wooden toothpick between the ends of his or her fingers as shown in the upper photograph. Ask that person to try to break the toothpick by pressing down with the first and third fingers. Now repeat the procedure, but this time have the person hold the toothpick as shown in the lower photograph. Explain to your family why the toothpick was easier to break on the second try. How were the positions of the forces and fulcrum different in each case?

What Is Work?

Key Ideas

- Work is done on an object when a force causes that object to move some distance.
- The amount of work done on an object is equal to the force on the object in the direction of its motion multiplied by the distance the object moves.

$$Work = Force \times Distance$$

Key Terms

work
joule

Mechanical Advantage and Efficiency

Key Ideas

- A machine makes work easier by changing the direction or amount of force needed to accomplish a task.
- The efficiency of a machine is the percentage of the input work that is changed to output work.

$$Efficiency = \frac{Output\ work}{Input\ work} \times 100\%$$

- The mechanical advantage of a machine is obtained by dividing the output force by the input force.

$$Mechanical\ advantage = \frac{Output\ force}{Input\ force}$$

- The ideal mechanical advantage of a machine is the mechanical advantage that it would have if there were no friction.

Key Terms

machine
input force
output force
mechanical advantage
efficiency
actual mechanical advantage
ideal mechanical advantage

Simple Machines

Key Ideas

- There are six basic kinds of simple machines: the inclined plane, the wedge, the screw, the lever, the wheel and axle, and the pulley.
- A compound machine is a machine that is made from two or more simple machines.

Key Terms

inclined plane
wedge
screw
lever
fulcrum
wheel and axle
pulley
compound machine
gears

Machines in the Human Body

Integrating Life Science

Key Ideas

- Most of the machines in your body are levers that consist of bones with muscles attached to them.
- When you bite into something, your front teeth use the principle of the wedge.

Key Term

tendon

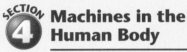

Organizing Information

Compare/Contrast Table Complete a compare/contrast table similar to the one shown below. For each of three other basic types of simple machines, you should show how to calculate the ideal mechanical advantage and give an example. (For more on compare/contrast tables, see the Skills Handbook.)

Simple Machine	Mechanical Advantage	Example
Inclined Plane	*Length of incline ÷ Height of incline*	*Ramp*

CHAPTER 4 ASSESSMENT

Reviewing Content

For more review of key concepts, see the Interactive Student Tutorial CD-ROM.

Multiple Choice

Choose the letter of the answer that best completes each statement.

1. The amount of work done on an object is obtained by multiplying
   a. input force and output force.
   b. force and distance.
   c. time and force.
   d. efficiency and work.
2. One way a machine can make work easier for you is by
   a. decreasing the amount of work you do.
   b. changing the direction of your force.
   c. increasing the amount of work required for a task.
   d. decreasing the friction you encounter.
3. The output force is greater than the input force for a
   a. nutcracker.
   b. fishing pole.
   c. single fixed pulley.
   d. rake.
4. An example of a second-class lever is a
   a. seesaw. b. shovel.
   c. paddle. d. wheelbarrow.
5. An example of a compound machine is a
   a. screwdriver. b. crowbar.
   c. bicycle. d. ramp.

True or False

If the statement is true, write true. If it is false, change the underlined word or words to make the statement true.

6. If none of the force on an object is in the direction of the object's <u>motion</u>, no work is done.
7. <u>Friction</u> reduces the efficiency of a machine.
8. The comparison between output work and input work is <u>ideal mechanical advantage</u>.
9. A <u>pulley</u> can be thought of as an inclined plane wrapped around a central cylinder.
10. Your front teeth act as a <u>fulcrum</u> when you bite into something.

Checking Concepts

11. The mythical god Atlas was supposed to hold the stationary Earth on his shoulders. Was Atlas performing any work? Explain your answer.
12. Suppose that you do 1,000 joules of work when you operate an old can opener. However, the can opener does only 500 joules of work in opening the can. What is the efficiency of the can opener?
13. The actual mechanical advantage of a machine is 3. If you exert an input force of 5 N, what output force is exerted by the machine?
14. Which has a greater ideal mechanical advantage, a ramp that is 12 m long and 2 m high or a ramp that is 6 m long and 2 m high? Explain your answer.
15. When you let water into a bathtub, what kind of machine helps you open the tap?
16. Describe a lever in your body. Locate the input force, output force and fulcrum.
17. **Writing to Learn** You are a brilliant inventor. Recently you completed your most outstanding project—an odd-looking, but very important machine. Write an explanation describing your machine, how you built it, what it is made of, and what it does. You may wish to illustrate your explanation.

Thinking Critically

18. **Applying Concepts** To open a door, you push on the part farthest from the hinges. Why would it be harder to open the door if you pushed on the center?
19. **Classifying** What type of simple machine would be used to lower an empty bucket into a well and then lift the bucket full of water?
20. **Relating Cause and Effect** Describe the relationship between friction and the efficiency of a machine.
21. **Inferring** Why would sharpening a knife or ax blade improve its mechanical advantage?

Applying Skills

Use the illustration to answer Questions 22–25.

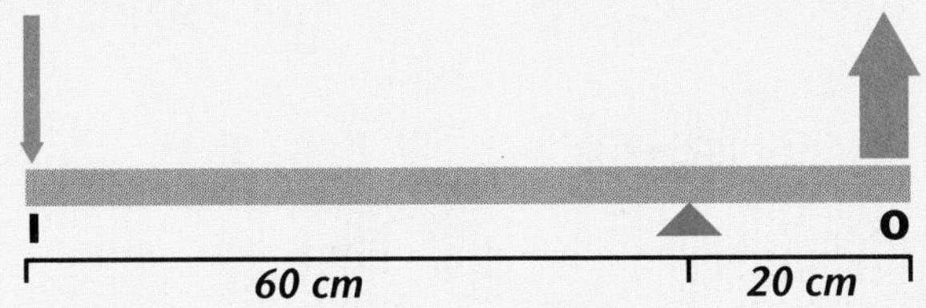

22. **Calculating** The figure shows the distance from the fulcrum to the input force (point I) and from the fulcrum to the output force (point O). Use the distance to calculate the ideal mechanical advantage of the lever.
23. **Predicting** What would the ideal mechanical advantage be if the distance from the fulcrum to the input force were 20 cm, 40 cm, or 80 cm?
24. **Graphing** Use your answers to Questions 22 and 23 to graph the distance from the fulcrum to the input force on the *x*-axis and the ideal mechanical advantage of the lever on the *y*-axis.
25. **Interpreting Data** What does your graph show you about the relationship between the ideal mechanical advantage of a first-class lever and the distance between the fulcrum and the input force.

Performance Assessment

CHAPTER PROJECT 4

Project Wrap Up Ask a classmate to review your project with you. Does your machine lift the loaded can 5 cm? Is it made up of two or more simple machines? Check all measurements and calculations. When you demonstrate your nifty lifting machine to the class, explain why you built it as you did. Describe any other designs that you considered along the way.

Reflect and Record If you were just beginning this project, you could use the knowledge you've gained to build an even better machine. Draw diagrams and write a short paragraph in your journal to explain how you would improve the machine you built.

Test Preparation

Use these questions to prepare for standardized tests.

Use the diagram to answer Questions 26–28.

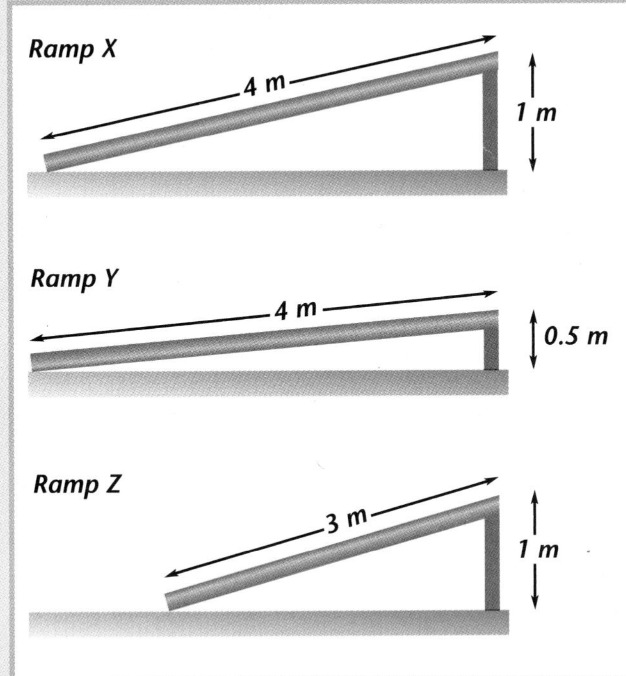

26. Which ramp has the greatest ideal mechanical advantage?
    a. X
    b. Y
    c. Z
    d. X and Y are the same.
27. To increase the ideal mechanical advantage of a ramp, you can
    a. increase the length and the height by the same amount.
    b. increase the length or decrease the height.
    c. decrease the length or increase the height.
    d. decrease the length and the height by the same amount.
28. What would the ideal mechanical advantage of Ramp Z become if the height were changed to 0.5 m and the length remained the same?
    a. 1.5
    b. 3.5
    c. 6
    d. 15

CHAPTER 5

Energy and Power

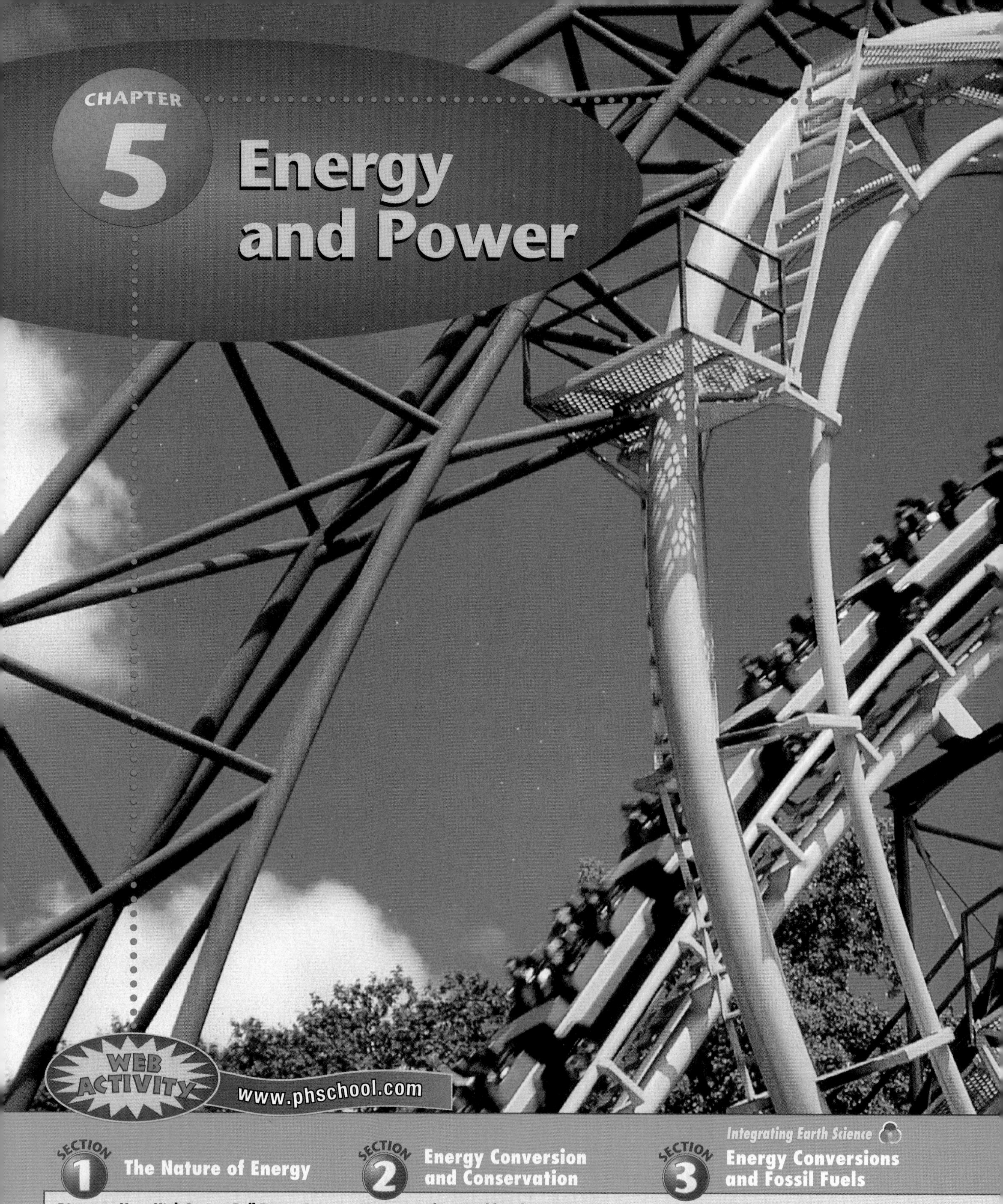

WEB ACTIVITY
www.phschool.com

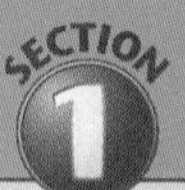

SECTION 1 The Nature of Energy

Discover **How High Does a Ball Bounce?**
Skills Lab **Soaring Straws**

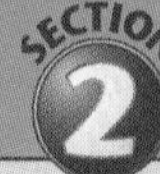

SECTION 2 Energy Conversion and Conservation

Discover **What Would Make a Card Jump?**
Try This **Pendulum Swing**

Integrating Earth Science

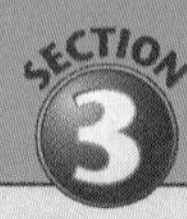

SECTION 3 Energy Conversions and Fossil Fuels

Discover **What Is a Fuel?**
Sharpen Your Skills **Graphing**

PROJECT 5

Roller Coaster!

Slowly, but steadily, you climb the mighty hill. Up, up, up, and then whoosh—you plunge swiftly down the other side. You curve left, then right, and then up again.

This thrilling roller coaster ride is brought to you courtesy of energy. In this chapter you will learn about energy, the forms it takes, and how it is transformed and conserved. You will use what you learn to design and construct your own roller coaster.

Your Goal To design and construct a roller coaster that uses kinetic and potential energy to move.

Your project must

- be no wider than 2 meters and be easily disassembled and reassembled
- have a first hill with a height of 1 meter and have at least two additional hills
- have a car that moves along the entire track without stopping
- follow the safety guidelines in Appendix A

Get Started If you or any of your classmates have ridden a roller coaster, share your experiences. Brainstorm the characteristics of a good roller coaster. Consider how fast the roller coaster moves and how its speed changes throughout the ride.

Check Your Progress You'll be working on this project as you study this chapter. To keep your project on track, look for Check Your Progress boxes at the following points.

Section 1 Review, page 145: Experiment with different hill heights and inclines.

Section 3 Review, page 157: Describe how your vehicle moves along its tracks in terms of potential and kinetic energy.

Section 4 Review, page 162: Add turns and loops to determine their effect.

Wrap Up At the end of the chapter (page 165), you will show how your roller coaster car can move up and down at least three hills once you release it.

The cars on a roller coaster like this one may reach speeds of more than 100 kilometers per hour.

SECTION 4 Power

The Nature of Energy

DISCOVER — ACTIVITY

How High Does a Ball Bounce?

1. Hold a meter stick vertically, with the zero end on the ground.
2. Drop a tennis ball from the 50-centimeter mark and record the height to which it bounces.
3. Drop the tennis ball from the 100-centimeter mark and record the height to which it bounces.
4. Predict how high the ball will bounce if dropped from the 75-centimeter mark. Test your prediction.

Think It Over

Observing How does the height from which you drop the ball relate to the height to which the ball bounces?

GUIDE FOR READING

- **How are work and energy related?**
- **What are the two basic kinds of energy?**
- **What are some of the different forms of energy?**

Reading Tip **Before you read, list several familiar examples of energy. Add to your list as you read the section.**

Brilliant streaks of lightning flash across the night sky. The howl of the wind and the crashing of thunder drown out the sound of falling rain. Then a sound like a railroad locomotive approaches. As the sound grows louder, a small town experiences the power and fury of a tornado. Whirling winds of more than 250 kilometers per hour blow through the town. Roofs are lifted off of buildings. Cars are thrown about like toys. Then, in minutes, the tornado is gone.

The next morning, as rescuers survey the damage, a light breeze delicately carries falling leaves past the debris. How strange it is that the wind is violent enough to destroy buildings one night and barely strong enough to carry a leaf the next morning. Wind is just moving air, but it possesses energy. As you read on, you'll find out what energy is.

What Is Energy?

When wind moves a leaf, or even a house, it causes a change. In this case, the change is in the position of the object. Recall that work is done when a force moves an object through a distance. The ability to do work or cause change is called **energy.** So the wind has energy.

Figure 1 The energy of a tornado can devastate a town in minutes.

Figure 2 A bowling ball can do work because it is moving. *Applying Concepts What is the ability to do work called?*

When an object or organism does work on another object, some of its energy is transferred to that object. **You can think of work, then, as the transfer of energy.** When energy is transferred, the object upon which the work is done gains energy. Energy is measured in joules—the same units as work.

Kinetic Energy

There are two general kinds of energy. **The two kinds of energy are kinetic energy and potential energy.** Whether energy is kinetic or potential depends on whether an object is moving or not.

The examples you have read about so far have involved things that were moving. A moving object can collide with another object and move it some distance. In that way, the moving object does work. For example, a bowling ball knocks over a bowling pin.

Because the moving object can do work, it must have energy. The energy of motion is called **kinetic energy.** The word kinetic comes from the Greek word *kinetos*, which means "moving."

Mass and Velocity The kinetic energy of an object depends on both its mass and its velocity. Think about rolling a golf ball and a bowling ball so that they travel at the same velocity. Which ball would you have to roll more forcefully? You would have to exert a greater force on the bowling ball because it has more mass than the golf ball.

Since energy is transferred during work, the more work you do, the more energy you give to the ball. So a bowling ball has more kinetic energy than a golf ball traveling at the same velocity. Kinetic energy increases as mass increases.

What would you have to do to make the bowling ball move faster? You would have to throw it harder, or use a greater force.

Figure 3 Kinetic energy increases as mass and velocity increase. *Interpreting Diagrams* *List the three vehicles in order of increasing kinetic energy.*

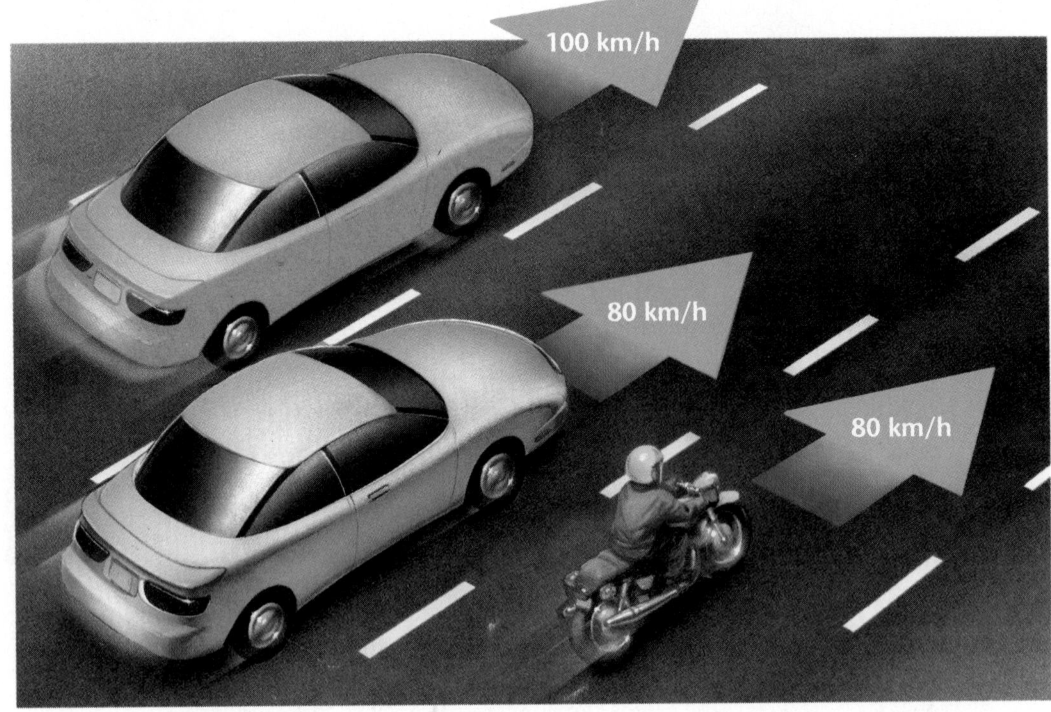

In other words, you have to do more work on the bowling ball to give it a greater velocity. Kinetic energy increases when velocity increases.

Calculating Kinetic Energy Kinetic energy depends on both mass and velocity. The mathematical relationship between kinetic energy, mass, and velocity is written as follows.

$$\text{Kinetic energy} = \frac{\text{Mass} \times \text{Velocity}^2}{2}$$

Do changes in velocity and mass have the same effect on kinetic energy? No—changing the velocity of an object will have a greater effect on its kinetic energy than changing its mass. This is because velocity is squared in the energy equation. For instance, doubling the mass of an object will double its kinetic energy. But doubling its velocity will quadruple its kinetic energy.

☑ *Checkpoint* *What is kinetic energy?*

Potential Energy

Sometimes when you transfer energy to an object, you change its position or shape. For example, you lift a book up to your desk or you compress a spring to wind a toy. Unlike kinetic energy, which is the energy of motion, potential energy is stored. It might be used later on when the book falls to the floor or the spring unwinds. Energy that is stored and held in readiness is called **potential energy.** This type of energy has the *potential* to do work.

Math TOOLBOX

Squared Numbers

A squared number is written with an exponent of 2. For example, you can write 2^2, 3^2, or 4^2. To find the value of a squared number, multiply the number by itself.

$2^2 = 2 \times 2 = 4$

$3^2 = 3 \times 3 = 9$

$4^2 = 4 \times 4 = 16$

Notice how fast the squared numbers increase. For example, although the numbers 2 and 3 only differ by one, their squares differ by five.

An archer gives potential energy to a bow by pulling it back. The stored energy can send an arrow whistling to its target. The potential energy associated with objects that can be stretched or compressed is called **elastic potential energy.**

You give a different type of potential energy to an object when you lift it. Potential energy that depends on height is **gravitational potential energy.**

The gravitational potential energy an object has is equal to the work done to lift it. Remember that Work = Force × Distance. The force is the force you use to lift the object, or its weight. The distance is the distance the object moves, or its height. This gives you the following formula.

Gravitational potential energy = Weight × Height

When weight is measured in newtons and height is measured in meters, the unit of energy is the newton-meter. This unit is also known as the joule (J). Recall from Chapter 4 that a joule is the amount of work you do when you exert a force of 1 newton to move an object a distance of 1 meter. Work and energy share the same unit because energy and work are so closely related.

Once you know weight and height, you can calculate gravitational potential energy. Suppose that a hiker climbs 40 meters up a hill and that he weighs 680 newtons. The hiker has gained 27,200 joules (680 newtons × 40 meters) of gravitational potential energy at the top of the climb.

The greater the weight of an object or the greater the height it is lifted, the greater its gravitational potential energy. The hiker would gain more gravitational potential energy by climbing to a greater height or by increasing weight, maybe by wearing a backpack.

What if you know the mass of an object instead of its weight? Then you multiply the mass of the object (in kilograms) by the acceleration of gravity (9.8 m/s^2) to find its weight in newtons. Now you can write a second formula for gravitational potential energy.

Gravitational potential energy = Mass × Gravitational acceleration × Height

Again, the unit of measure is the joule.

Figure 4 A rock poised for a fall has potential energy. *Inferring How did the rock get its potential energy?*

Figure 5 Energy is all around you in many different forms. The leaping frog is an example of mechanical energy, and the melting ice is an example of thermal energy. *Observing Which forms of energy are shown in the photographs of the sparkler, the sun, and the lightning?*

Different Forms of Energy

The examples of energy you have read about so far involve objects being moved or physically changed. But both kinetic energy and potential energy have a variety of different forms. **Some of the major forms of energy are mechanical energy, thermal energy, chemical energy, electrical energy, electromagnetic energy, and nuclear energy.**

Mechanical Energy The school bus you ride in, a frog leaping through the air, and even the sounds you hear all have mechanical energy. **Mechanical energy** is the energy associated with the motion or position of an object. Mechanical energy can occur as kinetic energy or potential energy.

Thermal Energy All matter is made up of small particles, called atoms and molecules. These particles have both potential energy and kinetic energy due to their arrangement and motion. **Thermal energy** is the total energy of the particles in a substance or material. When the thermal energy of an object increases, its particles move faster, making the temperature of the object rise. Ice cream melts when its thermal energy increases.

Chemical Energy Chemical compounds, such as chocolate, wood, and wax, store **chemical energy.** Chemical energy is potential energy stored in chemical bonds that hold chemical compounds together. Chemical energy is stored in the foods you eat and in a match that is used to light a candle. Chemical energy is even stored in the cells of your body.

Electrical Energy When you receive a shock from a metal doorknob, you experience electrical energy. Moving electric charges produce electricity, and the energy they carry is called **electrical energy.** You rely on electrical energy from batteries or power lines to run electrical devices such as radios, lights, and computers.

Electromagnetic Energy The light that you see each day is a form of **electromagnetic energy.** Electromagnetic energy travels in waves. These waves have some electrical properties and some magnetic properties. In addition to visible light, ultraviolet radiation, microwaves, and infrared radiation are all examples of electromagnetic energy.

Nuclear Energy Another type of potential energy, called **nuclear energy,** is stored in the nucleus of an atom and is released during nuclear reactions. One kind of nuclear reaction occurs when a nucleus splits (nuclear fission). Another kind occurs when nuclei fuse, or join together (nuclear fusion). These reactions release tremendous amounts of energy. Nuclear power plants use fission reactions to produce electricity. Nuclear fusion occurs in the sun and other stars.

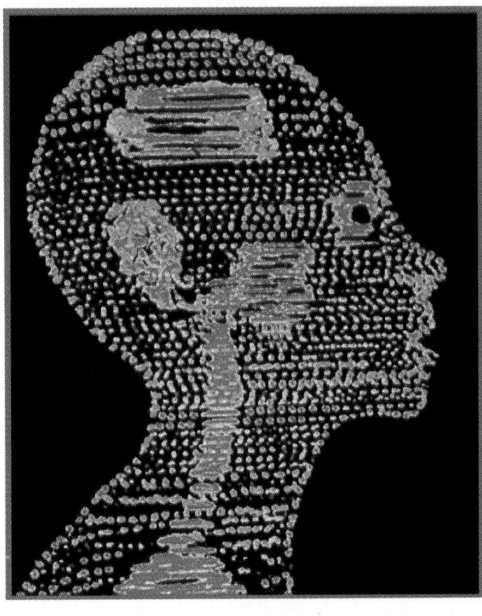

Figure 6 Electromagnetic energy is used to take a CT scan.

Section 1 Review

1. Are energy and work the same thing? Explain.
2. How are kinetic and potential energy different?
3. List the forms of energy and give an example of each.
4. **Thinking Critically Problem Solving** A boulder that weighs 200 N is poised at the edge of a 100-meter cliff. What is its gravitational potential energy? Draw a diagram showing how its potential energy changes as it falls to 50 m, 20 m, and 10 m.

Check Your Progress

CHAPTER PROJECT 5

Some materials that you can use to build a roller coaster track and car include marbles, rubber tubing, cardboard, and string. Experiment with different hill heights and inclines. (*Hint:* See how high you can make the second and third hills before the roller coaster car can no longer climb up the hills.) Think about how you can explain the types of energy involved as the roller coaster car moves.

Skills Lab

Controlling Variables

SOARING STRAWS

In this lab you will use the skill of controlling variables. You will investigate the relationship between the height reached by a rocket and the amount of stretch in a rubber band.

Problem

How does the gravitational potential energy of a straw rocket depend on the elastic potential energy of the rubber band launcher?

Materials

scissors
3 plastic straws
marker
balance
empty toilet paper tube
rubber band
meter stick
metric ruler
masking tape

Procedure  

1. Construct the rocket and launcher following the instructions below. Use a balance to find the mass of the rocket in grams. Record the mass.
2. Hold the launcher in one hand with your fingers over the ends of the rubber band. Load the launcher by placing the straw rocket on the rubber band and pulling down from the other end as shown in the photograph. Let go and launch the rocket straight up. **CAUTION:** *Be sure to aim the straw rocket into the air, not at classmates.*
3. In your notebook, make a data table similar to the one on the next page.
4. Have your partner hold a meter stick, or tape it to the wall, so that its zero end is even with the top of the rocket launcher. Measure the height, in meters, to which the rocket rises. If the rocket goes higher than a single meter stick, use two meter sticks.
5. You can measure the amount of stretch of the rubber band by noting where the markings on the rocket line up with the bottom of the launching cylinder. Launch the rocket using five different amounts of stretch. Record your measurements.

MAKING A ROCKET AND LAUNCHER

A. Cut a rubber band and tape it across the open end of a hollow cylinder, such as a toilet paper tube. The rubber band should be taut, but stretched only a tiny amount. This is the launcher.

B. Cut about 3 cm off a plastic straw.

C. Lay 2 full-length straws side by side on a flat surface with the 3-cm piece of straw between them. Arrange the straws so that their ends are even.

D. Tape the straws together side by side.

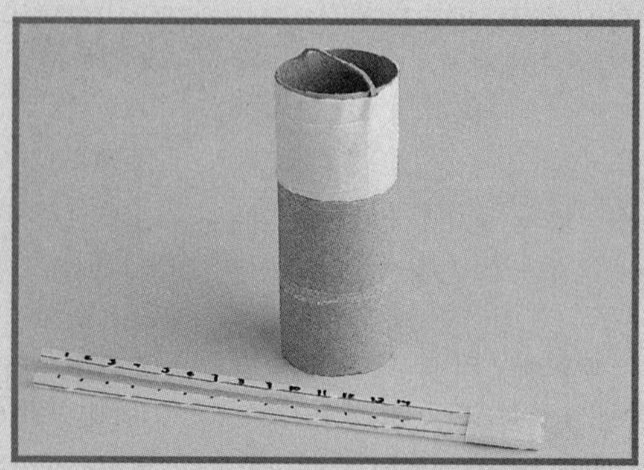

E. Starting from the untaped end, make marks every centimeter on one of the long straws. This is the rocket.

DATA TABLE

Amount of Stretch (cm)	Height (Trial 1) (m)	Height (Trial 2) (m)	Height (Trial 3) (m)	Average Height (m)	Gravitational Potential Energy (mJ)

6. For each amount of stretch, find the average height to which the rocket rises. Record the height in your data table.
7. Find the gravitational potential energy for each amount of stretch:

   Gravitational potential energy =
   Mass × Gravitational acceleration × Height

   You have measured the mass in grams. So the unit of energy is the millijoule (mJ), which is one thousandth of a joule. Record the results in your data table.

Analyze and Conclude

1. Which variable in your data table is the manipulated variable? The responding variable? How do you know?
2. Graph your results. Show gravitational potential energy on the vertical axis and amount of stretch on the horizontal axis.
3. What measurement is related to the elastic potential energy in this experiment?
4. Look at the shape of the graph. What conclusions can you reach about the relationship between the gravitational potential energy of the rocket and the elastic potential energy of the rubber band?
5. How do you think the amount of energy before the rocket was released compares to the amount of energy after the rocket was released? Account for any losses.
6. **Think About It** Besides the amount of stretch, what other variables might affect the height to which the straw rocket rises? Have you been able to control these variables in your experiment? Explain why or why not.

More to Explore

Use your launcher to investigate launches at angles other than straight up. Instead of manipulating the amount of stretch, hold that variable constant and manipulate the angle of launch. Measure both the heights and distances of the rocket. **CAUTION:** *Be careful not to aim the rocket near any of your classmates.*

Section 2 Energy Conversion and Conservation

Discover ACTIVITY

What Would Make a Card Jump?

1. Fold an index card in half.
2. In the edge opposite the fold, cut two slits that are about 2 cm long and 2 cm apart.
3. Keep the card folded and loop a rubber band through the slits. With the fold toward you, gently open the card like a tent and flatten it against your desk.
4. Predict what will happen to the card if you let go. Then test your prediction.

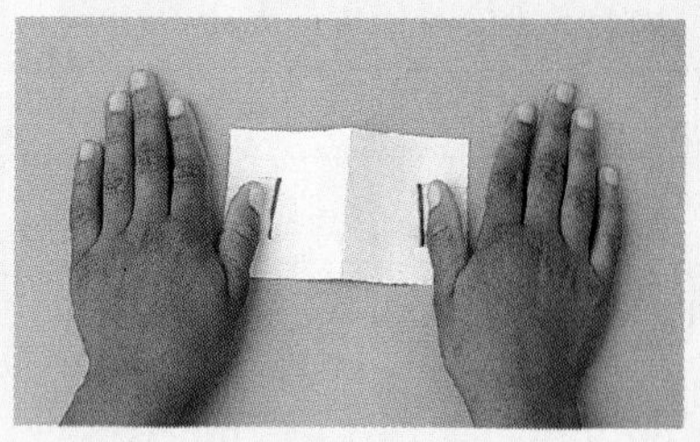

Think It Over

Forming Operational Definitions Describe what happened to the card. Define potential and kinetic energy in terms of the card and the rubber band.

Guide for Reading

- **How are different forms of energy related?**
- **What is the law of conservation of energy?**

Reading Tip **As you read, draw a flowchart to show each example of energy conversions.**

The spray of water bounces off your raincoat as you look up at the millions of liters of water plunging toward you. The roar of water is deafening. You hold on to the rail as you are rocked back and forth by the rough waves. Are you doomed? Fortunately not—you are on a sightseeing boat at the foot of the mighty Niagara Falls, located on the border between the United States and Canada. The waterfall carries the huge amount of water that drains from the upper Great Lakes. It is an awesome sight that has attracted visitors from all over the world for hundreds of years.

What many visitors don't know, however, is that Niagara Falls serves as much more than just a spectacular view. The Niagara Falls area is the center of a network of electrical power lines. Water that is diverted above the falls is used to generate electricity for much of the neighboring region.

Figure 7 Niagara Falls is more than 50 meters high.

The lamp and clock convert electrical energy to electromagnetic energy.

A water heater converts chemical energy in natural gas to thermal energy.

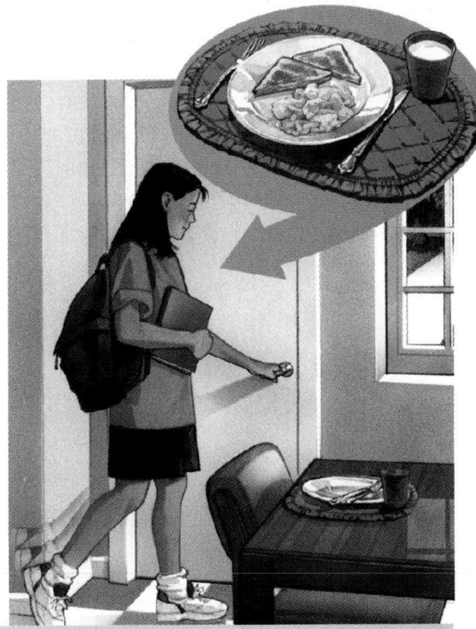
The student's body converts chemical energy in food to mechanical energy.

Figure 8 In just the first few minutes of the morning, this student experiences numerous energy conversions. Imagine how many more can be identified throughout the course of a single day!

Conversions Between Forms of Energy

What does water have to do with electricity? You may already know that the mechanical energy of moving water can be converted, or transformed, into electrical energy. A change from one form of energy to another is called an **energy conversion,** or an energy transformation. **Most forms of energy can be converted into other forms.**

You encounter energy conversions frequently. A toaster, for example, converts electrical energy to thermal energy. In an electric motor, electrical energy is converted to mechanical energy that can be used to run a machine.

Your body converts the chemical energy in the food you eat to the mechanical energy you need to move your muscles. Chemical energy in food is also converted to the thermal energy your body uses to maintain its temperature. Chemical energy is even converted to the electrical energy your brain uses to think.

Often a series of energy conversions is needed to do a task. Strike a match, for example, and the mechanical energy used to scratch the match is converted to thermal energy. The thermal energy causes the match to release stored chemical energy, which is converted to thermal energy and to the energy you see as light.

In a car engine another series of conversions occurs. Electrical energy produces a hot spark. The thermal energy of the spark releases chemical energy in the fuel. When the fuel burns, this chemical energy in turn becomes thermal energy. Thermal energy is converted to mechanical energy used to move the car, and to electrical energy that produces more sparks.

☑ *Checkpoint* *Give an example of an energy conversion.*

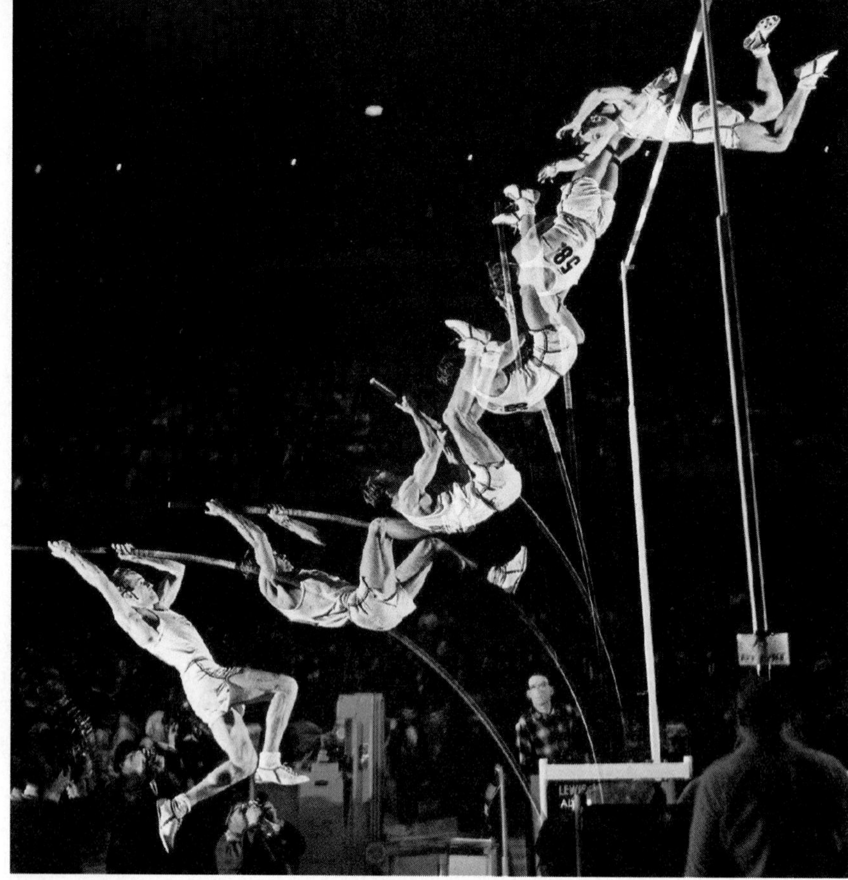

Figure 9 Energy conversions enable this athlete to vault more than six meters into the air. *Predicting What energy conversions will occur after the vaulter falls over the bar?*

Figure 10 When an object is tossed into the air, energy conversions take place.

Maximum potential energy

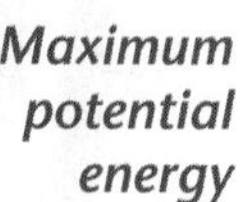

50% kinetic energy
50% potential energy

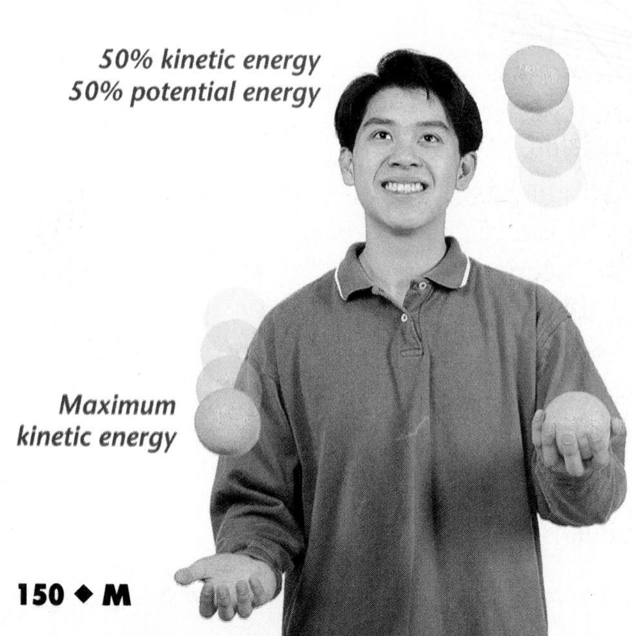

Maximum kinetic energy

Kinetic and Potential Energy

One of the most common conversions is the conversion of potential energy to kinetic energy. When you stretch a rubber band, you give it elastic potential energy. If you let it go, the rubber band flies across the room. When the rubber band is moving, it has kinetic energy. The potential energy of the stretched rubber band is converted to the kinetic energy of the moving rubber band.

Energy Conversion in Juggling Any object that rises or falls experiences a change in its kinetic and gravitational potential energy. Look at the orange in Figure 10. When it moves, the orange possesses kinetic energy. As it rises, it slows down. Its kinetic energy decreases. But because its height increases, its potential energy increases. At the highest point in its path, it stops moving. At this point, it no longer possesses kinetic energy, but it possesses potential energy. As the orange falls, the entire energy conversion is reversed—kinetic energy increases while potential energy decreases.

Energy Conversion in a Waterfall There is a conversion between potential and kinetic energy on a large scale at Niagara Falls, which you read about earlier. The water at the top of the falls has gravitational potential energy because it is higher than the bottom of the falls. But as the water falls, its height decreases and so it loses potential energy. At the same time, its kinetic energy increases because its velocity increases. Thus potential energy is converted into kinetic energy.

Energy Conversion in a Pole Vault As a pole vaulter runs, he has kinetic energy because he is moving. When he plants his pole to jump, the pole bends. His kinetic energy is converted to elastic potential energy in the pole. As the pole straightens out, the vaulter is lifted high into the air. The elastic potential energy of the pole is converted to the gravitational potential energy of the pole vaulter. Once over the bar, the vaulter's gravitational potential energy is converted into kinetic energy as he falls to the safety cushion below.

Energy Conversion in a Pendulum A continuous conversion between kinetic energy and potential energy takes place in a pendulum. At the highest point in its swing, the pendulum in Figure 11 has only gravitational potential energy. As the pendulum starts to swing downward, it speeds up and its gravitational potential energy changes to kinetic energy. At the bottom of its swing, all its energy is kinetic energy. Then, as it swings to the other side and slows down, it regains gravitational potential energy, and at the same time loses kinetic energy. At the top of its swing on the other side it again has only gravitational potential energy. And so the pattern of energy conversion continues.

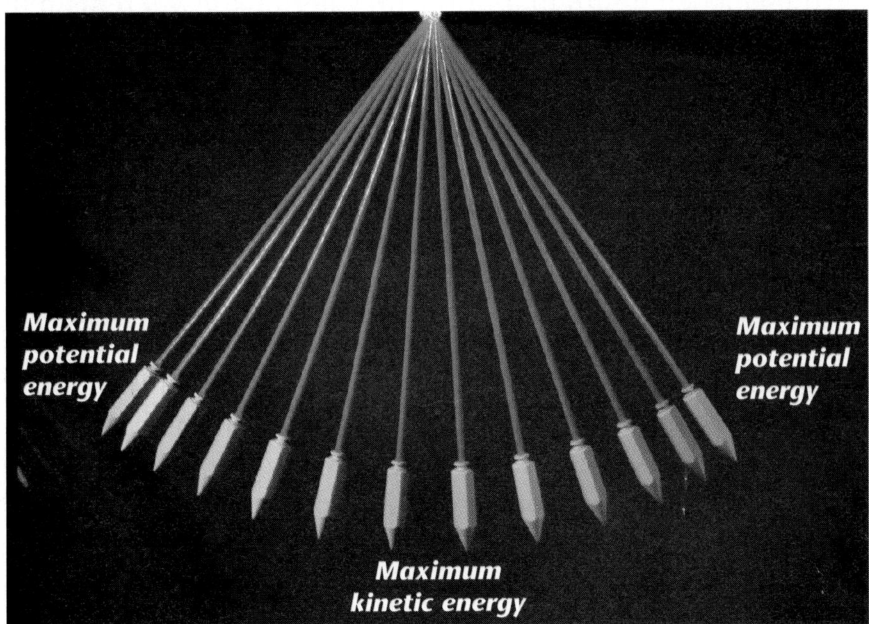

Figure 11 Conversions between kinetic energy and potential energy take place in a pendulum. *Interpreting Diagrams At what two points is potential energy greatest?*

Pendulum Swing

ACTIVITY

1. Set up a pendulum using washers or a rubber stopper, string, a ring stand, and a clamp.
2. Pull the pendulum back so that it makes a 45° angle with the vertical. Measure the height of the stopper. Then set it in motion and observe the height to which it swings.
3. Use a second clamp to reduce the length of the pendulum as shown. The pendulum will run into the second clamp at the bottom of its swing.

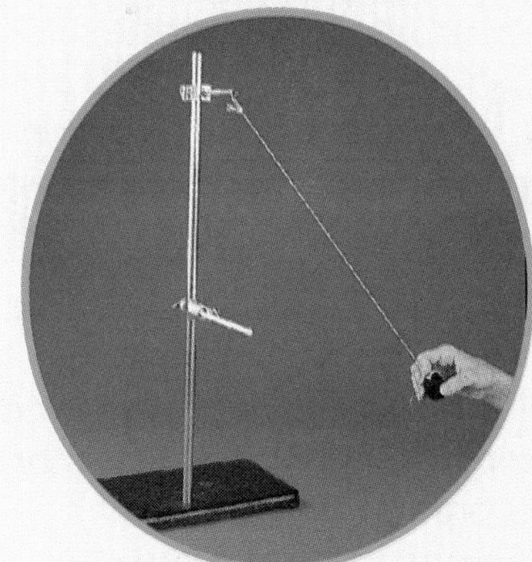

4. Pull the pendulum back to the same height as you did the first time. Predict the height to which the pendulum will swing. Then set it in motion and observe it.

Observing How high did the pendulum swing in each case? Explain your observations.

Figure 12 M. C. Escher's print "Waterfall" was done in 1961.

Visual Arts CONNECTION

The Dutch artist M. C. Escher produced many intriguing illustrations. Escher, who lived from 1898 to 1972, was most recognized for his use of illusions and repeating geometric patterns.

In Your Journal

Look at Escher's "Waterfall." Then look again. In your journal, write a description of the illustration. Did you see anything in the art during your second look that you didn't see at first glance? Is the law of conservation of energy followed or violated in the art? Explain your answer.

Conservation of Energy

If you set a pendulum in motion, do you think it will remain in motion forever? No, it will not. Does that mean that energy is destroyed over time? The answer is no. The **law of conservation of energy** states that when one form of energy is converted to another, no energy is destroyed in the process. **According to the law of conservation of energy, energy cannot be created or destroyed.** So the total amount of energy is the same before and after any process. All energy can be accounted for.

Energy and Friction So what happens to the kinetic energy of the pendulum? As the pendulum moves, it encounters friction at the pivot of the string and from the air through which it moves. When an object experiences friction, the motion (and thus the kinetic energy) of the atoms or molecules increases. This means its thermal energy increases. So the mechanical energy of the moving pendulum is converted to thermal energy. The pendulum slows down, but its energy is not destroyed.

The fact that friction converts mechanical energy to thermal energy should not surprise you. After all, you take advantage of such thermal energy when you rub your cold hands together to warm them up. The fact that mechanical energy is converted to thermal energy because of friction explains why no machine is 100 percent efficient. Recall from Chapter 4 that the work output of a machine is always less than the work input. Now you know that mechanical energy is converted to thermal energy in a machine.

Energy and Matter You might have heard of Albert Einstein's theory of relativity. Einstein's theory included a small change to the law of conservation of energy. He explained that energy can sometimes be created—by destroying matter! This process is not important for most of the energy conversions described in this chapter. But it is important in nuclear reactions, where huge amounts of energy are produced by destroying tiny amounts of matter. This discovery means that in some situations energy alone is not conserved. But scientists say that matter and energy together are always conserved. Just as different forms of energy can be converted to one another, matter can sometimes be converted to energy.

Figure 13 Albert Einstein published his theory of special relativity in 1905.

Conserving Energy

When you hear or read about conserving energy, don't get confused with the law of conservation of energy. Conserving energy means saving energy, or not wasting it. In other words, conserving energy means we should not waste fuels, such as gasoline, or our resources will be used up quickly. The law of conservation of energy in physical science, however, refers to a quantity that remains constant. In science, energy is always conserved because its total quantity does not change.

Section 2 Review

1. What is an energy conversion?
2. State the law of conservation of energy in your own words.
3. Describe the energy conversions that occur when a ball is dropped and bounces back up. Why do you think the ball bounces a little lower each time?
4. **Thinking Critically Applying Concepts** A roller coaster car with a mass of 500 kg is at the top of a hill that is 30 m high. Without friction, what would its kinetic energy be as it reached the bottom of the hill?

Science at Home

Straighten a wire hanger. Have your family members feel the wire and observe whether it feels cool or warm. Then hold the ends of the wire and bend it several times. **CAUTION:** *If the wire breaks, it can be sharp.* Do not bend it more than a few times. After bending the wire, have your family members feel it again. Ask them to explain how energy conversions can produce a change in temperature.

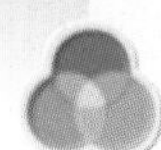

SECTION 3 Energy Conversions and Fossil Fuels

DISCOVER ACTIVITY

What Is a Fuel?

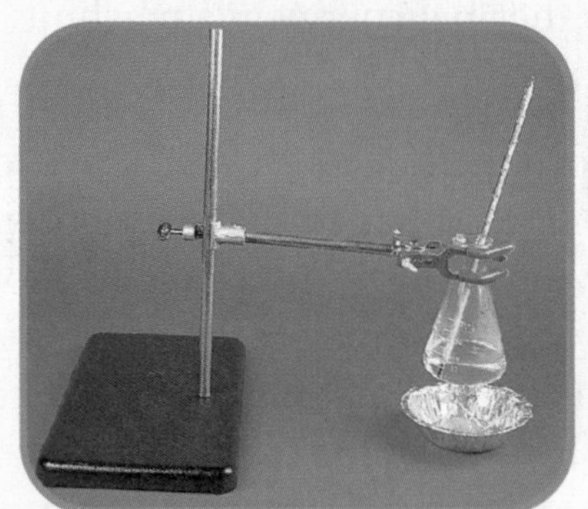

1. Put on your goggles. Attach a flask to a ring stand with a clamp. Then place a thermometer in the flask.
2. Add enough water to the flask to cover the thermometer bulb. Record the temperature of the water, and remove the thermometer.
3. Fold a wooden coffee stirrer in three places to look like a W.
4. Stand the bent coffee stirrer in a small aluminum pan so that the W is upright. Position the pan 4–5 cm directly below the flask.
5. Ignite the coffee stirrer at the center. **CAUTION:** *Be careful when using matches.*
6. When the coffee stirrer has stopped burning, find the temperature of the water again. Wait until the flask has cooled before cleaning up.

Think It Over

Forming Operational Definitions Gasoline in a car, kerosene in a lantern, and a piece of wood are all fuels. Based on your observations, what is a fuel?

GUIDE FOR READING

- **What is the source of the energy stored in fossil fuels?**
- **How is energy converted when fossil fuels are used?**

Reading Tip **Before you read, preview *Exploring Energy Conversions.* Write down any questions that you may have. Then look for answers as you read.**

Envision a lush, green, swampy forest. Ferns as tall as trees block the view as they rise up to 30 meters. Enormous dragonflies buzz through the warm, moist air. And huge cockroaches, some longer than your finger, crawl across the ground. Where is it? Actually, the question should be, When is it? The time is over 400 million years ago. That's even before the dinosaurs lived! What does this ancient forest have to do with you? You might be surprised to find out just how important this forest is to you.

Figure 14 The plants and animals in this painting of an ancient forest have become the fossil fuels you use today. *Applying Concepts* *What are fossil fuels?*

Figure 15 Fossil fuels such as coal store chemical potential energy. *Predicting How do you think the stored energy is utilized?*

Formation of Fossil Fuels

The plants of vast forests that once covered Earth provide you with energy you use today. This energy is stored in fuels. A fuel is a material that stores chemical potential energy. The gasoline used in your school bus, the propane used in a gas barbecue grill, and the chemicals used to launch a space shuttle are examples of fuels. Some of the fuels used today were formed hundreds of millions of years ago by geological processes. These fuels, which include coal, petroleum, and natural gas, are known as **fossil fuels.**

As you'll discover in *Exploring Energy Conversions* on page 156, coal was formed from the ancient forests you just read about. When ancient plants and animals died, they formed thick layers in swamps and marshes. Clay and sand sediments covered the plant and animal remains. Over time, more and more sediment piled up. The resulting pressure along with high temperatures turned the animal and plant remains into coal.

Energy is conserved. That means that fuels do not create energy. So if fossil fuels store energy, they must have gotten energy from somewhere else. But where did it come from? **Fossil fuels contain energy that came from the sun.** In fact, the sun is the source of energy for most of Earth's processes. Within the dense core of the sun, hydrogen atoms are moving at such high velocities that when they collide they join, or fuse, together to form helium atoms. During this process of nuclear fusion, nuclear energy is converted to electromagnetic energy. A portion of this energy reaches Earth.

When the sun's energy reaches Earth, plants, algae, and certain bacteria convert some of the light energy to chemical potential energy. This process is known as photosynthesis because the plants or bacteria synthesize, or make, complex chemicals. Some of this chemical energy is used for the plant's daily needs, and the rest is stored.

Graphing

ACTIVITY

The following list shows what percent of power used in a recent year in the United States came from each power source: coal, 23%; nuclear, 8%; oil, 39%; natural gas, 24%; water, 3%; and biofuels, 3%. Prepare a circle graph that presents these data. (See the Skills Handbook for more on circle graphs.)

What fuel source does the United States rely on most? What percent of total energy needs is met by coal, oil, and natural gas combined?

EXPLORING *Energy Conversions*

The energy you use to toast your bread may have had a very long history—hundreds of millions of years worth.

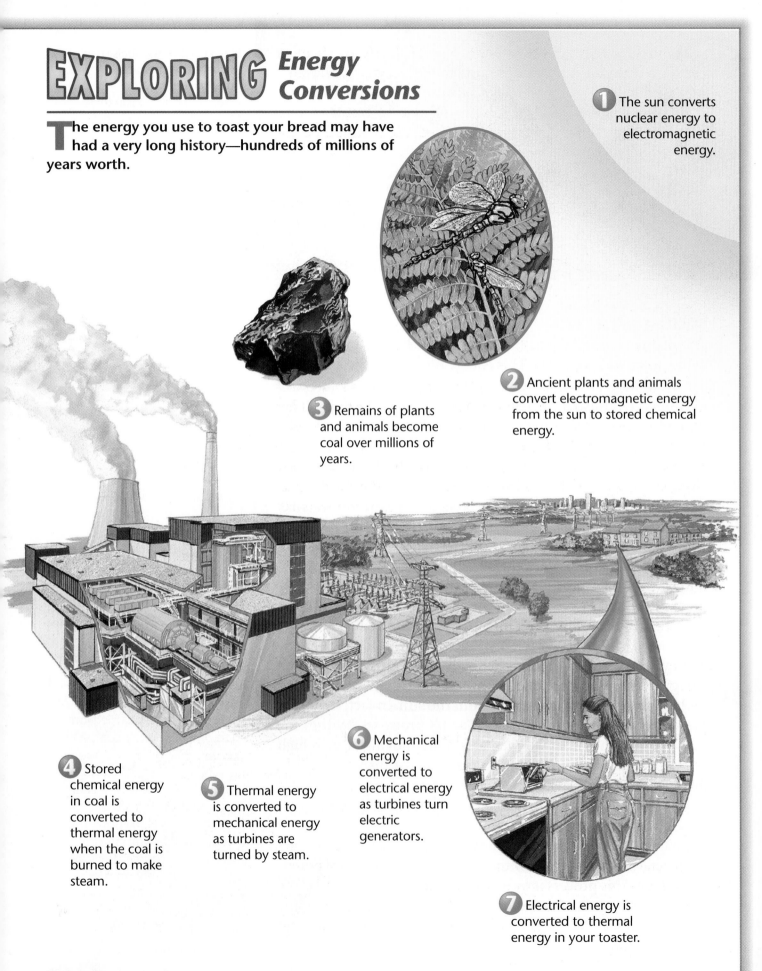

1 The sun converts nuclear energy to electromagnetic energy.

2 Ancient plants and animals convert electromagnetic energy from the sun to stored chemical energy.

3 Remains of plants and animals become coal over millions of years.

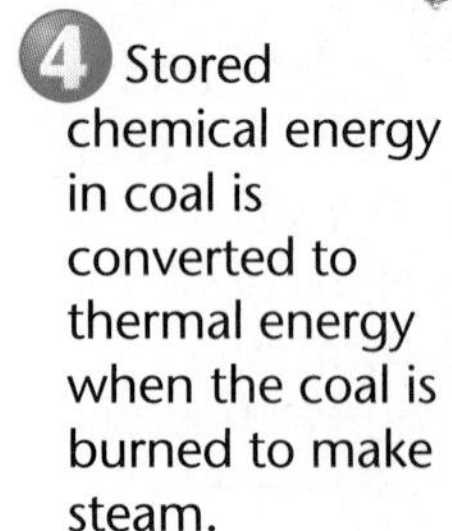

4 Stored chemical energy in coal is converted to thermal energy when the coal is burned to make steam.

5 Thermal energy is converted to mechanical energy as turbines are turned by steam.

6 Mechanical energy is converted to electrical energy as turbines turn electric generators.

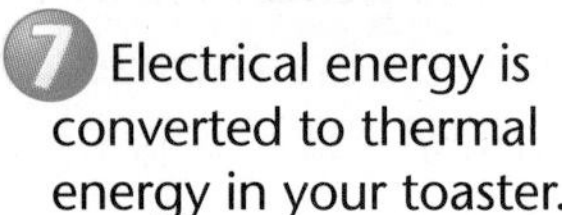

7 Electrical energy is converted to thermal energy in your toaster.

Animals that eat plants convert some of the stored chemical energy to chemical energy that is stored in their own cells. The rest is converted to other forms of energy, such as mechanical energy used in movement or thermal energy used to maintain body temperature.

When ancient animals and plants died, the chemical potential energy they had stored was trapped within them. This is the chemical potential energy that is found in coal.

☑ *Checkpoint* *What is the process that produces the sun's energy?*

Use of Fossil Fuels

Fossil fuels can be burned to release the potential chemical energy stored millions of years ago. The process of burning fuels is known as combustion. During combustion, the fuel's chemical potential energy is converted to thermal energy. This thermal energy can be used to heat water until the water boils and produces steam.

In modern coal-fired power plants, the steam is raised to a very high temperature in a boiler. When it leaves the boiler it has enough pressure to turn a turbine. A turbine is like a fan, with blades attached to a shaft. The pressure of the steam on the blades causes the turbine to spin very fast. In this process, the thermal energy of the steam is converted to the mechanical energy of the moving turbine. Turbines are in turn connected to generators. Generators are just electric motors made to run backward. When they are spun by turbines, they produce electricity. In other words, in a power plant mechanical energy is converted to electrical energy. This energy is then used to light your home and run other electrical devices, such as a toaster.

Section 3 Review

1. How is the chemical energy in fossil fuels related to the sun's energy?
2. How is the energy of coal released?
3. Describe the energy conversions involved in the formation of coal.
4. **Thinking Critically Making Judgments** What general statement can you make about the supply of fossil fuels, given what you know about their formation?

Check Your Progress

CHAPTER PROJECT 5

Experiment with different design ideas for your roller coaster vehicle. What variables affect how fast your vehicle moves? How do potential and kinetic energy change as you make modifications to your design? At what point does the vehicle have the greatest kinetic energy? The greatest potential energy? How does friction affect the performance of your roller coaster? How can you relate the law of conservation of energy to your design?

Section 4 Power

Discover Activity

Is Work Always the Same?

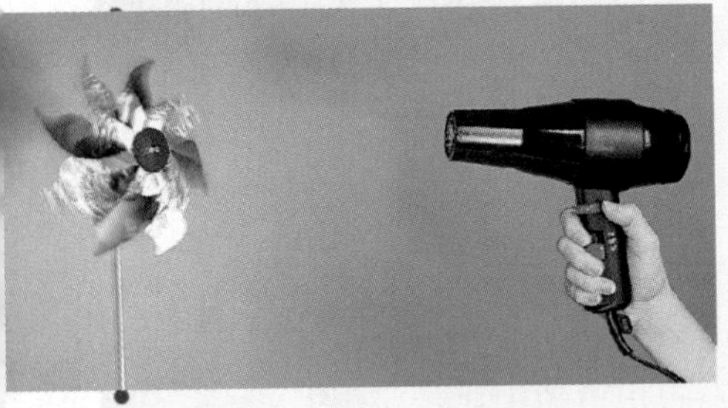

1. Obtain a pinwheel and a hair dryer with at least two different power settings.
2. Set the dryer on its lowest setting. Use it to blow the pinwheel. Observe the pinwheel's motion.
3. Set the dryer on its highest setting. Again, use it to blow the pinwheel. Observe the pinwheel's motion.

Think It Over

Inferring Explain why work is done in spinning the pinwheel. What differences can you identify between the two situations? Is the amount of work greater for the high or low speed?

GUIDE FOR READING

- **How do you calculate power?**
- **What is the difference between power and energy?**

Reading Tip **As you read, use your own words to describe the relationship among work, power, and energy.**

The ad for a sleek new sports car catches your eye as you read a magazine. Its manufacturer boasts that the car can go from 0 to 100 km/h in 5 seconds because it has a 320-horsepower engine. But what does a car have to do with horses? Maybe more than you think.

What Is Power?

A car does work to accelerate from rest. Some car engines do this work rapidly, while others do it more slowly. The faster an engine can do an amount of work, the more power the engine has. **Power** is the rate at which work is done or the amount of work done in a unit of time.

When you carry an object up some stairs, you do the same amount of work whether you walk or run up the stairs. (Work is the weight of the object times the height of the stairs.) But you exert more power when you run because you are doing the work faster.

You can think of power in another way. A device that is twice as powerful as another can do the same amount of work in half the time. Or it can do twice the work in the same time.

Calculating Power Whenever you know how fast work is done, you can calculate power. **Power is calculated by dividing the amount of work done by the amount of time taken to do the work.** This can be written as the following formula.

$$Power = \frac{Work}{Time}$$

Since work is equal to force times distance, you can rewrite the equation for power as follows.

$$\text{Power} = \frac{\text{Force} \times \text{Distance}}{\text{Time}}$$

When work is measured in joules and time in seconds, the unit of power is the joule per second (J/s). This unit is also known as the watt (W), in honor of James Watt, who made great improvements to the steam engine. One watt of power is produced when one joule of work is done in one second. In other words, 1 watt = 1 J/s.

A watt is a relatively small unit of power. For example, you produce about one watt of power if you raise a glass of water to your mouth in one second. Because a watt is so small, power is often measured in larger units. One kilowatt (kW) equals 1,000 watts. A washing machine uses about one kilowatt per hour when it is running. An electric power plant produces millions of kilowatts.

☑ *Checkpoint* *What is power?*

A crane lifts an 8,000-N beam 75 m to the top of a building in 30 s. How much power does the crane use?

Analyze. The force needed to lift the beam will be equal to its weight, 8,000 N. The distance and time are given, so the formula for power can be used.

Write the formula.

$$\text{Power} = \frac{\text{Force} \times \text{Distance}}{\text{Time}}$$

Substitute and solve.

$$\text{Power} = \frac{8{,}000 \text{ N} \times 75 \text{ m}}{30 \text{ s}}$$

$$\text{Power} = \frac{600{,}000 \text{ N}\cdot\text{m}}{30 \text{ s}} \text{ or } \frac{600{,}000 \text{ J}}{30 \text{ s}}$$

$$\text{Power} = 20{,}000 \text{ J/s} = 20{,}000 \text{ W or } 20 \text{ kW}$$

Think about it. The answer tells you that the crane used 20,000 W to lift the beam. That equals 20 kW.

Practice Problems

1. A motor exerts a force of 10,000 N to lift an elevator 6 m in 5 s. What is the power produced by the motor?
2. A tow truck exerts a force of 9,000 N to pull a car out of a ditch. It moves the car a distance of 6 m in 25 s. What is the power of the tow truck?

Power and Energy

Recall that work is the transfer of energy. Thus power can be defined in another way. **Power is the rate at which energy is transferred from one object to another or converted from one form to another.** For this reason, power is not limited to situations in which objects are moved. Power can be found whenever energy is being transferred or converted.

Real-World Lab

Careers in Science

Can You Feel the Power?

Imagine you are a physical therapist who wants to increase the power output of her patients. In this lab, you will simulate a simple exercise using a step.

Problem

How can you change how much power you expended while doing an exercise?

Skills Focus

measuring, calculating, interpreting data

Materials

calculator

meter stick

stopwatch or clock with a second hand

board, about 2.5 cm × 30 cm × 120 cm

8–10 books, each about 2 cm thick

Procedure

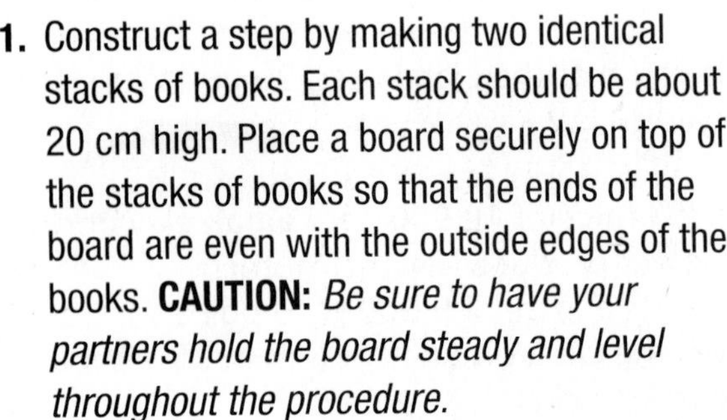

1. Construct a step by making two identical stacks of books. Each stack should be about 20 cm high. Place a board securely on top of the stacks of books so that the ends of the board are even with the outside edges of the books. **CAUTION:** *Be sure to have your partners hold the board steady and level throughout the procedure.*
2. Copy the data table into your notebook.
3. You do work every time you take a step.
   Work = Weight × Height
   a. Assume your weight is 400 N and your partners' weights are 425 N and 450 N.
   b. Measure the vertical distance in centimeters from the floor to the top of the board. Convert to meters by dividing by 100 and record this height in the data table.
4. Calculate the work you do in stepping up onto the board once. Then calculate the work you do in stepping up onto the board 20 times. Record both answers in your data table.
5. Step up onto the board with both feet and then step backwards off the board onto the floor. This up and down motion is one repetition. Make sure you are comfortable with the motion.
6. Have one partner time how long it takes you to do 20 repetitions performed at a constant speed. Count out loud to help the timer keep track of the number of repetitions. Record the time in your data table.
7. Calculate the power you expended to do 20 repetitions. (Power = Work ÷ Time.) Predict how your results will change if you step up and down at different speeds.

You know that a 100-watt light bulb is much brighter than a 40-watt light bulb. The wattage printed on a light bulb tells you its power. The power of a light bulb is the rate at which electrical energy is converted into electromagnetic energy (light) and thermal energy. A 100-watt light bulb converts electrical energy at a rate of 100 joules each second. A 100-watt bulb is brighter because it gives off more energy per second than a 40-watt bulb.

DATA TABLE

	Weight (N)	Height of Board (m)	Time for 20 Repetitions (s)	Work for 1 Repetition (J)	Work for 20 Repetitions (J)	Power (W)
Student 1 Trial 1						
Student 1 Trial 2						

8. Repeat Steps 6 and 7, but climb the step more slowly than you did the first time. Record the new data in the Trial 2 row of your data table.
9. Switch roles with your partners and repeat Steps 3 through 8 with a different weight from Step 3a.

Analyze and Conclude

1. Compare the amount of work you did during your first and second trials.
2. Compare the amount of power you produced during your first and second trials.
3. Did you and your partners all do the same amount of work? Explain your answer.
4. Did you and your partners all produce the same power during your trials? Explain your answer.
5. **Apply** Suggest how a physical therapist cou use music to change the power output of h patients. Why would a therapist want to change power outputs?

Design an Experime

Design an experiment to test t ways a physical therapist cou the power output of her patie your teache before beg experimen

Figure 16 One of Watt's engines (next to the chimney) is shown at work at a coal mine.

Horsepower

INTEGRATING TECHNOLOGY When people talk about engines for automobiles, they use another power unit instead of the watt. This unit is the horsepower. One horsepower is equal to 746 watts. (The horsepower is not an SI unit.)

The word horsepower was used by James Watt to advertise the advantages of his improved steam engine of 1769. Watt decided to relate his engine to the common source of power in his day—horses. He compared the amount of work his steam engine could do to the amount of work a horse could do hauling coal. He defined one horsepower as the amount of work a horse does to lift a 33,000-pound weight a distance of one foot in one minute.

tion 4 Review

for calculating power.
nd energy related?
do when you exert a force of
nce of 18 m in 4 seconds.
r you expend.
y **Problem Solving** The
fan converts 24,000 J of
minute (60 s). What is
motor?
omparing and
rsepower engine
l each hour as a
xplain this in terms

CHAPTER PROJECT 5

Check Your Progress

Add turns to the tracks on your roller coaster. What happens to the speed of the car as it rounds a turn? Are there certain locations along the tracks that are better for turns? Experiment with putting a vertical loop in the tracks. Where is the best place to put a loop? The roller coaster converts gravitational potential energy to kinetic energy. At what point in the car's trip is this rate of conversion greatest?

CHAPTER 5 STUDY GUIDE

Section 1 The Nature of Energy

Key Ideas

- Energy is the ability to do work or produce change.
- Energy is transferred from one object to another when work is done.
- Kinetic energy is the energy that an object has because of its motion. Potential energy is the energy an object has because of its position or condition.
- Six forms of energy are mechanical energy, thermal energy, chemical energy, electric energy, electromagnetic energy, and nuclear energy.

Key Terms

energy
kinetic energy
potential energy
elastic potential energy
gravitational potential energy
mechanical energy
thermal energy
chemical energy
electrical energy
electromagnetic energy
nuclear energy

Section 2 Energy Conversion and Conservation

Key Ideas

- An energy conversion or transformation occurs when energy changes from one form to another.
- In any process, no energy is lost. This is the law of conservation of energy.

Key Terms

energy conversion
law of conservation of energy

Section 3 Energy Conversions and Fossil Fuels

Key Ideas

- Energy from the sun is converted to chemical energy in plants and animals. Fossil fuels, such as coal and petroleum, were formed from the remains of ancient plants and animals.
- The energy in fossil fuels is released and transformed when the fuels are burned.

Key Term

fossil fuels

Section 4 Power

Integrating Mathematics

Key Ideas

- Power is the rate at which work is done, or the rate at which energy is transformed.
- Power is calculated by dividing the amount of work done (or energy converted) by the time it took. The unit of power is the watt: $1 \text{ W} = 1 \text{ J/s}$.

Key Term

power

Organizing Information

Concept Map Copy the concept map about energy onto a separate sheet of paper. Then complete it and add a title. (For more on concept maps, see the Skills Handbook.)

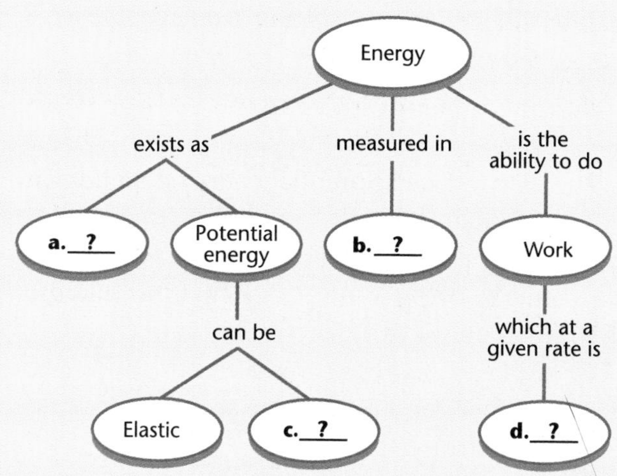

CHAPTER 5 ASSESSMENT

Reviewing Content

For more review of key concepts, see the Interactive Student Tutorial CD-ROM.

Multiple Choice

Choose the letter of the answer that best completes each statement.

1. Energy of motion is called
   a. elastic potential energy.
   b. kinetic energy.
   c. gravitational potential energy.
   d. chemical energy.
2. When you stretch a slingshot you give it
   a. kinetic energy.
   b. elastic potential energy.
   c. gravitational potential energy.
   d. power.
3. Whenever energy is transformed, some energy is converted to
   a. nuclear energy.
   b. electrical energy.
   c. thermal energy.
   d. mechanical energy.
4. Coal stores energy from the sun as
   a. chemical energy.
   b. electromagnetic energy.
   c. mechanical energy.
   d. electrical energy.
5. The rate at which work is done is called
   a. energy. b. efficiency.
   c. power. d. conservation.

True or False

If the statement is true, write true. If it is false, change the underlined word or words to make the statement true.

6. Kinetic energy is due to the <u>position</u> of an object.
7. Gravitational potential energy depends on <u>weight</u> and height.
8. Green plants convert the electromagnetic energy of the sun into <u>mechanical</u> energy.
9. The SI unit of <u>power</u> is the joule.
10. A device that has three times the <u>power</u> of another can do the same amount of work in one third the time.

Checking Concepts

11. Describe the difference between kinetic energy and potential energy.
12. For each of the following, decide which forms of energy are present: a leaf falls from a tree; a candle burns; a rubber band is wrapped around a newspaper.
13. An eagle flies from its perch in a tree to the ground to capture its prey. Describe its energy transformations as it descends.
14. When you walk upstairs, how are you obeying the law of conservation of energy?
15. One chef places a pie in the oven at a low setting so that it is baked in one hour. Another chef places a pie in the oven at a high setting so that the pie bakes in half an hour. Is the amount of transformed energy the same in each case? Is the power the same?
16. **Writing to Learn** As you saw in the figure on page 145, you can find different forms of energy all around you. Imagine you are writing your own biography. Pick three major events in your life. Write a paragraph about the form of energy that was most important in each event.

Thinking Critically

17. **Calculating** A 1300-kg car travels at 11 m/s. What is its kinetic energy?
18. **Problem Solving** A 500-N girl walks down a flight of stairs so that she is 3 m below her starting level. What is the change in the girl's gravitational potential energy?
19. **Applying Concepts** You turn on an electric fan to cool off. Describe the energy conversions involved.
20. **Relating Cause and Effect** A motorcycle, an automobile, and a bus are all traveling at the same speed. Which has the least kinetic energy? The greatest kinetic energy? Explain your answer.

Applying Skills

Use the illustration of a golfer taking a swing to answer the Questions 21–23. The golf club starts at point A and ends at point E.

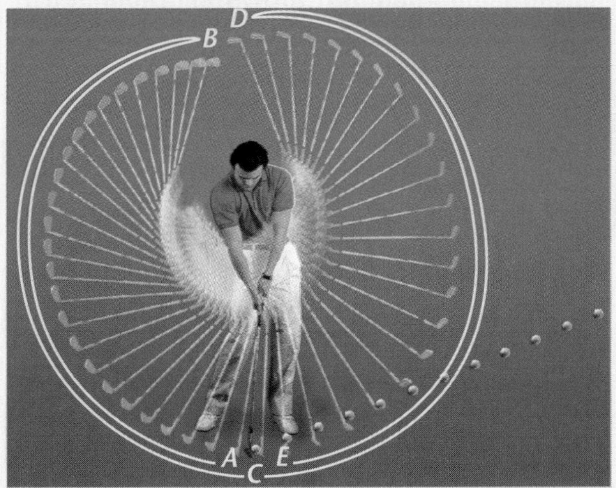

21. **Inferring** At which point(s) does the golf club have the greatest potential energy? At which point(s) does it have the greatest kinetic energy?
22. **Communication** Describe the energy conversions from point *A* to point *E*.
23. **Drawing Conclusions** The kinetic energy of the club at point *C* is more than the potential energy of the club at point *B*. Does this mean that the law of conservation of energy is violated?

Performance Assessment

Project Wrap Up Present your roller coaster to the class. Explain how you selected your materials, as well as the effect of hill height, incline, turns, and loops on the motion of the roller coaster. You should also explain how energy is converted as the roller coaster moves along the tracks. Point out an interesting feature of your roller coaster.

Reflect and Record In your journal, explain how you might improve your roller coaster. Think about what you knew about kinetic and potential energy before the project began, and what you know now. Which features would you change? Which would you keep the same?

Test Preparation

Use these questions to prepare for standardized tests.

Use the diagram to answer Questions 24–26.

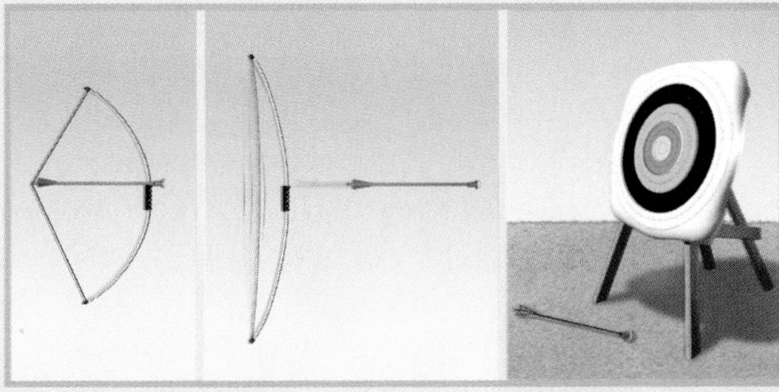

24. What type of energy did the arrow have as it moved through the air?
    a. potential
    b. kinetic
    c. electromagnetic
    d. chemical
25. Where did the energy of the arrow come from?
    a. It always had the energy.
    b. It gained energy from the air as it moved.
    c. Energy was stored in the arrow when the bow was pulled back.
    d. Energy transferred to the bow as it was pulled back was transferred to the arrow.
26. What might have caused the arrow to fall short of the target?
    a. It did not have enough energy because the archer did not pull the bow back far enough.
    b. It had too much energy because the archer pulled the bow back too far.
    c. Its kinetic energy was converted to gravitational potential energy as it moved.
    d. Its kinetic energy was converted to potential energy as it moved.

CHAPTER 6

Thermal Energy and Heat

Bright colors in this thermogram show areas that radiate the most heat.

www.phschool.com

SECTION 1 **Temperature and Thermal Energy**

Discover **How Cold Is the Water?**

SECTION 2 **The Nature of Heat**

Discover **What Does It Mean to Heat Up?**
Sharpen Your Skills **Inferring**
Try This **Feel the Warmth**
Skills Lab **Just Add Water**

Integrating Chemistry

SECTION 3 **Thermal Energy and States of Matter**

Discover **What Happens to Heated Metal?**
Sharpen Your Skills **Observing**

PROJECT 6

In Hot Water

This unusual image is not from a cartoon or horror movie. It's a thermogram of a house. A thermogram is an image formed by heat given off by an object. You might be very interested in a thermogram of your own house, because it can help you find expensive heat losses.

In this chapter, you will find out what heat is and how it relates to thermal energy and temperature. As you read the chapter, you will use what you learn to construct a device that will insulate a container of hot water.

Your Goal To build a container for a 355-mL (12-oz) aluminum can that keeps water hot.

Your project must

- reduce the loss of thermal energy from the container
- be constructed from available raw materials rather than be a ready-made insulating container
- have insulation no thicker than 3 cm
- not use electricity or heating chemicals
- follow the safety guidelines in Appendix A

Get Started With a group of classmates, brainstorm different materials that prevent heat loss. Consider such questions as the following: What properties do the materials seem to have in common? Which materials are easy to get? How can you find out which materials best prevent heat loss?

Check Your Progress You'll be working on this project as you study this chapter. To keep your project on track, look for Check Your Project boxes at the following points.

Section 2 Review, page 177: Perform experiments to determine the best insulating materials and keep a log of your results.

Section 4 Review, page 190: Build and test the device.

Wrap Up At the end of the chapter (page 193), you will test the performance of your insulating device.

Uses of Heat

Discover **What Happens at the Pump?**
Try This **Shake It Up**

Temperature and Thermal Energy

DISCOVER

How Cold Is the Water?

1. Fill a plastic bowl with cold water, another with warm water, and a third with water at room temperature. Label each bowl.
2. Line up the three bowls. Place your right hand in the cold water and your left hand in the warm water.
3. After about a minute, place both your hands in the third bowl at the same time.

Think It Over

Observing How did the water in the third bowl feel when you touched it? Did it feel the same on both hands? If not, can you explain why?

GUIDE FOR READING

- **What are the three common temperature scales?**
- **How does temperature differ from thermal energy?**

Reading Tip **As you read, use the headings to make an outline about temperature and thermal energy. Leave space to add definitions as you read.**

The radio weather report says that today's high temperature will be 25 degrees. What should you wear? Do you need a coat and a scarf to keep warm, or only shorts and a T-shirt? What you decide depends on the temperature scale. On one scale, 25 degrees is below freezing, while on another scale 25 degrees is quite comfortable.

Temperature

You don't need a science book to tell you that the word *hot* means higher temperatures or the word *cold* means lower temperatures. You wear different clothes on a hot day than on a cold day. When scientists think about temperature, however, they are considering the particles that make up matter.

Matter is made up of tiny particles called atoms and molecules. These particles are always in motion even if the object they make up isn't moving at all. As you recall, the energy of motion is called kinetic energy, so all particles of matter have kinetic energy. The faster particles move, the more kinetic energy they have. **Temperature** is a measure of the average kinetic energy of the individual particles in an object.

Figure 1 The particles of hot cocoa move faster than those of cold chocolate milk. *Applying Concepts Which drink has particles with greater average kinetic energy?*

Look at the mug of hot cocoa and the glass of cold chocolate milk in Figure 1. The hot cocoa has a higher temperature than the cold chocolate. Its particles are moving faster, so they have greater average kinetic energy. If the chocolate milk is heated, its particles will move faster, so their kinetic energy will increase. This means that the temperature of the milk will rise.

Temperature Scales

If you did the Discover activity, you know that whether something feels hot or cold depends on what you compare it to. Walking into an air-conditioned building on a hot day can give you a chill. You need a few minutes to get comfortable with the indoor temperature. Since you can't rely on your sense of touch, you need a scale to measure temperature accurately. **The three common scales for measuring temperature are the Fahrenheit, Celsius, and Kelvin scales.**

Fahrenheit Scale In the United States, the most common temperature scale is called the **Fahrenheit scale.** On this scale, the number 32 is assigned to the temperature at which water freezes. The number 212 is assigned to the temperature at which water boils. The interval between these two temperatures is divided into 180 equal intervals called degrees Fahrenheit (°F).

Celsius Scale The temperature scale used in most of the world is the **Celsius scale.** On this scale, the number 0 is assigned to the temperature at which water freezes. The number 100 is assigned to the temperature at which water boils. The interval between freezing and boiling is divided into 100 equal parts, called degrees Celsius (°C).

Kelvin Scale The temperature scale commonly used in physical science is the **Kelvin scale.** Units on the Kelvin scale are the same size as those on the Celsius scale, and are called kelvins (K).

Figure 2 This illustration compares the three temperature scales. *Comparing and Contrasting How do the three temperature scales differ from one another?*

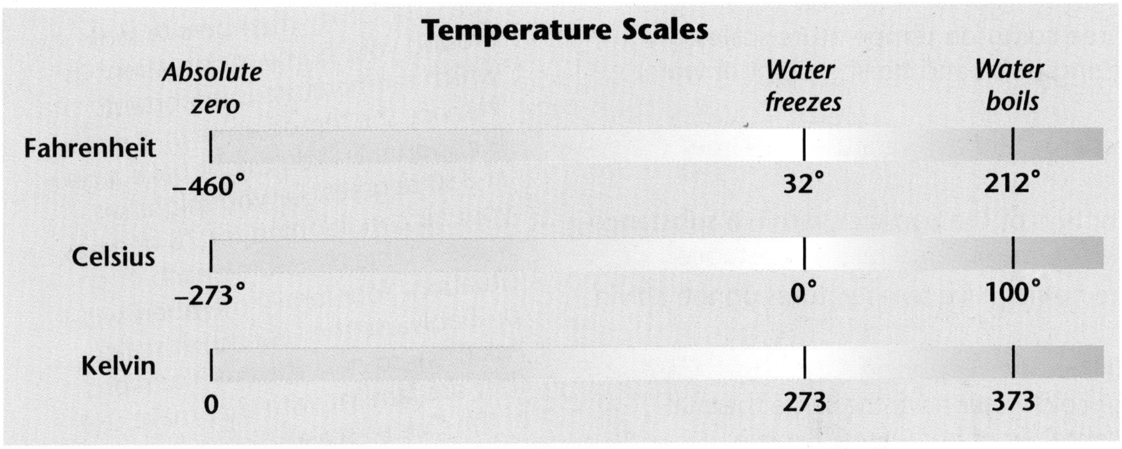

Temperature Scales

	Absolute zero	*Water freezes*	*Water boils*
Fahrenheit	–460°	32°	212°
Celsius	–273°	0°	100°
Kelvin	0	273	373

Figure 3 A large pot of hot cocoa can have the same temperature as a small cup of cocoa. *Comparing and Contrasting* *Do both containers have the same thermal energy?*

Any temperature on the Kelvin scale can be changed to Celsius degrees by subtracting 273 from it. So the freezing point of water on the Kelvin scale is 273 K and the boiling point is 373 K.

Why is the number 273 so special? Experiments have led scientists to conclude that –273°C is the lowest temperature possible. At this temperature, called **absolute zero,** no more energy can be removed from matter. The Kelvin scale is defined so that zero on the Kelvin scale is absolute zero.

☑ *Checkpoint* ***What three points define the common temperature scales?***

Thermal Energy

The total energy of all of the particles in a substance or material is called thermal energy, or sometimes internal energy. Even if two samples of matter are at the same temperature, they do not necessarily have the same total energy.

The more particles a substance has at a given temperature, the more thermal energy it has. For example, 2 liters of hot cocoa at 75°C has more thermal energy than 0.15 liter at 75°C. **So temperature is a measure of the average kinetic energy of the individual particles of matter. Thermal energy is the total energy of all of the particles.**

Thermal energy does not depend on just temperature and the number of particles in a substance. It also depends on how the particles are arranged. In Section 3 you will learn about how thermal energies differ for solids, liquids, and gases.

Section 1 Review

1. Name the three common temperature scales. Give the freezing point and boiling point of water for each.
2. Are thermal energy and temperature the same? Explain.
3. How is the motion of the particles within a substance related to the thermal energy of the substance?
4. Why are there no negative temperatures on the Kelvin scale?
5. **Thinking Critically** **Applying Concepts** Can a container of cold water have the same thermal energy as a container of hot water? Explain.

Science at Home

Ask your family members to look around your home for situations in which temperature is important. Perhaps the temperature in the oven is important—you might bake a cake at 350 degrees. Or you might set your air conditioning for 78 degrees. Make a table describing each situation. Your family members will probably use the Fahrenheit scale. Ask them to describe any situations they are familiar with that make use of the Celsius scale.

SECTION 2 The Nature of Heat

DISCOVER — ACTIVITY

What Does It Mean to Heat Up?

1. Obtain several utensils made of different materials, such as silver, stainless steel, plastic, and wood.
2. Stand the utensils in a beaker so that they do not touch each other.
3. Press a small gob of frozen butter on the handle of each utensil. Make sure that when the utensils stand on end, the butter is at the same height on each.
4. Pour hot water into the beaker until it is about 6 cm below the butter. Watch the utensils for the next several minutes. What do you see happening?

5. The utensils will be greasy. Wipe them off and wash them in soapy water.

Think It Over

Observing What happened to the butter? Did the same thing happen on every utensil? How can you account for your observations?

GUIDE FOR READING

- How is heat related to thermal energy?
- What are the three forms of heat transfer?
- How is specific heat related to thermal energy?

Reading Tip **Before you read, define heat in your own words. Make any necessary corrections to your definition as you read the section.**

Blacksmithing is hot work. A piece of iron held in the forge becomes warmer and begins to glow as thermal energy from the fire travels along it. At the same time, the blacksmith feels hot air rising from the forge and his face and arms begin to feel warmer. Each of these movements of energy is a form of heat. **Heat** is the movement of thermal energy from a substance at a higher temperature to another at a lower temperature.

Figure 4 This blacksmith uses heat to soften a piece of iron before he hammers it into shape.

Sharpen your Skills

Inferring ACTIVITY

You pull some clothes out of the dryer as soon as they are dry. You grab your shirt without a problem, but when you pull out your jeans, you quickly drop them. The metal zipper is too hot to touch! What can you infer about which material in your jeans conducts thermal energy better? Explain.

Notice that the scientific definition of heat is different from its everyday use. In a conversation, you might hear someone say that an object contains heat. Matter, however, contains not heat but thermal energy. Only when thermal energy is transferred is it called heat. **Heat is thermal energy moving from a warmer object to a cooler object.** Recall from Chapter 5 that work also involves the transfer of mechanical energy. So work and heat are both energy transfers, and they are both measured with the same unit—joules.

How Is Heat Transferred?

There are three ways that heat can move. **Heat is transferred by conduction, convection, and radiation.** The blacksmith experienced all three.

Conduction In the process of **conduction,** heat is transferred from one particle of matter to another without the movement of matter itself. Think of a metal spoon in a pot of water being heated on an electric stove. The fast-moving particles of the hot electric coil collide with the slow-moving particles of the cool pot. Heat is transferred, causing the slower particles to move faster. Then the particles of the pot collide with the particles of the water, which in turn collide with the particles at one end of the spoon. As the particles move faster, the metal spoon becomes hotter. This process of conduction is repeated all along the metal until the entire spoon becomes hot.

In Figure 5, the horseshoes in a blacksmith's forge glow red as heat is transferred to the metal from the forge. This transfer of heat throughout the horseshoes is due to conduction.

Figure 5 The entire horseshoe becomes hot even though only its underside touches the hot forge. *Inferring By what method is heat transferred through the metal?*

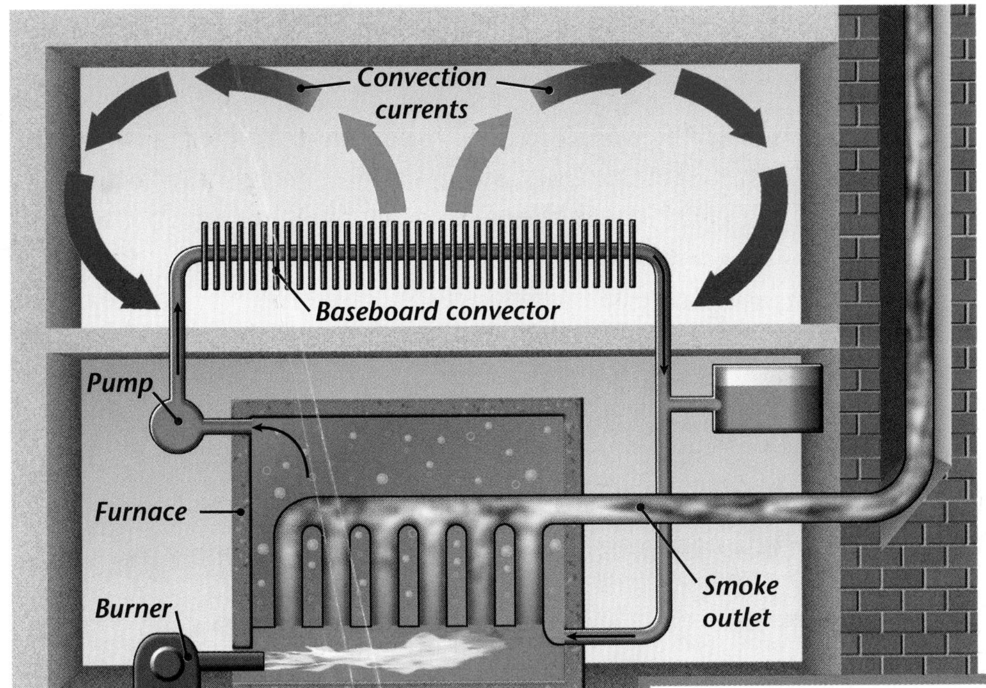

Figure 6 Just as convection currents move heat throughout the liquid in a pot, convection currents move heat from the baseboard throughout the room.

Convection If you watch a pot of hot water on a stove, you will see the water moving. **Convection** is the movement that transfers heat within the water. In convection, heat is transferred by the movement of currents within a fluid (a liquid or gas).

When the water at the bottom of the pot is heated, its particles move faster, and they also move farther apart. As a result, the heated water becomes less dense. Recall from Chapter 3 that a less dense fluid will float on top of a more dense one. So the heated water rises. The surrounding cooler water flows into its place. This flow creates a circular motion known as a **convection current,** as shown in Figure 6.

Convection currents are used to transfer heated air throughout a building. As the air near the baseboard heater in Figure 6 is heated, it becomes less dense and rises. When the warm air rises, the surrounding cool air flows into its place.

INTEGRATING EARTH SCIENCE Convection currents occur in the environment as well. A soaring bird, such as a hawk, takes advantage of this fact and rides updrafts where warm air rises. In fact, convection currents transfer air heated by the sun throughout Earth's atmosphere. They produce the global winds that form Earth's weather.

☑ *Checkpoint* *How does convection transfer heat?*

Figure 7 Radiation from the heat lamps above keeps food warm in a cafeteria.

Feel the Warmth

How is heat transferred from a light bulb?

1. Turn on a lamp without the shade. Wait about a minute.
2. Hold the palm of your hand about 10 cm from the side of the bulb for about 15 seconds. Remove it sooner if it gets too warm.
3. Now hold the palm of your hand about 10 cm above the top of the bulb for about 15 seconds.

Drawing Conclusions In which location did your hand feel warmer? Explain your observations in terms of heat transfer.

Radiation **Radiation** is the transfer of energy by electromagnetic waves. You can feel radiation from a bonfire or a heat lamp across a distance of several meters. And of course a blacksmith feels the radiation from his forge. There is an important difference between radiation and the processes of conduction and convection. Radiation does not require matter to transfer thermal energy. All of the sun's energy that reaches Earth travels through millions of kilometers of empty space.

Heat Moves One Way

If two substances have different temperatures, heat will flow from the warmer object to the colder one. When heat flows into a substance, the thermal energy of the substance increases. As the thermal energy increases, its temperature increases. At the same time, the temperature of the substance giving off heat decreases. Heat will flow from one substance to the other until the two substances have the same temperature. A bowl of hot oatmeal cools to room temperature if you don't eat it quickly.

What happens to something cold, like ice cream? The ingredients used to make it, such as milk and sugar, are not nearly as cold as the finished ice cream. In an ice cream maker, the ingredients are put into a metal can that is packed in ice. You might think that the ice transfers cold to the ingredients in the can. But this is not the case. There is no such thing as "coldness." Instead, the ingredients grow colder as thermal energy flows from them to the ice. Heat transfer occurs in only one direction.

☑ *Checkpoint* ***In what direction does heat move?***

Conductors and Insulators

Have you ever stepped from a rug to a tile floor on a cold morning? The tile floor feels colder than the rug. Yet if you measured their temperatures, they would be the same—room temperature. The difference between them has to do with how materials conduct heat.

A material that conducts heat well is called a **conductor.** Metals such as silver and stainless steel are good conductors. A metal spoon conducts heat faster than a wooden or plastic spoon. A material that does not conduct heat well is called an **insulator.** Wood, wool, straw, paper, and cork are good insulators. Gases, such as air, are also good insulators.

A good conductor, such as a tile floor, will feel cool to the touch because it transfers heat away from your skin easily. An insulator such as a rug, on the other hand, slows the transfer of heat from your skin, so it feels warmer.

Clothes and blankets are insulators that slow the transfer of heat out of your body. Mammals and birds have natural insulation. Birds have feathers that trap air under them, and mammals such as walruses have a layer of fat called blubber.

A well-insulated building is comfortable inside whether the weather is hot or cold outdoors. Insulation prevents heat from entering the building in hot weather and prevents heat from escaping in cold weather. Fiberglass is a common insulating material in buildings. It is made of a tangle of thin glass fibers that trap air. Air is a poor conductor of heat, and trapped air cannot transfer heat by convection. So fiberglass slows the transfer of heat through the walls or roof.

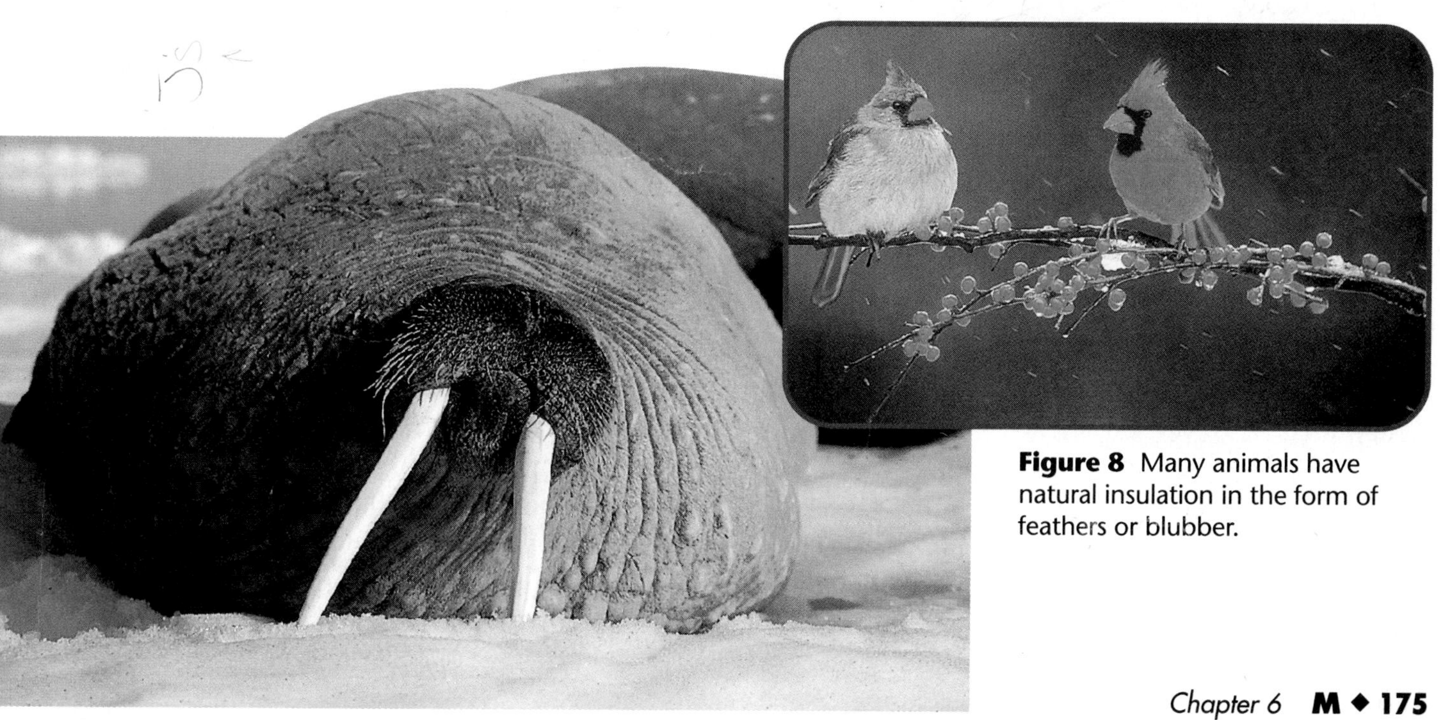

Figure 8 Many animals have natural insulation in the form of feathers or blubber.

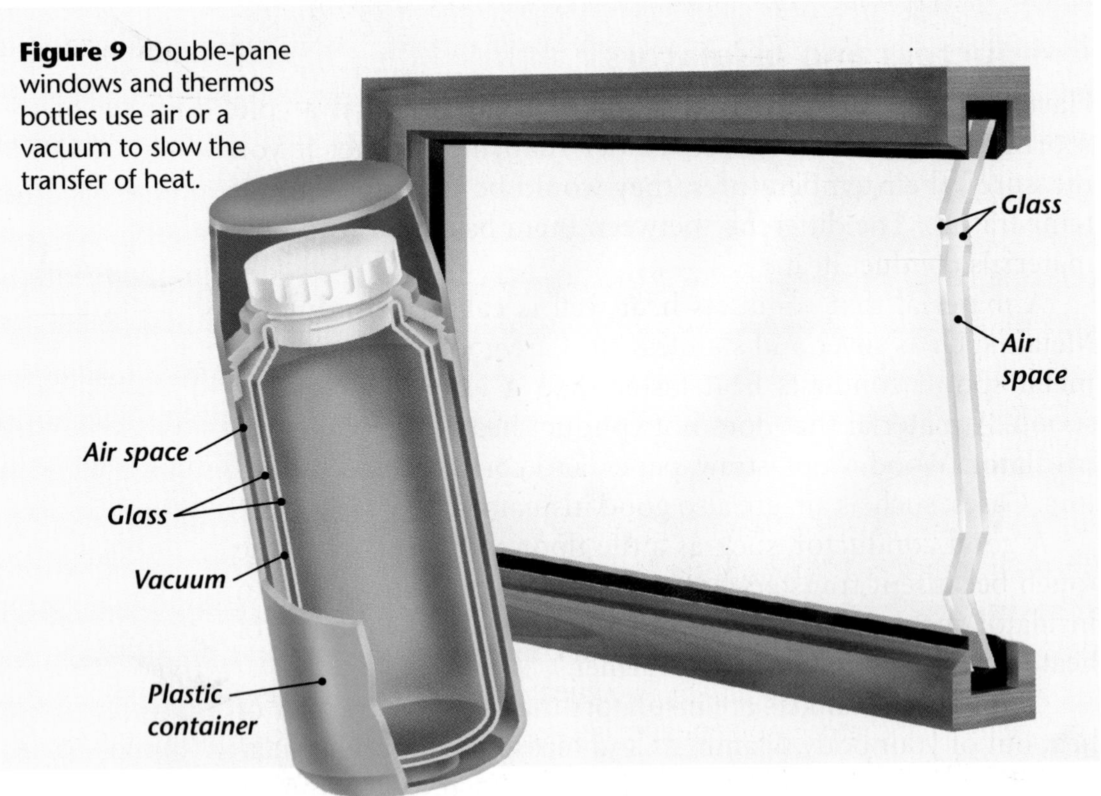

Figure 9 Double-pane windows and thermos bottles use air or a vacuum to slow the transfer of heat.

Much of the heat transfer in a house occurs through the windows. For this reason, insulating windows are made up of two panes of glass with a thin space of air between them. The air trapped between the glass panes does not transfer heat well. Thermos bottles use the same principle. They contain a vacuum, which is a better insulator than air.

Figure 10 This table lists the specific heats of several substances. *Problem Solving How much more energy is required to raise the temperature of 1 kg of iron than is needed to raise the temperature of 1 kg of copper by the same amount?*

Specific Heat of Common Substances

Substance	Specific Heat (J/(kg·K))
Aluminum	903
Brass	376
Copper	385
Glass	664
Ice	2,060
Iron	450
Sand	670
Silver	235
Water	4,180

Specific Heat

Imagine running across hot sand toward the ocean's edge. You run to the water's edge, but you don't go any farther—the water is too cold. How can the sand be so hot and the water so cold? After all, they were both heated by the sun. The answer is that water requires more heat to raise its temperature than sand does.

When an object is heated its temperature rises. But the temperature does not rise at the same rate for all objects. The amount of heat required to raise the temperature depends on the chemical makeup of the material. Different materials need more or less heat to change their temperature by the same amount.

Scientists have defined a quantity to measure the relationship between heat and temperature change. The amount of energy required to raise the temperature of 1 kilogram of a substance by 1 kelvin is called its **specific heat.** The unit of measure for specific heat is joules per kilogram-kelvin (J/(kg·K)). Look at the specific heats of the substances listed in Figure 10.

Figure 11 Bright summer sun has made the beach sand painfully hot. But a few meters away, the ocean water is still cool.

Notice that the specific heat of water is quite high. One kilogram of water requires 4,180 joules of energy to raise its temperature 1 kelvin. Materials with a high specific heat can absorb a great deal of thermal energy without a great change in temperature.

The energy gained or lost by an object is related to the mass, change in temperature, and specific heat of the material. You can calculate thermal energy changes with the following formula.

Change in energy =
Mass × Specific heat × Change in temperature

How much heat is required to raise the temperature of 5 kilograms of water 10 kelvins?

Heat absorbed = (5 kg)(4,180 J/(kg·K))(10 K) = 209,000 J

You need to transfer 209,000 joules to the water to increase its temperature by 10 kelvins.

Section 2 Review

1. How does heat differ from thermal energy?
2. Describe the three kinds of heat transfer.
3. What is specific heat?
4. **Thinking Critically** **Problem Solving** How much thermal energy is gained by 10 kg of silver if it is heated from 21°C to 35°C?
5. **Thinking Critically** **Applying Concepts** Before homes were heated, people often placed hot water bottles in their beds at bedtime. Why is water a good choice?

CHAPTER PROJECT 6

Check Your Progress

Prepare a short summary of your experimental plan. How will you test insulating ability? (*Hint:* What variables do you want to keep constant? How can you make sure you control these?) Think about how you can design a fair test to compare the relative insulating abilities of each material. How often will you record the temperature? Then carry out your tests.

Skills Lab

Interpreting Data

Just Add Water

If you add hot water to cold water, what will happen? In this lab, you'll make a device that measures changes in thermal energy. It is called a calorimeter. You will use the skill of interpreting data to calculate the thermal energy transferred.

Problem

When hot and cold water are mixed, how much thermal energy is transferred from the hot water to the cold water?

Materials

hot tap water
balance
scissors
pencil
4 plastic foam cups
2 thermometers or temperature probes
beaker of water kept in an ice bath

Procedure

1. Predict how the amount of thermal energy lost by hot water will be related to the amount of thermal energy gained by cold water.
2. Copy the data table into your notebook.
3. Follow the instructions in the box to make two calorimeters. Find the mass of each empty calorimeter (including the cover) on a balance and record each mass in your data table.

Making a Calorimeter

A. Label a plastic foam cup with the letter C ("C" stands for cold water).
B. Cut 2 to 3 cm from the top of a second plastic foam cup. Invert the second cup inside the first. Label the cover with a C also. The cup and cover are your cold-water calorimeter.
C. Using a pencil, poke a hole in the cover large enough for a thermometer to fit into snugly.
D. Repeat Steps A, B, and C with two other plastic foam cups. This time, label both cup and cover with an H. This is your hot-water calorimeter.

4. From a beaker of water that has been sitting in an ice bath, add water (no ice cubes) to the cold-water calorimeter. Fill it about one-third full. Put the cover on, find the total mass, and record the mass in your data table.
5. Add hot tap water to the hot-water calorimeter. **CAUTION:** *Hot tap water can cause burns.* Fill the calorimeter about one-third full. Put the cover on, find the total mass, and record the mass in your data table.

DATA TABLE

	Mass of Empty Cup (g)	Mass of Cup and Water (g)	Mass of Water (g)	Starting Temp. (°C)	Final Temp. (°C)	Change in Temp. (°C)
Cold Water Calorimeter						
Hot Water Calorimeter						

6. Calculate the mass of the water in each calorimeter. Record the results in your data table.
7. Put thermometers through the holes in the covers of both calorimeters. Wait a minute or two and then record the temperatures. If you are using temperature probes, see your teacher for instructions.
8. Remove both thermometers and covers. Pour the water from the cold-water calorimeter into the hot-water calorimeter. Put the cover back on the hot-water calorimeter, and insert a thermometer. Record the final temperature as the final temperature for both calorimeters.

Analyze and Conclude

1. What is the temperature change of the cold water? Record your answer in the data table.
2. What is the temperature change of the hot water? Record your answer in the data table.
3. Calculate the amount of thermal energy that enters the cold water by using the formula for the transfer of thermal energy. The specific heat of water is 4.18 J/(g·K), so you use the following formula.
   Thermal energy transferred =
   4.18 J/(g·K) × Mass of cold water × Temperature change of cold water
   Remember that a change of 1°C is equal to a change of 1 K.
4. Now use the formula to calculate the thermal energy leaving the hot water.
5. What unit should you use for your results for Questions 3 and 4?
6. Was your prediction from Step 1 confirmed? How do you know?
7. **Think About It** What sources of error might have affected your results? How could the lab be redesigned in order to reduce the errors?

Design an Experiment

How would your results be affected if you started with much more hot water than cold? If you used more cold water than hot? Make a prediction. Then design a procedure to test your prediction. Get your teacher's approval, and try your new procedure.

SCIENCE AND SOCIETY

Insulation — And a Breath of Clean Air

People want to save money. They also want to conserve the fossil fuels—oil, coal, and natural gas—used to heat and cool buildings. So, since the 1970s, new homes, offices, and schools have been built to be energy-efficient. Builders have constructed large, square buildings with thick insulation, less outside wall space, and smaller, airtight windows. These features slow the transfer of thermal energy into and out of buildings.

Limiting the transfer of thermal energy, however, often means limiting the transfer of air. As a result, viruses, bacteria, and pollutants are not carried away by fresh outdoor air. People who live and work in these buildings sometimes develop illnesses. These illnesses cost billions of dollars a year in medical expenses and lost work.

The Issues

How Can Indoor Air Be Made Cleaner?

Limiting indoor pollutants—or getting rid of them altogether—is a major way of reducing building-related illness. Toward this end, builders can construct buildings with materials and insulation that do not pollute the air. They can use natural wood, for instance, instead of plastics and particle board, which give off irritating chemicals. Indoor air can be filtered. Walls, floors, and carpets can be cleaned frequently. Machines that give off irritating chemicals, such as copiers, can be placed in specially ventilated rooms. In this way, pollution can be kept out of the air that most people in the building breathe.

How Can Ventilation Be Improved?

Good ventilation requires at least 10 liters per second of fresh air for each person. If less fresh air comes in, some people may get illnesses or eye, nose, and throat irritations. There are several ways to increase ventilation. In some buildings, machines such as fans and blowers are used to move air in and out. People in those buildings must be careful not to block air vents with furniture or equipment. Special attention must be paid to ventilation during times of increased pollution, such as when a room is being painted.

Increasing air flow into buildings means using more energy for heating and air conditioning. So the energy savings from efficient buildings are reduced. To make up for this loss, people can wear heavier clothing in winter. They can set their thermostats lower and use less energy for heating. They can also wear lighter clothes in summer, and use less energy for air conditioning.

Another way to obtain clean air while conserving energy is called energy recovery ventilation. Heat is transferred from stale, but warm, indoor air to fresh, but cold, outdoor air. The air goes out but the energy stays inside.

You Decide

1. Identify the Problem
In your own words, describe the problem caused by thick layers of insulation.

2. Analyze the Options
List five different options for reducing building-related illnesses. How would each option affect the amount of fuel needed for heating?

3. Find a Solution
You're building a new school. Make a checklist of steps to take to prevent illness but still keep heating costs down.

SECTION 3 Thermal Energy and States of Matter

DISCOVER ACTIVITY

What Happens to Heated Metal?

1. Wrap one end of a one-meter-long metal wire around a clamp on a ring stand.
2. Tie the other end through several washers. Adjust the clamp so that the washers swing freely, but nearly touch the floor.
3. Light a candle. Hold the candle with an oven mitt, and heat the wire. **CAUTION:** *Be careful near the flame, and avoid dripping hot wax on yourself.* Predict how heat from the candle will affect the wire.
4. With your hand in the oven mitt, swing the wire. Observe any changes in the motion of the washers.
5. Blow out the candle and allow the wire to cool. After several minutes, swing the wire again and observe its motion.

Think It Over

Inferring Based on your observations, what can you conclude about the effect of heating a solid?

GUIDE FOR READING

- **What causes matter to change state?**
- **Why does matter expand when it is heated?**

Reading Tip **As you read, take notes on how each illustration helps to explain the text.**

Throughout the day, temperatures at an orange grove drop steadily. The anxious farmer awaits the updated weather forecast. The news is not good. The temperature is expected to fall even further during the night. Low temperatures could wipe out the entire crop. He considers picking the crop early, but the oranges are not yet ripe.

Instead, the farmer tells his workers to haul in long water hoses. He has them spray the orange trees with water. As the temperature drops, the water turns to ice. The ice keeps the oranges warm!

How can ice possibly keep anything warm? The answer has to do with how thermal energy is transferred as water becomes ice.

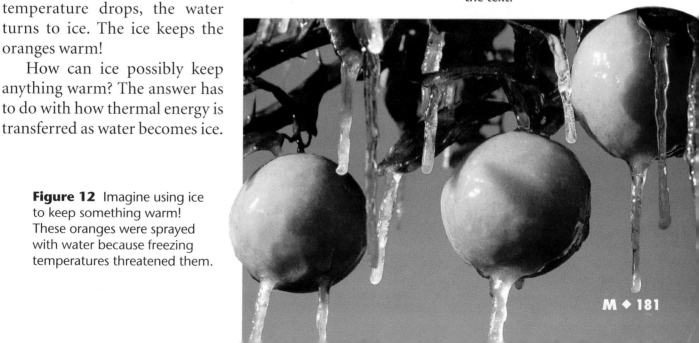

Figure 12 Imagine using ice to keep something warm! These oranges were sprayed with water because freezing temperatures threatened them.

Figure 13 Matter exists in three states—solid, liquid, and gas. *Comparing and Contrasting How does the motion of the particles relate to the state of matter?*

Three States of Matter

What happens when you hold an ice cube in your hand? It melts. The solid and the liquid are both the same substance—water. Water can exist in three different forms. In fact, most matter exists in three **states**—solid, liquid, and gas. Although the chemical composition of a substance remains the same, the arrangement of the particles that make up the matter differ from one state to another.

Solids An ice cube, a coin, a book, and the crystal of fluorite shown above are all solids. The particles that make up a solid are packed together in relatively fixed positions. Particles of a solid cannot move out of their positions. They can only vibrate back and forth. This is why solids retain a fixed shape and volume.

Liquids Water, orange juice, and the molten steel shown at the left are all liquids. The particles that make up a liquid are close together, but they are not held together as tightly as those of a solid. Because liquid particles can move around, liquids don't have a definite shape. But liquids do have a definite volume.

Gases Air, helium, and the neon used in colored signs are all gases. In a gas, the particles are moving so fast that they don't even stay close together. Gases expand to fill all the space available. They do not have a fixed shape or volume.

Changes of State

The physical change from one state of matter to another is called a **change of state.** A change of state occurs most often between the solid and liquid states, and between the liquid and gas states.

The state of a substance depends on the amount of thermal energy it possesses. The more thermal energy a substance has, the faster its particles move. Since a gas has more thermal energy than a liquid, the particles of a gas move faster than the particles of the same substance in the liquid or solid state. Particles in a liquid are freer to move around than particles in the solid state.

Matter will change from one state to another if thermal energy is absorbed or released. Figure 14 is a graph of changes of state. Thermal energy is shown on the horizontal axis and temperature is shown on the vertical axis. You can see that as thermal energy increases, a substance changes from a solid to a liquid and then to a gas. A substance changes from a gas to a liquid and then to a solid as thermal energy is removed from it.

The flat regions of the graph show conditions under which thermal energy is changing but temperature remains the same. Under these conditions matter is changing from one state to another. During a change of state, the addition or loss of thermal energy changes the arrangement of the particles. However, the average kinetic energy of those particles does not change. Since temperature is a measure of average kinetic energy, the temperature does not change as a substance changes state.

Solid–Liquid Changes of State

On the lower left portion of the graph in Figure 14, matter goes through changes between the solid and liquid states. These changes are known as melting and freezing.

Melting The change of state from a solid to a liquid is called **melting.** Melting occurs when a solid absorbs thermal energy. As the thermal energy of the solid increases, the rigid structure of its particles begins to break down. The particles become freer to move around. The temperature at which a solid changes to a liquid is called the **melting point.**

☑ *Checkpoint* *What is a change of state?*

Language Arts CONNECTION

All around you, you can observe substances in different states of matter. You can also observe matter changing from one state to another.

In Your Journal

Write a one-page description of a scene in which the state of matter changes. Here are some ideas: a glass of lemonade with ice cubes, a pond freezing in winter, a puddle of water on hot pavement, water boiling on a stove, or rain falling on a desert. Write about how the scene would affect your senses of sight, smell, touch, taste, and hearing.

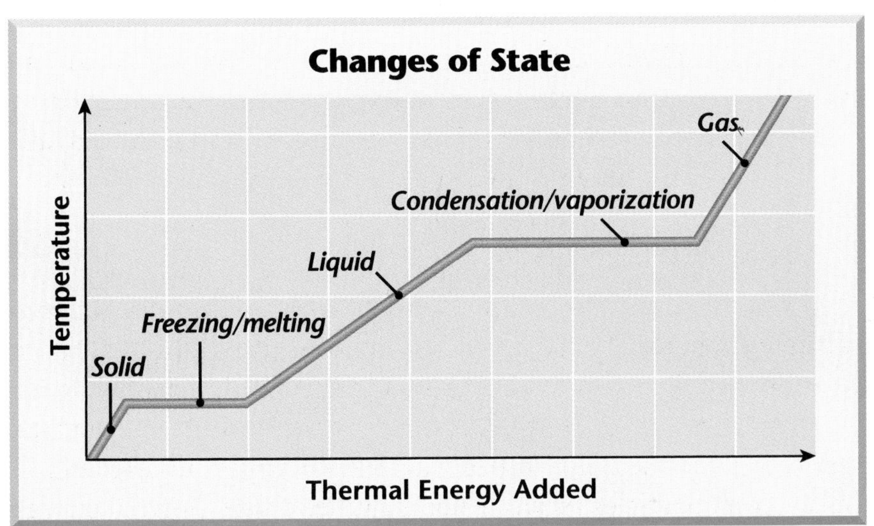

Figure 14 This graph shows how thermal energy and temperature change as a pure substance changes from one state to another.

Sharpen your Skills

Observing ACTIVITY

Put a teakettle on a stove or a lab burner, and bring the water to a boil. Look carefully at the steam coming out of the spout. **CAUTION:** *Steam and boiling water can cause serious burns.* What state of matter is the steam that you see? What is present, but not visible, in the small space between the steam and the spout?

Freezing The change of state from a liquid to a solid is called **freezing.** Freezing occurs when a substance loses thermal energy. The temperature at which a substance changes from a liquid to a solid is called its **freezing point.** For a given substance, the freezing point and the melting point are the same. The only difference between the two is whether the substance is gaining or releasing thermal energy.

The fact that freezing involves a release of energy explains why the farmer had his workers spray the orange trees with water. The liquid water released thermal energy as it froze. Some of this thermal energy was transferred to the oranges, and kept them from freezing.

Liquid–Gas Changes of State

The upper right portion of Figure 14 shows changes between the liquid and gas states of matter. These changes are known as vaporization and condensation.

Vaporization The process by which matter changes from the liquid to the gas state is called **vaporization.** During this process, particles in a liquid absorb thermal energy. This causes the particles to move faster. Eventually they move fast enough to escape the liquid, as gas particles.

If vaporization takes place at the surface of a liquid, it is called **evaporation.** At higher temperatures, vaporization can occur below the surface of a liquid as well. This process is called **boiling.** When a liquid boils, gas bubbles formed within the liquid rise to the surface. The temperature at which a liquid boils is called its **boiling point.**

Condensation You have seen that beads of water appear on the outside of a cold drinking glass or on the bathroom mirror after you take a shower. This occurs because water vapor that is

Figure 15 Water vapor in the air begins to condense soon after sunset. *Applying Concepts As it condenses, does water absorb or release thermal energy?*

Figure 16 Joints on bridges and spaces in sidewalks allow for the expansion and contraction of matter. *Applying Concepts What happens to the spaces in the expansion joint as the bridge gets warmer?*

present in the air loses thermal energy when it comes in contact with the cold glass. When a gas loses a sufficient amount of thermal energy, it will change into a liquid. A change from the gas state to the liquid state is called **condensation.**

☑ *Checkpoint* *What is the difference between boiling and evaporation of a liquid?*

Thermal Expansion

Have you ever loosened a tight jar lid by holding it under a stream of hot water? This works because the metal lid expands a little. Do you know why? **As the thermal energy of a substance increases, its particles spread out and the substance expands.** This is true even when the substance is not changing state. The expanding of matter when it is heated is known as **thermal expansion.**

When a substance is cooled, thermal energy is released. This means that the motion of the particles slows down and the particles move closer together. So as a substance is cooled, it contracts, or decreases in size.

Thermometers You are already familiar with one application of thermal expansion—a thermometer. In a common thermometer, a liquid such as mercury or alcohol is sealed within a glass tube. As the liquid is heated, it expands and climbs up the tube. As the liquid is cooled, it contracts and flows down in the tube.

Expanding Teeth Your teeth also expand and contract with changes in temperature. If you have a filling, the material used for the filling must expand and contract with your tooth. If it didn't, the filling could cause the tooth to crack, or the filling could loosen. So dentists use fillings that have the same expansion properties as teeth.

INTEGRATING HEALTH

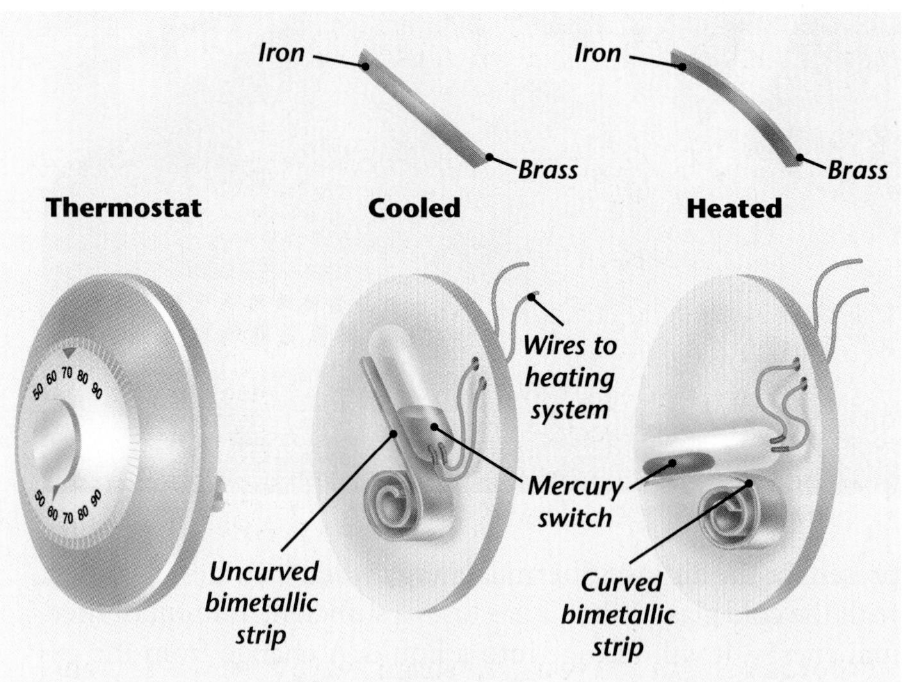

Figure 17 A bimetallic strip controls many thermostats. When it cools, the strip straightens and rises, allowing mercury to flow into contact with the wires. When the strip warms up, it curves downward, breaking the circuit. *Relating Cause and Effect What causes the bimetallic strip to curve and uncurve?*

Thermostats Thermal expansion is used in **thermostats,** or heat-regulating devices. Many thermostats contain **bimetallic strips,** which are strips of two different metals joined together. Different metals expand at different rates. When the bimetallic strip is heated, one side expands more than the other. This causes the strip to bend into a curve.

The movement of the strip operates a switch. If the switch is connected to a furnace or other heating system, the thermostat will turn the heating system on and off. In addition to home heating systems, thermostats are used on such devices as air conditioners, ovens, toasters, and electric blankets.

Section 3 Review

1. How does thermal energy produce a change from one state of matter to another?
2. What is thermal expansion?
3. What happens to the temperature of a substance during a change of state? What happens to thermal energy during a change of state?
4. How does a thermostat make use of thermal expansion?
5. **Thinking Critically Applying Concepts** Why do cookbooks recommend that you poke holes in a potato before baking it?

Science at Home

Blow up two medium-size balloons so that they are the same size. Have a family member use a measuring tape to measure the circumference of the balloons. Then ask them to place one of the balloons in the freezer for fifteen to twenty minutes. Remove the balloon from the freezer and measure both balloons again. Explain how changes in thermal energy cause the change in circumference.

Section 4 Uses of Heat

Discover Activity

What Happens at the Pump?

1. Obtain a bicycle pump and a deflated basketball or soccer ball.
2. Feel the pump with your hand. Note if it feels cool or warm.
3. Use the pump to inflate the ball to the recommended pressure.

4. As soon as you stop pumping, feel the pump again. Observe any changes in temperature.

Think It Over

Developing Hypotheses Propose an explanation for any changes that you observed.

Guide for Reading

- How is thermal energy related to heat engines and refrigerators?

Reading Tip Before you read, preview the illustrations showing how engines work. Write down any questions you have, and answer them as you read.

For more than 100 years, the steam locomotive was a symbol of power and speed. It first came into use in the 1830s, and was soon hauling hundreds of tons of freight faster than a horse could gallop. Yet today, trains are pulled by diesel locomotives that are far more efficient. You will probably see a steam locomotive only as a tourist attraction.

Heat Engines

To power a coal-burning steam locomotive, a fireman shovels coal into a roaring fire. Heat is then transferred from the fire to water in the boiler. But how can heat move a train?

The thermal energy of the coal fire must be converted to the mechanical energy, or energy of motion, of the moving train. You already know about the reverse process, the conversion of mechanical energy to thermal energy. It happens when you rub your hands together to make them warm.

The conversion of thermal energy to mechanical energy requires a device called a **heat engine.** Heat engines usually make use of combustion. **Combustion** is the process of burning a fuel, such as coal or gasoline. During combustion, chemical energy that is stored in fuel is converted to thermal energy. **Heat engines convert thermal energy to mechanical energy.** Heat engines are classified according to whether combustion takes place outside the engine or inside the engine.

Shake It Up

How does work relate to temperature?

1. Place a handful of dry sand in a metal container that has a cover.
2. Measure the temperature of the sand with a thermometer.
3. Cover the can and shake it vigorously for a minute or two.
4. Predict any change in the temperature of the sand. Was your prediction correct?

Classifying Identify any energy conversions and use them to explain your observations.

External Combustion Engines In an **external combustion engine,** the fuel is burned outside the engine. A steam engine is an example of an external combustion engine. The combustion of wood, coal, or oil heats water in a boiler outside the engine. As its thermal energy increases, the water turns to water vapor, or steam. The steam is then passed through a valve into the engine where it pushes against a metal plunger called a piston. The piston moves back and forth in a tube called a cylinder.

Figure 18 shows how steam can do work, such as moving the wheels of a locomotive. Steam enters at the right end of the cylinder, pushing the piston to the left. Steam then enters at the left end of the cylinder and pushes the piston back. This type of external combustion engine can also move the propellers of a steamship. Modern steam engines are more efficient than old-fashioned piston steam engines. But in both types of engine, thermal energy is converted to mechanical energy.

Internal Combustion Engines In an **internal combustion engine,** the fuel is burned in cylinders inside the engine. Diesel and gasoline engines, which power most automobiles, are both examples of internal combustion engines. A piston inside a cylinder moves up and down, turning a crankshaft. The motion of the crankshaft is transferred to the wheels of the car.

Each up or down movement by a piston is called a stroke. Most diesel and gasoline engines are four-stroke engines, as shown in *Exploring a Four-Stroke Engine.* Automobile engines usually have four, six, or eight cylinders. The four-stroke process occurs in each cylinder, and is repeated many times each second.

☑ *Checkpoint* ***What happens during the process of combustion?***

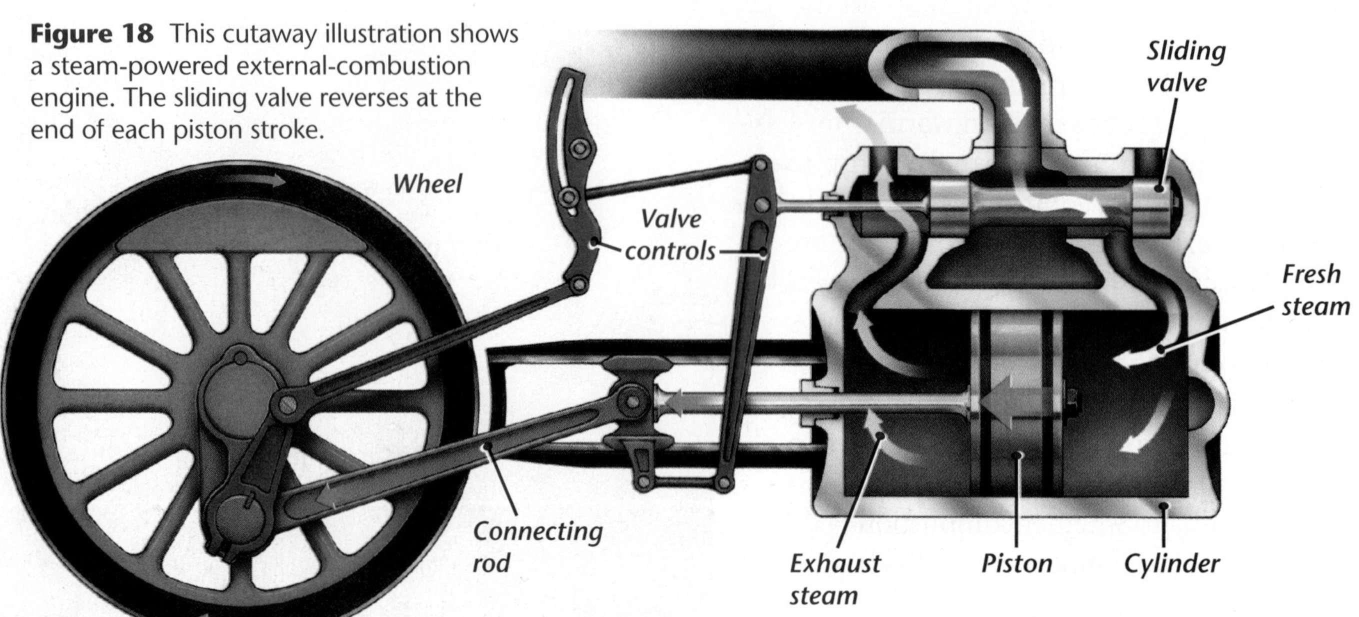

Figure 18 This cutaway illustration shows a steam-powered external-combustion engine. The sliding valve reverses at the end of each piston stroke.

EXPLORING a Four-Stroke Engine

Most automobiles use four-stroke heat engines. These four strokes occur repeatedly in each cylinder in the engine.

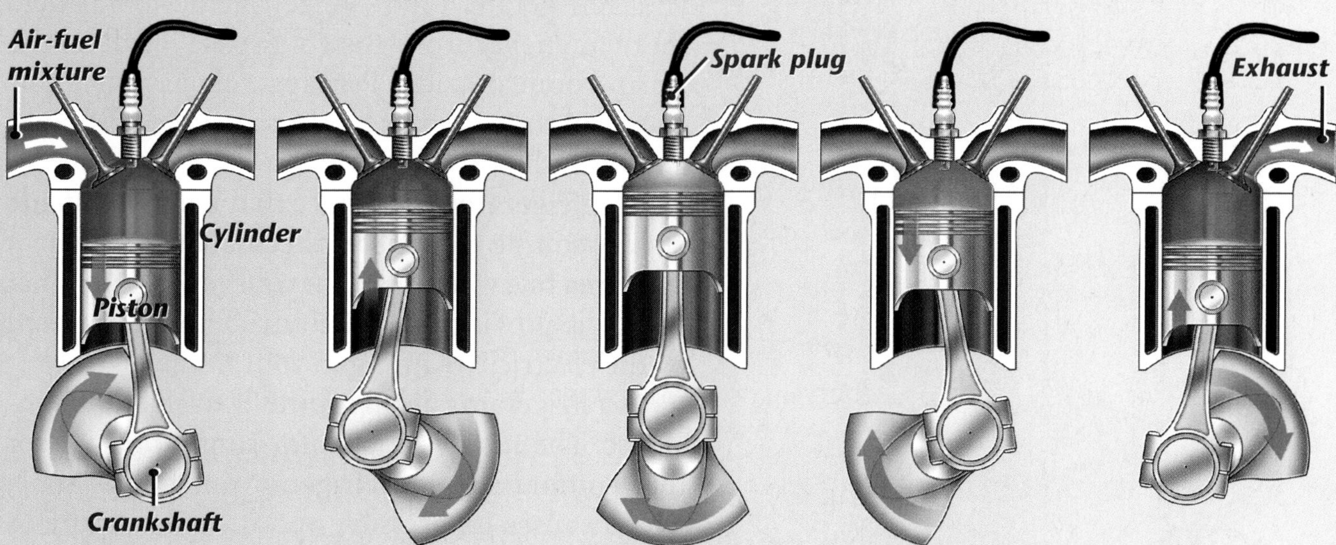

Intake Stroke
A mixture of fuel and air is drawn into the cylinder as the piston moves down.

Compression Stroke
The mixture is squeezed, or compressed, into a smaller space as the piston moves back up.

Ignition
When the piston is almost at the top of the cylinder, a spark plug ignites the mixture. Stored chemical energy is converted to thermal energy, which heats the gas.

Power Stroke
As the heated gas expands, it pushes the piston down. The piston, in turn, moves the crankshaft. Thus thermal energy is converted to mechanical energy.

Exhaust Stroke
The piston moves back up, pushing the heated gas out. This makes room for new fuel and air, so that the cycle can be repeated.

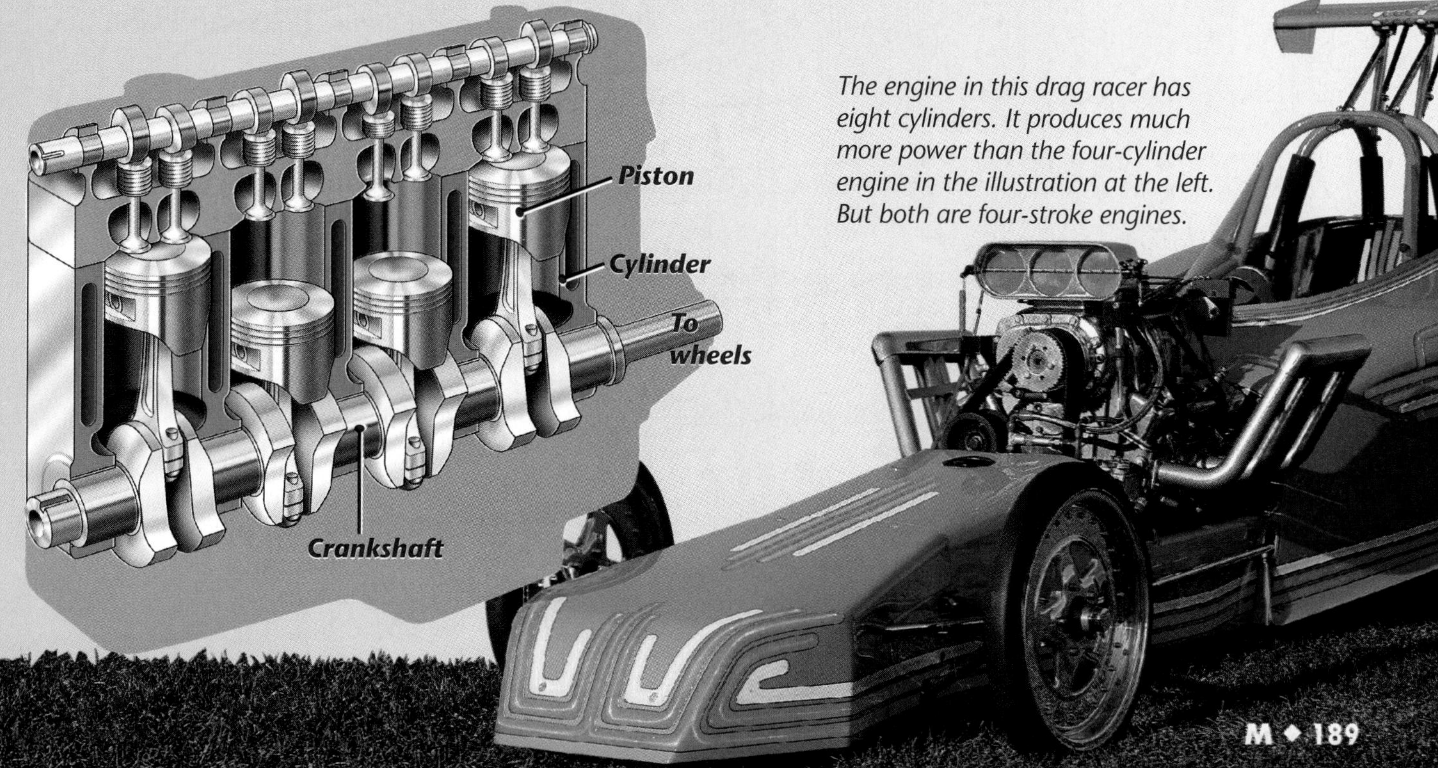

The engine in this drag racer has eight cylinders. It produces much more power than the four-cylinder engine in the illustration at the left. But both are four-stroke engines.

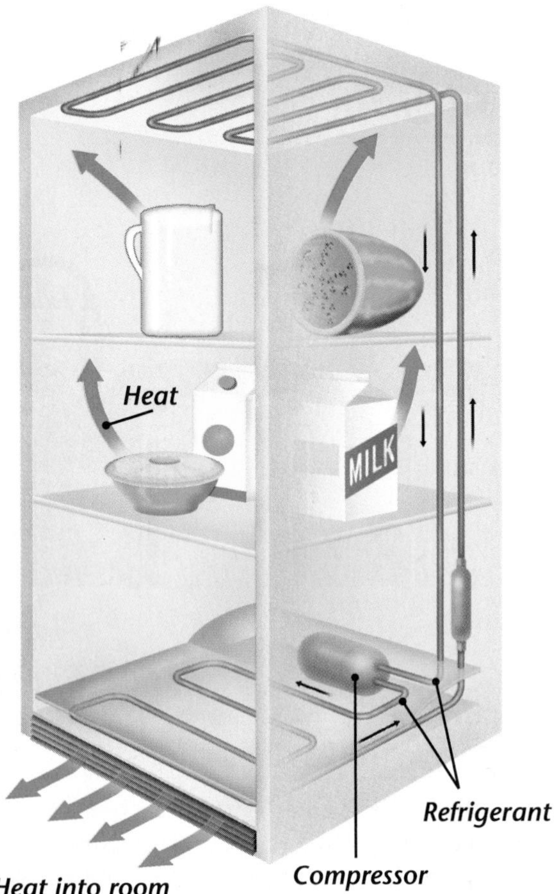

Figure 19 This diagram shows the basic parts of a refrigerator. *Interpreting Diagrams How are changes of state used to cool food?*

Refrigerators

Energy conversion can also be used to keep food cool. Does that seem surprising? After all, heat naturally flows from a warm body to a cold body—not the other way around. So how can you refrigerate food? A refrigerator transfers thermal energy from the cold space inside to the warm room outside. Perhaps you have felt this energy in the warm air blown out at the bottom of a refrigerator.

A refrigerator is a device that uses an outside energy source to transfer thermal energy from a cool area to a warm area. In your refrigerator, that energy is provided by an electric motor, powered by the electricity coming to your home.

A refrigerator also requires a refrigerant substance. The refrigerator motor runs a compressor that compresses the refrigerant in the gas state, which causes its pressure and its temperature to rise. When this happens, the gas gives off thermal energy. This heat is transferred to the outside air. As the gas loses thermal energy, it changes from a gas to a liquid. The liquid is then allowed to evaporate. As it evaporates, it cools. The cold gas is then pumped through tubes inside the walls of the refrigerator. There the gas absorbs heat from inside the refrigerator. And so thermal energy is transferred from the space inside the refrigerator to the gas. The gas then returns to the compressor, and the whole cycle begins again.

An air conditioner operates in the same way. But it cools the area inside a building and transfers thermal energy to the air outdoors.

Section 4 Review

1. What is a heat engine?
2. Describe the process that occurs in a refrigerator.
3. What are the parts of the four-stroke cycle?
4. **Thinking Critically Comparing and Contrasting** What are the two types of heat engines? How are they alike? How are they different?

Check Your Progress

CHAPTER PROJECT 6

Build and test your container. Remember that you need to be able to get to the aluminum can at the beginning of the test so that hot water can be poured into it. You must also be able to measure the temperature of the water at the end of the test.

CHAPTER 6 STUDY GUIDE

Section 1 Temperature and Thermal Energy

Key Ideas

- Temperature is a measure of the average kinetic energy of each particle within an object.
- Three temperature scales are Fahrenheit, Celsius, and Kelvin.
- Thermal energy is the total energy of the particles that make up an object.

Key Terms

temperature
Fahrenheit scale
Celsius scale
Kelvin scale
absolute zero

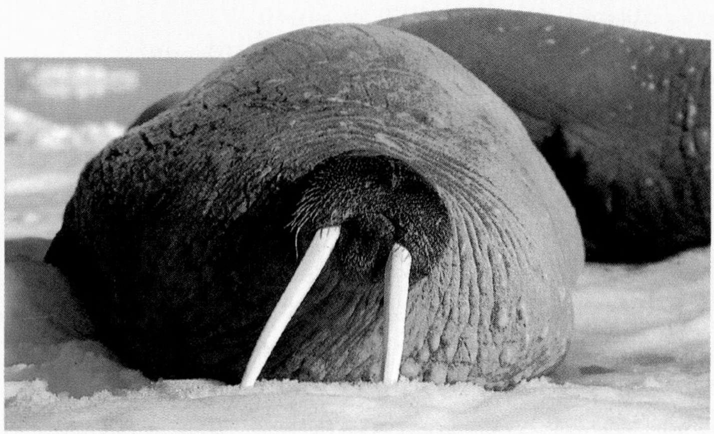

Section 2 The Nature of Heat

Key Ideas

- Heat is a transfer of thermal energy from an object at a higher temperature to an object at a lower temperature.
- Heat is transferred by conduction, convection, and radiation.
- A conductor transfers heat well, whereas an insulator does not.
- The amount of heat necessary to raise a unit of mass of a substance by a specific unit of temperature is called the specific heat.

Key Terms

heat
conduction
convection
convection current
radiation
conductor
insulator
specific heat

Section 3 Thermal Energy and States of Matter

INTEGRATING CHEMISTRY

Key Idea

- Matter can undergo a change of state when thermal energy is added or removed.

Key Terms

state
change of state
melting
melting point
freezing
freezing point
vaporization
evaporation
boiling
boiling point
condensation
thermal expansion
thermostat
bimetallic strip

Section 4 Uses of Heat

Key Ideas

- A heat engine converts thermal energy to mechanical energy that can do work.
- A refrigerator transfers thermal energy from a cool region to a warm region.

Key Terms

heat engine
combustion
external combustion engine
internal combustion engine

Organizing Information

Concept Map Copy the thermal energy concept map onto a separate sheet of paper. Then complete it and add a title. (For more on concept maps, see the Skills Handbook.)

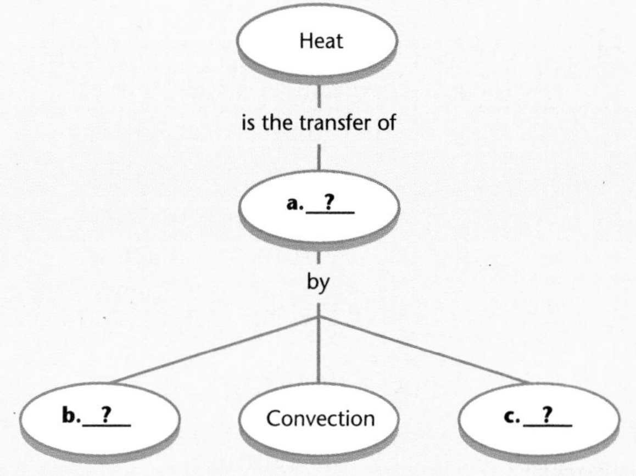

Reviewing Content

For more review of key concepts, see the Interactive Student Tutorial CD-ROM.

Multiple Choice

Choose the letter of the answer that best completes each statement.

1. The average kinetic energy of the particles of an object is its
   a. heat content. **b.** temperature.
   c. specific heat. **d.** thermal energy.
2. The process by which heat moves from one end of a solid to the other is called
   a. convection. **b.** conduction.
   c. radiation. **d.** insulation.
3. If you want to know the amount of heat needed to raise the temperature of 2 kg of steel by 10°C, you need to know steel's
   a. temperature. **b.** thermal energy.
   c. heat content. **d.** specific heat.
4. The change of state that occurs when a gas becomes a liquid is called
   a. evaporation.
   b. boiling.
   c. freezing.
   d. condensation.
5. Heat engines convert thermal energy to
   a. chemical energy.
   b. electrical energy.
   c. mechanical energy.
   d. radiant energy.

True or False

If the statement is true, write true. If it is false, change the underlined word or words to make the statement true.

6. The temperature reading of zero on the <u>Celsius</u> scale is equal to absolute zero.
7. Heat transfer by <u>radiation</u> can occur in a vacuum.
8. In order to decrease the amount of thermal energy that moves from one place to another, you would use a <u>conductor</u>.
9. When a substance melts, the temperature of the substance <u>increases</u>.
10. In an <u>external</u> combustion engine, the fuel is burned inside the cylinder.

Checking Concepts

11. What happens to the particles of a solid as the thermal energy of the solid increases?
12. When you heat a pot of water on the stove, a convection current is formed. Explain how this happens.
13. When night falls on a summer day, the air temperature drops by 10°C. Will the temperature of the water in a nearby lake change by the same amount? Explain why or why not.
14. How can you add thermal energy to a substance without increasing its temperature?
15. When molten steel becomes solid, is energy absorbed or released by the steel?
16. Describe how a thermostat controls the temperature in a building.
17. **Writing to Learn** Haiku is a form of poetry that began in Japan. A haiku has three lines. The first and third lines have five syllables each. The second line has seven syllables. Write a haiku describing how you might feel on a frosty winter morning or a sweltering summer afternoon.

Thinking Critically

18. **Problem Solving** Suppose a mercury thermometer contains 2 grams of mercury. If the thermometer's reading changes from 25°C to 40°C, how much heat was needed? The specific heat of mercury is 140 J/(kg·K).
19. **Relating Cause and Effect** Why is the air pressure in a car's tires different before and after the car has been driven for an hour?
20. **Applying Concepts** Telephone lines are allowed to sag when they are hung. Can you think of a reason why?
21. **Relating Cause and Effect** A refrigerator is running in a small room. The refrigerator door is open, but the room does not grow any cooler. Use the law of conservation of energy to explain why the temperature does not drop.

Applying Skills

Use the drawing of three containers of water to answer Questions 22–24.

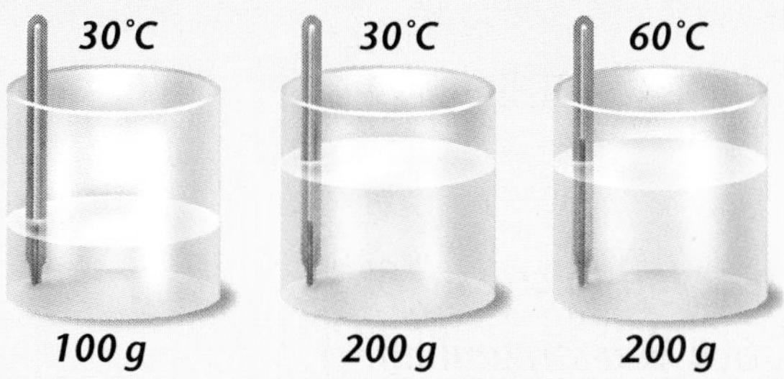

22. **Interpreting Data** Compare the average motion of the molecules in the three containers. Explain your answer.
23. **Drawing Conclusions** Compare the total amount of thermal energy in the three containers. Explain your answer.
24. **Calculating** Determine how much heat you would need to raise the temperature of each container by 1°C. (See Figure 10 on page 176.) Show your work.

Performance Assessment

Project Wrap Up Talk with your classmates about their designs. When you've had a chance to look them over, predict the final water temperature for each device. Record the starting temperature for each one, including your own. Record the final temperatures at the end of the demonstrations.

Reflect and Record In your journal, answer the following questions: Which insulating materials seemed to work the best? Which design worked best?

Test Preparation

Use these questions to prepare for standardized tests.

Read the passage. Then answer Questions 25–27.

Water has quite a high specific heat. This property of water affects the climate in many places. Because of the high specific heat of water, the temperature of ocean water does not vary much from summer to winter. In winter in many parts of Earth, the temperature of the ocean water is higher than the average air temperature. So the water warms the air that moves over it. In summer, the water is usually cooler than the air, so the water cools the air that moves over it.

During the winter on the west coast of the United States, air warmed by Pacific Ocean water blows onto land. In the summer, air cooled by the water blows onto land. As a result, the city of Portland, Oregon, is warmer in the winter and cooler in the summer than the city of Minneapolis, Minnesota, which is at about the same latitude as Portland. Because Minneapolis is farther from the ocean than Portland, its air is less affected by the temperature of the ocean water.

25. What is this passage mostly about?
    - **a.** how latitude affects temperature
    - **b.** why the southern states are warmer than the northern states
    - **c.** how the oceans affect the coastal climates
    - **d.** how the specific heat of water compares to other materials
26. Since the specific heat of water is higher than that of land
    - **a.** the temperature of land rises less than that of water given the same amount of energy.
    - **b.** the temperature of water rises less than that of land given the same amount of energy.
    - **c.** land absorbs more energy than water for the same temperature change.
    - **d.** water is always warmer than land.
27. Why is Portland, Oregon, cooler than Minneapolis, Minnesota, in the summer?
    - **a.** Winds carry warm air to Minneapolis.
    - **b.** Winds carry cool air to Portland.
    - **c.** Minneapolis is lower in latitude.
    - **d.** Portland is lower in latitude.

BRIDGES

FROM VINES TO STEEL

HAVE YOU EVER . . .

balanced on a branch or log to cross a brook?

jumped from rock to rock in a streambed?

swung on a vine or rope over a river?

Then you have used the same ways that early people used to get over obstacles. Fallen trees, twisted vines, and natural stones formed the first bridges.

Bridges provide easy ways of getting over difficult obstacles. For thousands of years, bridges have also served as forts for defense, scenes of great battles, and homes for shops and churches. They have also been sites of mystery, love, and intrigue. They span history—linking cities, nations, and empires and encouraging trade and travel.

But bridges have not always been as elaborate as they are today. The earliest ones were made of materials that were free and plentiful. In deep forests, people used beams made from small trees. In tropical regions where vegetation was thick, people wove together vines and grasses, then hung them to make walkways over rivers and gorges.

No matter what the structures or materials, bridges reflect the people who built them. Each of the ancient civilizations of China, Egypt, Greece, and Rome designed strong, graceful bridges to connect and control its empire.

The Roman arch bridge Ponte Sant'Angelo in Rome

The Balance of Forces

What keeps a bridge from falling down? How does it support its own weight and the weight of people and traffic on it? Builders found the answers by considering the various forces that act on a bridge.

The weight of the bridge and the traffic on it are called the *load*. When a heavy truck crosses a beam bridge, the weight of the load forces the beam to curve downward. This creates a tension force that stretches the bottom of the beam. At the same time, the load also creates a compression force at the top of the beam.

Since the bridge doesn't collapse under the load, there must be upward forces to balance the downward forces. In simple beam bridges, builders attached the beam to the ground or to end supports called abutments. To cross longer spans or distances, they construct piers under the middle span. Piers and abutments are structures that act as upward forces—reaction forces.

Another type of bridge, the arch bridge, supports its load by compression. A heavy load on a stone arch bridge squeezes or pushes the stones together, creating compression throughout the structure. Weight on the arch bridge pushes down to the ends of the arch. The side walls and abutments act as reaction forces.

Early engineers discovered that arch bridges made of stone could span wider distances than simple beam bridges. Arch bridges were also stronger and more durable. Although the Romans were not the first to build arch bridges, they perfected the form in their massive, elegant structures. Early Roman arch bridges were built without mortar, or "glue." The arch held together because the stones were skillfully shaped to work in compression. After nearly 2,000 years, some of these Roman arch bridges are still standing.

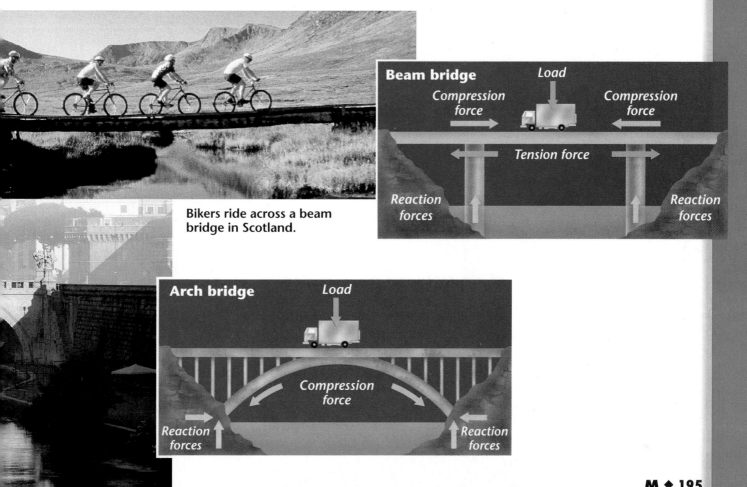

Bikers ride across a beam bridge in Scotland.

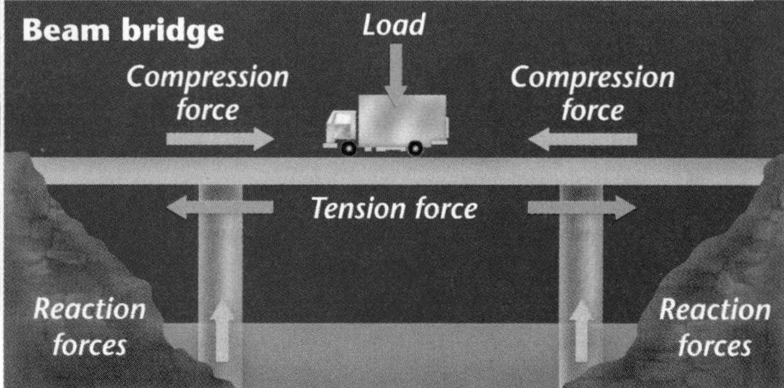

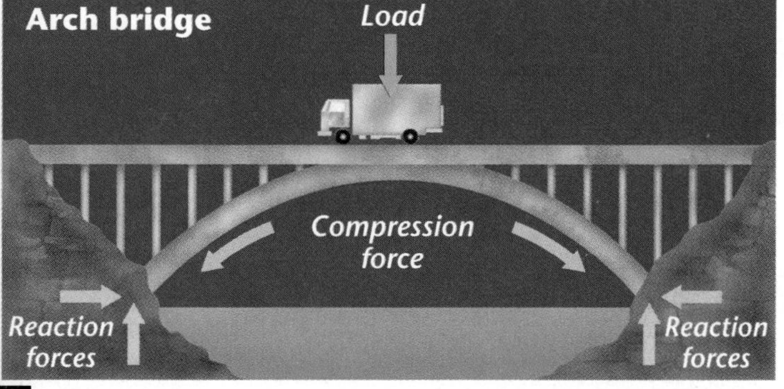

Science

The Golden Age of Bridges

In the 1800s in the United States, the invention of the steam locomotive and the expansion of railroads increased the demand for bridges. Trains pulling heavy freight needed strong, flat bridges. Builders began to use cast iron instead of stone and wood. By the late 1800s, they were using steel, which was strong and relatively lightweight.

The use of new building materials was not the only change. Engineers began designing different types of bridges as well. They found that they could build longer, larger bridges by using a suspension structure.

Suspension bridges are modern versions of long, narrow, woven bridges found in tropical regions. These simple, woven suspension bridges can span long distances. Crossing one of these natural structures is like walking a tightrope. The weight of people and animals traveling over the bridge pushes down on the ropes, stretching them and creating tension forces.

Modern suspension bridges follow the same principles of tension as do woven bridges. A suspension bridge is strong in tension. In suspension bridges, parallel cables are stretched the entire length of the bridge—over giant towers. The cables are anchored at each end of the bridge. The roadway hangs from the cables, attached by wire suspenders. The weight of the bridge and the load on it act to pull apart or stretch the cables. This pulling apart creates tension force.

The towers act as supports for the bridge cables. The abutments that anchor the cables exert reaction forces as well. So forces in balance keep a suspension bridge from collapsing.

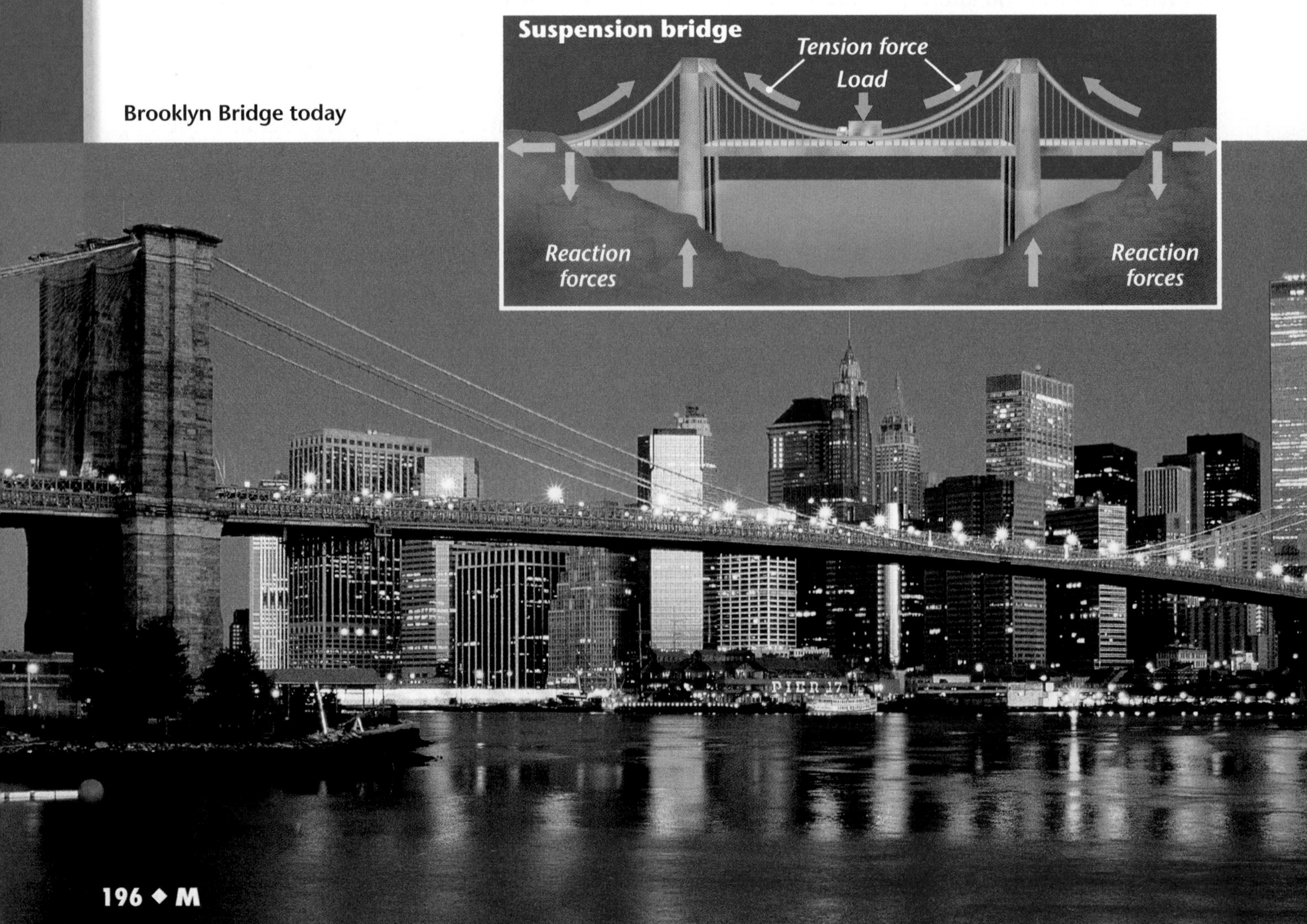

Brooklyn Bridge today

A Great Engineering Feat

When it opened in 1883, the Brooklyn Bridge was the longest suspension bridge in the world—one half span longer than any other. It connected Brooklyn and Manhattan. Yet when the idea was first proposed, people said it couldn't be done.

In the mid-1800s, many people from Brooklyn had jobs across the East River in Manhattan. But the only way to get there was by ferry. Fierce ocean tides, stormy weather, and ice chunks in winter could make the journey risky. In 1868 John Augustus Roebling, a German immigrant engineer, was hired to build a bridge.

An engineering genius, Roebling designed a suspension bridge using four cables stretched over two giant granite towers. Roebling was the first engineer to design bridge cables of strong, flexible steel instead of cast iron.

Each cable, about 16 inches in diameter, would contain nearly 5,300 wires. After the cables were in place, 1,500 smaller suspension cables would be attached to the main cables to support the roadway. It's not surprising that people didn't believe that it could be done.

It was impossible to lift heavy cables over the towers. So builders had to reel wire back and forth across the East River to create the cables. There are 3,515 miles of wire for each cable! To "spin the cables" John Roebling invented a traveling wheel that could carry the wire in a continuous loop, from one side of the river over the towers to the other side and back. It's an invention that is still used today.

Each of the smaller cables that hang from the four main cables of the Brooklyn Bridge is made up of seven bundles of seven steel wires.

Science Activity

Work in groups to make a suspension bridge, using 2 chairs, a wooden plank, rope, and some books.

- Place 2 chairs back to back and stretch 2 ropes over the backs of the chairs. Hold the ropes at both ends.
- Tie 3 pieces of rope to the longer ropes. Place the plank through the loops.
- With a partner, hold the ropes tightly at each end. Load books on top of the plank to see how much it will hold.

Why is it important to anchor the ropes tightly at each end?

Social Studies

Against All Odds

When John Roebling was hired in 1868 to build the Brooklyn Bridge, he was already an experienced suspension bridge engineer. He had plans for the bridge that he'd been working on since 1855.

But before bridge construction even began in 1869, John Roebling died in a bridge-related accident. Fortunately, he had worked out his bridge design to the last detail. His son, Colonel Washington Roebling, who was also a skilled engineer, dedicated himself to carrying out his father's plans.

The construction dragged on for 14 years and cost nearly 30 lives. Colonel Roebling himself became so disabled that he was forced to direct construction from his home. Using a telescope, Colonel Roebling followed every detail. His remarkable, energetic wife, Emily Warren Roebling, learned enough engineering principles to deliver and explain his orders to the workers.

The dedication of the Roebling family—John (left), Washington (center), and Emily (right)—ensured the success of the Brooklyn Bridge.

Workers building the Brooklyn Bridge

As soon as the giant towers were up, workers unrolled the steel wire back and forth across the towers to weave the cables. The next step was to twist the wires together. But the workmen were terrified of hanging so high on the bridge and refused to work. Finally, Frank Farrington, the chief mechanic, crossed the river on a small chair dangling from a wheel that ran across an overhead line. Farrington completed his journey to the roar of the crowd. This feat was billed as the greatest trapeze act of all time. Somewhat reassured, the builders returned to work. But it took two more years to string the cables. The bridge was one of the greatest engineering achievements of its time.

In the end, the Brooklyn Bridge project succeeded only because of the determination and sacrifices of the Roebling family. It became the model for hundreds of other suspension bridges.

Social Studies Activity

How do you think the Brooklyn Bridge changed the lives of New Yorkers? In groups, research the history of another famous bridge. Present your findings to your class along with drawings and photos. Find out

- ◆ when and why the bridge was built
- ◆ the type of bridge
- ◆ how peoples' lives changed after it was built—include effects on trade, travel, and population
- ◆ how landforms affected the bridge building
- ◆ about events connected to the bridge

The New York Times *May 25, 1883*

Two Great Cities United

The Brooklyn bridge was successfully opened yesterday. The pleasant weather brought visitors by the thousands from all around. Spectators were packed in masses through which it was almost impossible to pass, and those who had tickets to attend the ceremonies had hard work to reach the bridge. Every available house-top and window was filled, and an adventurous party occupied a tall telegraph pole. It required the utmost efforts of the police to keep clear the necessary space.

After the exercises at the bridge were completed the Brooklyn procession was immediately re-formed and the march was taken up to Col. Roebling's residence. From the back study on the second floor of his house Col. Roebling had watched through his telescope the procession as it proceeded along from the New York side until the Brooklyn tower was reached. Mrs. Roebling received at her husband's side and accepted her share of the honors of the bridge.

For blocks and blocks on either side of the bridge there was scarcely a foot of room to spare. Many persons crossed and re-crossed the river on the ferry boats, and in that way watched the display. Almost every ship along the river front was converted into a grand stand.

The final ceremonies of the opening of the great bridge began at eight o'clock, when the first rocket was sent from the center of the great structure, and ended at 9 o'clock, when a flight of 500 rockets illuminated the sky. The river-front was one blaze of light, and on the yachts and smaller vessels blue fires were burning and illuminating dark waters around them.

This historic painting shows fireworks at the opening of the Brooklyn Bridge in 1883.

Story adapted from *The New York Times,* May 25, 1883.

Language Arts Activity

A reporter's goal is to inform and entertain the reader. Using a catchy opening line draws interest. Then the reader wants to know the facts—what, who, where, when, why, and how (5 Ws and H).

You are a school reporter. Write about the opening of a bridge in your area. It could be a highway overpass or a bridge over water, a valley, or railroad tracks.

- Include some of the 5 Ws and H.
- Add interesting details and descriptions.

Mathematics

Bridge Geometry

As railroad traffic increased in the late 1800s, truss bridges became popular. Designed with thin vertical and diagonal supports to add strength, truss bridges were really reinforced beam bridge structures. Many of the early wood truss bridges couldn't support the trains that rumbled over them. Cast iron and steel trusses soon replaced wood trusses.

Using basic triangular structures, engineers went to work on more scientific truss bridge designs. The accuracy of the design is crucial to handling the stress from heavy train loads and constant vibrations. As in all bridge structures, each steel piece has to be measured and fitted accurately—including widths, lengths, angles, and points of intersection and attachment.

Forces Acting on Geometric Shapes

A basic triangle in a truss bridge is strong because its shape cannot be distorted.

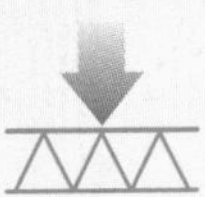
A triangle in a truss bridge can support a heavy load with its relatively small weight.

A square or rectangle is not as strong as a triangle.

It can collapse into a parallelogram under a heavy load.

Look closely at the truss patterns. In drawing bridge plans, engineers use geometric shapes.

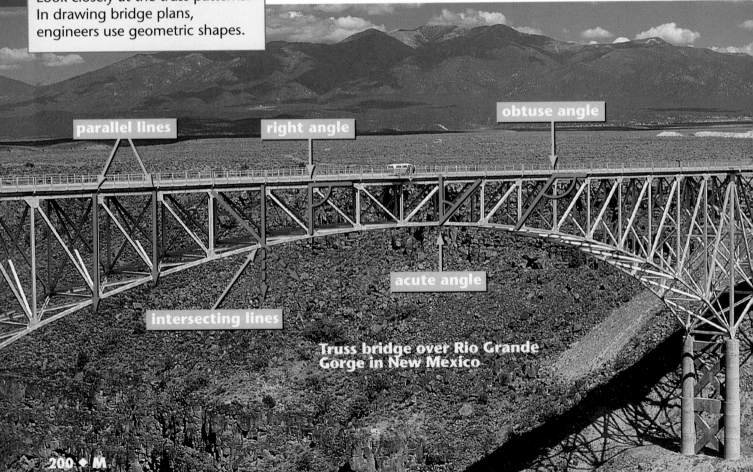

parallel lines

right angle

obtuse angle

acute angle

intersecting lines

Truss bridge over Rio Grande Gorge in New Mexico

Math Activity

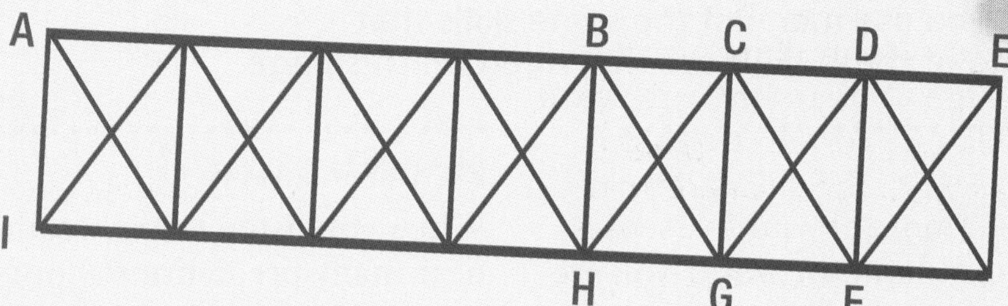

The chief building engineer has asked you to draw up exact plans for a new truss bridge. How well will you do as an assistant? You will soon find out by answering these questions:

1. Which lines are parallel?
2. Which lines intersect?
3. What kind of figure is formed by ABHI?
4. What kind of figure is formed by HCF?
5. What kind of angle is BGF—obtuse or right?
6. What kind of angle is CHG?
7. What kind of triangle is BHG? What makes it this kind of triangle?
8. Why is a triangle stronger than a square?

Tie It Together

Bridge the Gap

Work in small groups to build a model of a bridge out of a box of spaghetti and a roll of masking tape. Meet as a group to choose the type of bridge you will build. Each bridge should be strong enough to hold a brick. You can build—

- a beam bridge
- a truss bridge
- an arch bridge
- a suspension bridge (This one is challenging.)

After drawing a sketch of the bridge design, assign jobs for each team member. Then

- decide how long the bridge span will be
- measure and cut the materials
- build the roadway first for beam, truss, and suspension bridges
- build the arch first in an arch bridge

When your bridge is complete, display it in the classroom. Test the strength of each bridge by placing a brick on the roadway. Discuss the difference in bridge structures. Determine which bridge design is the strongest.

Think Like a Scientist

Although you may not know it, you think like a scientist every day. Whenever you ask a question and explore possible answers, you use many of the same skills that scientists do. Some of these skills are described on this page.

Observing

When you use one or more of your five senses to gather information about the world, you are **observing.** Hearing a dog bark, counting twelve green seeds, and smelling smoke are all observations. To increase the power of their senses, scientists sometimes use microscopes, telescopes, or other instruments that help them make more detailed observations.

An observation must be an accurate report of what your senses detect. It is important to keep careful records of your observations in science class by writing or drawing in a notebook. The information collected through observations is called evidence, or data.

Inferring

When you interpret an observation, you are **inferring,** or making an inference. For example, if you hear your dog barking, you may infer that someone is at your front door. To make this inference, you combine the evidence—the barking dog—and your experience or knowledge—you know that your dog barks when strangers approach—to reach a logical conclusion.

Notice that an inference is not a fact; it is only one of many possible interpretations for an observation. For example, your dog may be barking because it wants to go for a walk. An inference may turn out to be incorrect even if it is based on accurate observations and logical reasoning. The only way to find out if an inference is correct is to investigate further.

Predicting

When you listen to the weather forecast, you hear many predictions about the next day's weather—what the temperature will be, whether it will rain, and how windy it will be. Weather forecasters use observations and knowledge of weather patterns to predict the weather. The skill of **predicting** involves making an inference about a future event based on current evidence or past experience.

Because a prediction is an inference, it may prove to be false. In science class, you can test some of your predictions by doing experiments. For example, suppose you predict that larger paper airplanes can fly farther than smaller airplanes. How could you test your prediction?

Use the photograph to answer the questions below.

Observing Look closely at the photograph. List at least three observations.

Inferring Use your observations to make an inference about what has happened. What experience or knowledge did you use to make the inference?

Predicting Predict what will happen next. On what evidence or experience do you base your prediction?

Classifying

Could you imagine searching for a book in the library if the books were shelved in no particular order? Your trip to the library would be an all-day event! Luckily, librarians group together books on similar topics or by the same author. Grouping together items that are alike in some way is called **classifying.** You can classify items in many ways: by size, by shape, by use, and by other important characteristics.

Like librarians, scientists use the skill of classifying to organize information and objects. When things are sorted into groups, the relationships among them become easier to understand.

ACTIVITY

Classify the objects in the photograph into two groups based on any characteristic you choose. Then use another characteristic to classify the objects into three groups.

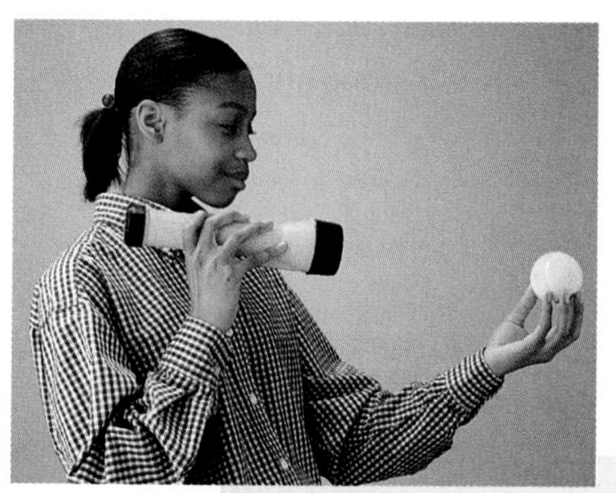

Making Models

Have you ever drawn a picture to help someone understand what you were saying? Such a drawing is one type of model. A model is a picture, diagram, computer image, or other representation of a complex object or process. **Making models** helps people understand things that they cannot observe directly.

Scientists often use models to represent things that are either very large or very small, such as the planets in the solar system, or the parts of a cell. Such models are physical models—drawings or three-dimensional structures that look like the real thing. Other models are mental models—mathematical equations or words that describe how something works.

ACTIVITY

This student is using a model to demonstrate what causes day and night on Earth. What do the flashlight and the tennis ball in the model represent?

Communicating

Whenever you talk on the phone, write a letter, or listen to your teacher at school, you are communicating. **Communicating** is the process of sharing ideas and information with other people. Communicating effectively requires many skills, including writing, reading, speaking, listening, and making models.

Scientists communicate to share results, information, and opinions. Scientists often communicate about their work in journals, over the telephone, in letters, and on the Internet. They also attend scientific meetings where they share their ideas with one another in person.

ACTIVITY

On a sheet of paper, write out clear, detailed directions for tying your shoe. Then exchange directions with a partner. Follow your partner's directions exactly. How successful were you at tying your shoe? How could your partner have communicated more clearly?

Making Measurements

When scientists make observations, it is not sufficient to say that something is "big" or "heavy." Instead, scientists use instruments to measure just how big or heavy an object is. By measuring, scientists can express their observations more precisely and communicate more information about what they observe.

Measuring in SI

The standard system of measurement used by scientists around the world is known as the International System of Units, which is abbreviated as SI (in French, *Système International d'Unités*). SI units are easy to use because they are based on multiples of 10. Each unit is ten times larger than the next smallest unit and one tenth the size of the next largest unit. The table lists the prefixes used to name the most common SI units.

Common SI Prefixes

Prefix	Symbol	Meaning
kilo-	k	1,000
hecto-	h	100
deka-	da	10
deci-	d	0.1 (one tenth)
centi-	c	0.01 (one hundredth)
milli-	m	0.001 (one thousandth)

Length To measure length, or the distance between two points, the unit of measure is the **meter (m).** The distance from the floor to a doorknob is approximately one meter. Long distances, such as the distance between two cities, are measured in kilometers (km). Small lengths are measured in centimeters (cm) or millimeters (mm). Scientists use metric rulers and meter sticks to measure length.

Common Conversions

1 km = 1,000 m
1 m = 100 cm
1 m = 1,000 mm
1 cm = 10 mm

ACTIVITY

The larger lines on the metric ruler in the picture show centimeter divisions, while the smaller, unnumbered lines show millimeter divisions. How many centimeters long is the shell? How many millimeters long is it?

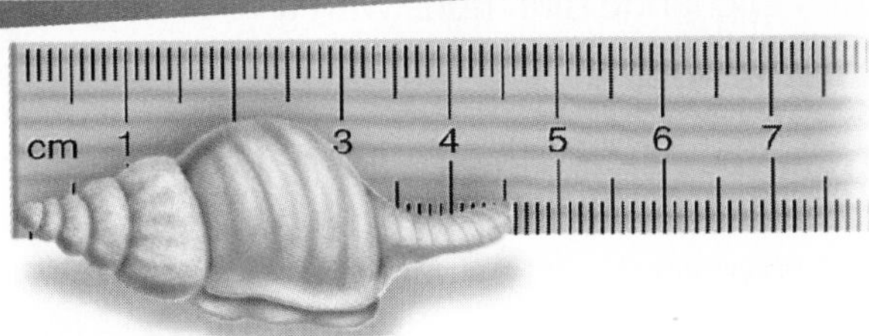

Liquid Volume To measure the volume of a liquid, or the amount of space it takes up, you will use a unit of measure known as the **liter (L).** One liter is the approximate volume of a medium-size carton of milk. Smaller volumes are measured in milliliters (mL). Scientists use graduated cylinders to measure liquid volume.

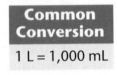

Common Conversion

1 L = 1,000 mL

ACTIVITY

The graduated cylinder in the picture is marked in milliliter divisions. Notice that the water in the cylinder has a curved surface. This curved surface is called the *meniscus*. To measure the volume, you must read the level at the lowest point of the meniscus. What is the volume of water in this graduated cylinder?

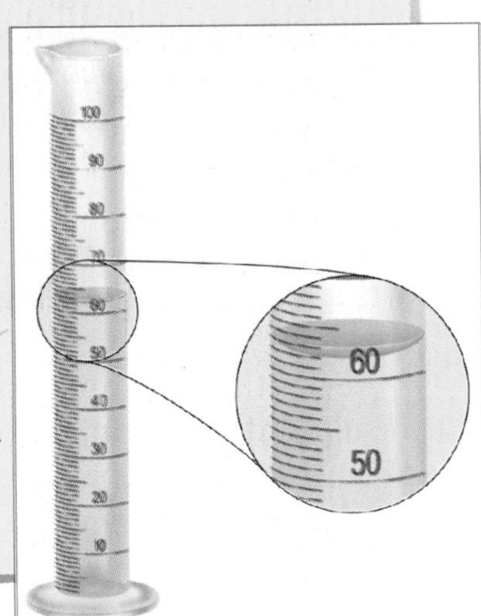

Mass To measure mass, or the amount of matter in an object, you will use a unit of measure known as the **gram (g)**. One gram is approximately the mass of a paper clip. Larger masses are measured in kilograms (kg). Scientists use a balance to find the mass of an object.

Common Conversion

1 kg = 1,000 g

ACTIVITY

The mass of the apple in the picture is measured in kilograms. What is the mass of the apple? Suppose a recipe for applesauce called for one kilogram of apples. About how many apples would you need?

Temperature

To measure the temperature of a substance, you will use the **Celsius scale.** Temperature is measured in degrees Celsius (°C) using a Celsius thermometer. Water freezes at 0°C and boils at 100°C.

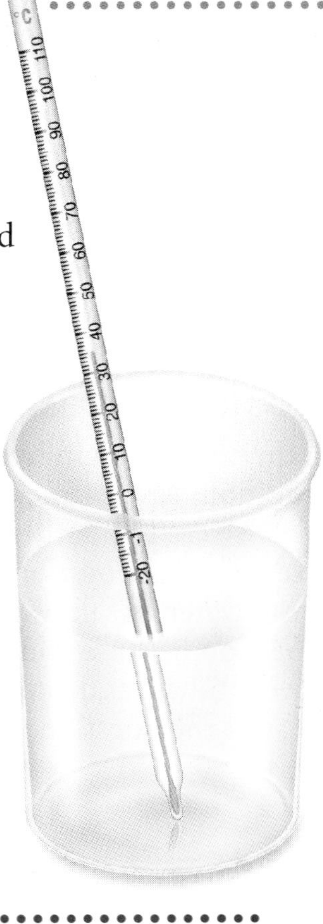

ACTIVITY

What is the temperature of the liquid in degrees Celsius?

Converting SI Units

To use the SI system, you must know how to convert between units. Converting from one unit to another involves the skill of **calculating**, or using mathematical operations. Converting between SI units is similar to converting between dollars and dimes because both systems are based on multiples of ten.

Suppose you want to convert a length of 80 centimeters to meters. Follow these steps to convert between units.

1. Begin by writing down the measurement you want to convert—in this example, 80 centimeters.
2. Write a conversion factor that represents the relationship between the two units you are converting. In this example, the relationship is *1 meter = 100 centimeters.* Write this conversion factor as a fraction, making sure to place the units you are converting from (centimeters, in this example) in the denominator.
3. Multiply the measurement you want to convert by the fraction. When you do this, the units in the first measurement will cancel out with the units in the denominator. Your answer will be in the units you are converting to (meters, in this example).

Example

80 centimeters = ___?___ meters

$$80 \text{ centimeters} \times \frac{1 \text{ meter}}{100 \text{ centimeters}} = \frac{80 \text{ meters}}{100}$$

$$= 0.8 \text{ meters}$$

ACTIVITY

Convert between the following units.

1. 600 millimeters = ___?___ meters
2. 0.35 liters = ___?___ milliliters
3. 1,050 grams = ___?___ kilograms

Conducting a Scientific Investigation

In some ways, scientists are like detectives, piecing together clues to learn about a process or event. One way that scientists gather clues is by carrying out experiments. An experiment tests an idea in a careful, orderly manner. Although experiments do not all follow the same steps in the same order, many follow a pattern similar to the one described here.

Posing Questions

Experiments begin by asking a scientific question. A scientific question is one that can be answered by gathering evidence. For example, the question "Which freezes faster—fresh water or salt water?" is a scientific question because you can carry out an investigation and gather information to answer the question.

Developing a Hypothesis

The next step is to form a hypothesis. A **hypothesis** is a possible explanation for a set of observations or answer to a scientific question. In science, a hypothesis must be something that can be tested. A hypothesis can be worded as an *If… then…* statement. For example, a hypothesis might be *"If I add salt to fresh water, then the water will take longer to freeze."* A hypothesis worded this way serves as a rough outline of the experiment you should perform.

Designing an Experiment

Next you need to plan a way to test your hypothesis. Your plan should be written out as a step-by-step procedure and should describe the observations or measurements you will make.

Two important steps involved in designing an experiment are controlling variables and forming operational definitions.

Controlling Variables In a well-designed experiment, you need to keep all variables the same except for one. A **variable** is any factor that can change in an experiment. The factor that you change is called the **manipulated variable.** In this experiment, the manipulated variable is the amount of salt added to the water. Other factors, such as the amount of water or the starting temperature, are kept constant.

The factor that changes as a result of the manipulated variable is called the responding variable. The **responding variable** is what you measure or observe to obtain your results. In this experiment, the responding variable is how long the water takes to freeze.

An experiment in which all factors except one are kept constant is a **controlled experiment.** Most controlled experiments include a test called the control. In this experiment, Container 3 is the control. Because no salt is added to Container 3, you can compare the results from the other containers to it. Any difference in results must be due to the addition of salt alone.

Forming Operational Definitions

Another important aspect of a well-designed experiment is having clear operational definitions. An **operational definition** is a statement that describes how a particular variable is to be measured or how a term is to be defined. For example, in this experiment, how will you determine if the water has frozen? You might decide to insert a stick in each container at the start of the experiment. Your operational definition of "frozen" would be the time at which the stick can no longer move.

EXPERIMENTAL PROCEDURE

1. *Fill 3 containers with 300 milliliters of cold tap water.*
2. *Add 10 grams of salt to Container 1; stir. Add 20 grams of salt to Container 2; stir. Add no salt to Container 3.*
3. *Place the 3 containers in a freezer.*
4. *Check the containers every 15 minutes. Record your observations.*

Interpreting Data

The observations and measurements you make in an experiment are called data. At the end of an experiment, you need to analyze the data to look for any patterns or trends. Patterns often become clear if you organize your data in a data table or graph. Then think through what the data reveal. Do they support your hypothesis? Do they point out a flaw in your experiment? Do you need to collect more data?

Drawing Conclusions

A conclusion is a statement that sums up what you have learned from an experiment. When you draw a conclusion, you need to decide whether the data you collected support your hypothesis or not. You may need to repeat an experiment several times before you can draw any conclusions from it. Conclusions often lead you to pose new questions and plan new experiments to answer them.

ACTIVITY

Is a ball's bounce affected by the height from which it is dropped? Using the steps just described, plan a controlled experiment to investigate this problem.

Thinking Critically

Has a friend ever asked for your advice about a problem? If so, you may have helped your friend think through the problem in a logical way. Without knowing it, you used critical-thinking skills to help your friend. Critical thinking involves the use of reasoning and logic to solve problems or make decisions. Some critical-thinking skills are described below.

Comparing and Contrasting

When you examine two objects for similarities and differences, you are using the skill of **comparing and contrasting.** Comparing involves identifying similarities, or common characteristics. Contrasting involves identifying differences. Analyzing objects in this way can help you discover details that you might otherwise overlook.

ACTIVITY

Compare and contrast the two animals in the photo. First list all the similarities that you see. Then list all the differences.

Applying Concepts

When you use your knowledge about one situation to make sense of a similar situation, you are using the skill of **applying concepts.** Being able to transfer your knowledge from one situation to another shows that you truly understand a concept. You may use this skill in answering test questions that present different problems from the ones you've reviewed in class.

ACTIVITY

You have just learned that water takes longer to freeze when other substances are mixed into it. Use this knowledge to explain why people need a substance called antifreeze in their car's radiator in the winter.

Interpreting Illustrations

Diagrams, photographs, and maps are included in textbooks to help clarify what you read. These illustrations show processes, places, and ideas in a visual manner. The skill called **interpreting illustrations** can help you learn from these visual elements. To understand an illustration, take the time to study the illustration along with all the written information that accompanies it. Captions identify the key concepts shown in the illustration. Labels point out the important parts of a diagram or map, while keys identify the symbols used in a map.

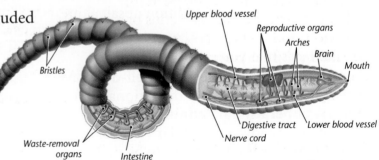

Upper blood vessel
Reproductive organs
Arches
Brain
Mouth
Bristles
Digestive tract
Lower blood vessel
Nerve cord
Waste-removal organs
Intestine

▲ **Internal anatomy of an earthworm**

Study the diagram above. Then write a short paragraph explaining what you have learned.

Relating Cause and Effect

If one event causes another event to occur, the two events are said to have a cause-and-effect relationship. When you determine that such a relationship exists between two events, you use a skill called **relating cause and effect.** For example, if you notice an itchy, red bump on your skin, you might infer that a mosquito bit you. The mosquito bite is the cause, and the bump is the effect.

It is important to note that two events do not necessarily have a cause-and-effect relationship just because they occur together. Scientists carry out experiments or use past experience to determine whether a cause-and-effect relationship exists.

ACTIVITY You are on a camping trip and your flashlight has stopped working. List some possible causes for the flashlight malfunction. How could you determine which cause-and-effect relationship has left you in the dark?

Making Generalizations

When you draw a conclusion about an entire group based on information about only some of the group's members, you are using a skill called **making generalizations.** For a generalization to be valid, the sample you choose must be large enough and representative of the entire group. You might, for example, put this skill to work at a farm stand if you see a sign that says, "Sample some grapes before you buy." If you sample a few sweet grapes, you may conclude that all the grapes are sweet—and purchase a large bunch.

ACTIVITY A team of scientists needs to determine whether the water in a large reservoir is safe to drink. How could they use the skill of making generalizations to help them? What should they do?

Making Judgments

When you evaluate something to decide whether it is good or bad, or right or wrong, you are using a skill called **making judgments.** For example, you make judgments when you decide to eat healthful foods or to pick up litter in a park. Before you make a judgment, you need to think through the pros and cons of a situation, and identify the values or standards that you hold.

ACTIVITY Should children and teens be required to wear helmets when bicycling? Explain why you feel the way you do.

Problem Solving

When you use critical-thinking skills to resolve an issue or decide on a course of action, you are using a skill called **problem solving.** Some problems, such as how to convert a fraction into a decimal, are straightforward. Other problems, such as figuring out why your computer has stopped working, are complex. Some complex problems can be solved using the trial and error method—try out one solution first, and if that doesn't work, try another. Other useful problem-solving strategies include making models and brainstorming possible solutions with a partner.

Organizing Information

As you read this textbook, how can you make sense of all the information it contains? Some useful tools to help you organize information are shown on this page. These tools are called ***graphic organizers*** because they give you a visual picture of a topic, showing at a glance how key concepts are related.

Concept Maps

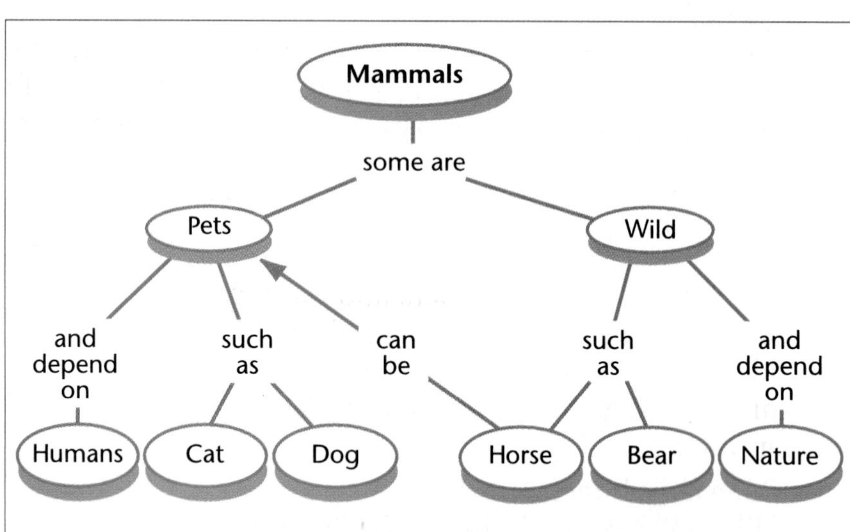

Concept maps are useful tools for organizing information on broad topics. A concept map begins with a general concept and shows how it can be broken down into more specific concepts. In that way, relationships between concepts become easier to understand.

A concept map is constructed by placing concept words (usually nouns) in ovals and connecting them with linking words. Often, the most general concept word is placed at the top, and the words become more specific as you move downward. Often the linking words, which are written on a line extending between two ovals, describe the relationship between the two concepts they connect. If you follow any string of concepts and linking words down the map, it should read like a sentence.

Some concept maps include linking words that connect a concept on one branch of the map to a concept on another branch. These linking words, called cross-linkages, show more complex interrelationships among concepts.

Compare/Contrast Tables

Compare/contrast tables are useful tools for sorting out the similarities and differences between two or more items. A table provides an organized framework in which to compare items based on specific characteristics that you identify.

To create a compare/contrast table, list the items to be compared across the top of a table. Then list the characteristics that will form the basis of your comparison in the left-hand column. Complete the table by filling in information about each characteristic, first for one item and then for the other.

Characteristic	Baseball	Basketball
Number of Players	9	5
Playing Field	Baseball diamond	Basketball court
Equipment	Bat, baseball, mitts	Basket, basketball

Venn Diagrams

Another way to show similarities and differences between items is with a Venn diagram. A Venn diagram consists of two or more circles that partially overlap. Each circle represents a particular concept or idea. Common characteristics, or similarities, are written within the area of overlap between the two circles. Unique characteristics, or differences, are written in the parts of the circles outside the area of overlap.

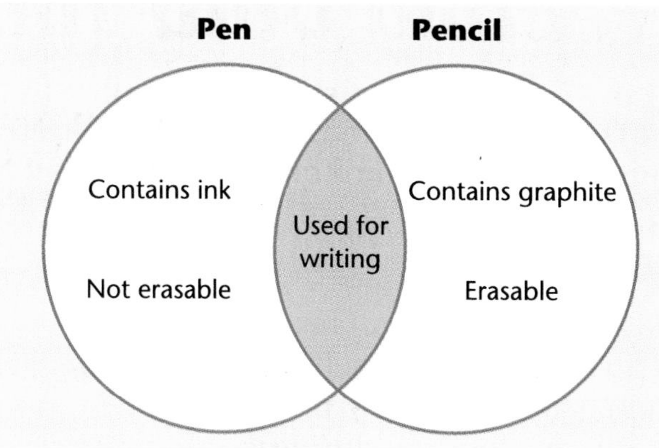

To create a Venn diagram, draw two overlapping circles. Label the circles with the names of the items being compared. Write the unique characteristics in each circle outside the area of overlap. Then write the shared characteristics within the area of overlap.

Flowcharts

A flowchart can help you understand the order in which certain events have occurred or should occur. Flowcharts are useful for outlining the stages in a process or the steps in a procedure.

To make a flowchart, write a brief description of each event in a box. Place the first event at the top of the page, followed by the second event, the third event, and so on. Then draw an arrow to connect each event to the one that occurs next.

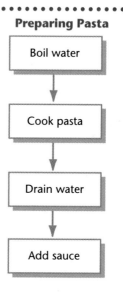

Preparing Pasta

Boil water → Cook pasta → Drain water → Add sauce

Cycle Diagrams

A cycle diagram can be used to show a sequence of events that is continuous, or cyclical. A continuous sequence does not have an end because, when the final event is over, the first event begins again. Like a flowchart, a cycle diagram can help you understand the order of events.

To create a cycle diagram, write a brief description of each event in a box. Place one event at the top of the page in the center. Then, moving in a clockwise direction around an imaginary circle, write each event in its proper sequence. Draw arrows that connect each event to the one that occurs next, forming a continuous circle.

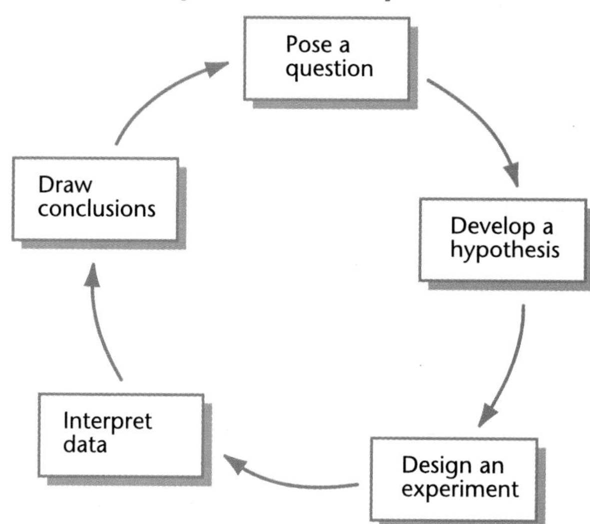

Steps in a Science Experiment

Creating Data Tables and Graphs

How can you make sense of the data in a science experiment? The first step is to organize the data to help you understand them. Data tables and graphs are helpful tools for organizing data.

Data Tables

You have gathered your materials and set up your experiment. But before you start, you need to plan a way to record what happens during the experiment. By creating a data table, you can record your observations and measurements in an orderly way.

Suppose, for example, that a scientist conducted an experiment to find out how many Calories people of different body masses burn while doing various activities. The data table shows the results.

CALORIES BURNED IN 30 MINUTES OF ACTIVITY

Body Mass	Experiment 1 Bicycling	Experiment 2 Playing Basketball	Experiment 3 Watching Television
30 kg	60 Calories	120 Calories	21 Calories
40 kg	77 Calories	164 Calories	27 Calories
50 kg	95 Calories	206 Calories	33 Calories
60 kg	114 Calories	248 Calories	38 Calories

Notice in this data table that the manipulated variable (body mass) is the heading of one column. The responding variable (for Experiment 1, the number of Calories burned while bicycling) is the heading of the next column. Additional columns were added for related experiments.

Bar Graphs

To compare how many Calories a person burns doing various activities, you could create a bar graph. A bar graph is used to display data in a number of separate, or distinct, categories. In this example, bicycling, playing basketball, and watching television are three separate categories.

To create a bar graph, follow these steps.

1. On graph paper, draw a horizontal, or x-, axis and a vertical, or y-, axis.
2. Write the names of the categories to be graphed along the horizontal axis. Include an overall label for the axis as well.
3. Label the vertical axis with the name of the responding variable. Include units of measurement. Then create a scale along the axis by marking off equally spaced numbers that cover the range of the data collected.
4. For each category, draw a solid bar using the scale on the vertical axis to determine the appropriate height. For example, for bicycling, draw the bar as high as the 60 mark on the vertical axis. Make all the bars the same width and leave equal spaces between them.
5. Add a title that describes the graph.

Calories Burned by a 30-kilogram Person in Various Activities

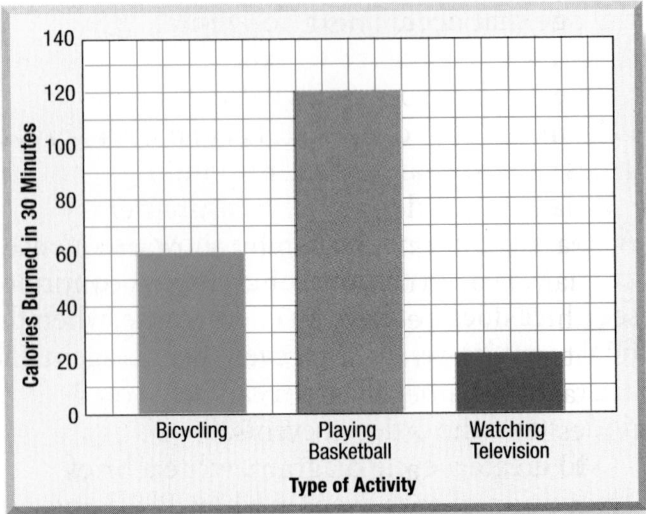

Line Graphs

To see whether a relationship exists between body mass and the number of Calories burned while bicycling, you could create a line graph. A line graph is used to display data that show how one variable (the responding variable) changes in response to another variable (the manipulated variable). You can use a line graph when your manipulated variable is *continuous*, that is, when there are other points between the ones that you tested. In this example, body mass is a continuous variable because there are other body masses between 30 and 40 kilograms (for example, 31 kilograms). Time is another example of a continuous variable.

Line graphs are powerful tools because they allow you to estimate values for conditions that you did not test in the experiment. For example, you can use the line graph to estimate that a 35-kilogram person would burn 68 Calories while bicycling.

Effect of Body Mass on Calories Burned While Bicycling

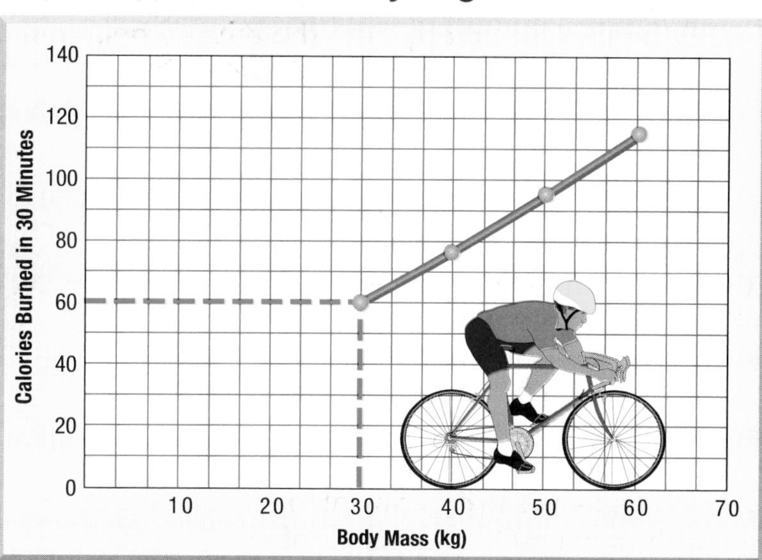

To create a line graph, follow these steps.

1. On graph paper, draw a horizontal, or *x*-, axis and a vertical, or *y*-, axis.
2. Label the horizontal axis with the name of the manipulated variable. Label the vertical axis with the name of the responding variable. Include units of measurement.
3. Create a scale on each axis by marking off equally spaced numbers that cover the range of the data collected.
4. Plot a point on the graph for each piece of data. In the line graph above, the dotted lines show how to plot the first data point (30 kilograms and 60 Calories). Draw an imaginary vertical line extending up from the horizontal axis at the 30-kilogram mark. Then draw an imaginary horizontal line extending across from the vertical axis at the 60-Calorie mark. Plot the point where the two lines intersect.
5. Connect the plotted points with a solid line. (In some cases, it may be more appropriate to draw a line that shows the general trend of the plotted points. In those cases, some of the points may fall above or below the line. Also, not all graphs are linear. It may be more appropriate to draw a curve to connect the points.)
6. Add a title that identifies the variables or relationship in the graph.

ACTIVITY

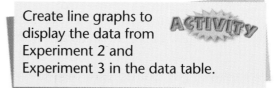

Create line graphs to display the data from Experiment 2 and Experiment 3 in the data table.

ACTIVITY

You read in the newspaper that a total of 4 centimeters of rain fell in your area in June, 2.5 centimeters fell in July, and 1.5 centimeters fell in August. What type of graph would you use to display these data? Use graph paper to create the graph.

Circle Graphs

Like bar graphs, circle graphs can be used to display data in a number of separate categories. Unlike bar graphs, however, circle graphs can only be used when you have data for *all* the categories that make up a given topic. A circle graph is sometimes called a pie chart because it resembles a pie cut into slices. The pie represents the entire topic, while the slices represent the individual categories. The size of a slice indicates what percentage of the whole a particular category makes up.

The data table below shows the results of a survey in which 24 teenagers were asked to identify their favorite sport. The data were then used to create the circle graph at the right.

FAVORITE SPORTS

Sport	Number of Students
Soccer	8
Basketball	6
Bicycling	6
Swimming	4

To create a circle graph, follow these steps.

1. Use a compass to draw a circle. Mark the center of the circle with a point. Then draw a line from the center point to the top of the circle.
2. Determine the size of each "slice" by setting up a proportion where x equals the number of degrees in a slice. (NOTE: A circle contains 360 degrees.) For example, to find the number of degrees in the "soccer" slice, set up the following proportion:

$$\frac{\text{students who prefer soccer}}{\text{total number of students}} = \frac{x}{\text{total number of degrees in a circle}}$$

$$\frac{8}{24} = \frac{x}{360}$$

Cross-multiply and solve for x.

$$24x = 8 \times 360$$
$$x = 120$$

The "soccer" slice should contain 120 degrees.

Sports That Teens Prefer

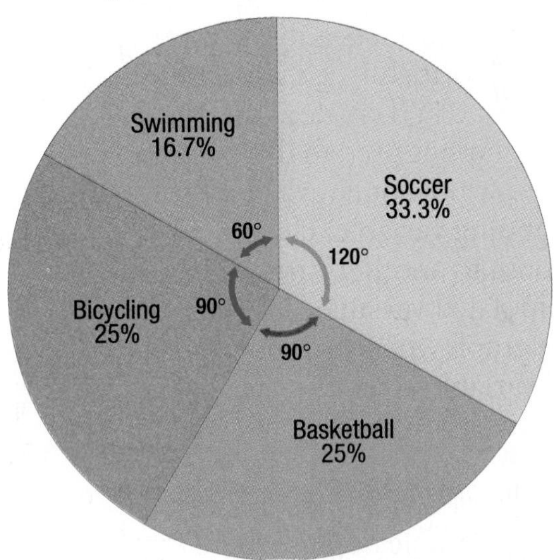

3. Use a protractor to measure the angle of the first slice, using the line you drew to the top of the circle as the 0° line. Draw a line from the center of the circle to the edge for the angle you measured.
4. Continue around the circle by measuring the size of each slice with the protractor. Start measuring from the edge of the previous slice so the wedges do not overlap. When you are done, the entire circle should be filled in.
5. Determine the percentage of the whole circle that each slice represents. To do this, divide the number of degrees in a slice by the total number of degrees in a circle (360), and multiply by 100%. For the "soccer" slice, you can find the percentage as follows:

$$\frac{120}{360} \times 100\% = 33.3\%$$

6. Use a different color to shade in each slice. Label each slice with the name of the category and with the percentage of the whole it represents.
7. Add a title to the circle graph.

ACTIVITY

In a class of 28 students, 12 students take the bus to school, 10 students walk, and 6 students ride their bicycles. Create a circle graph to display these data.

Laboratory Safety

Safety Symbols

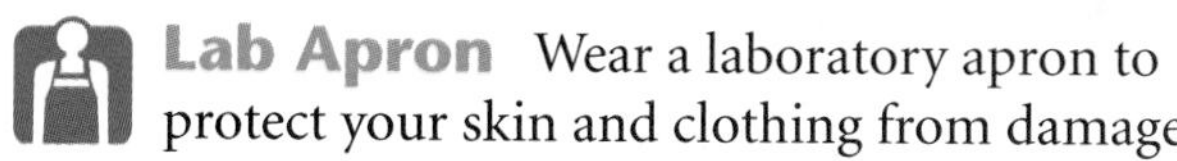
These symbols alert you to possible dangers in the laboratory and remind you to work carefully.

Safety Goggles Always wear safety goggles to protect your eyes in any activity involving chemicals, flames or heating, or the possibility of broken glassware.

Lab Apron Wear a laboratory apron to protect your skin and clothing from damage.

Breakage You are working with materials that may be breakable, such as glass containers, glass tubing, thermometers, or funnels. Handle breakable materials with care. Do not touch broken glassware.

Heat-resistant Gloves Use an oven mitt or other hand protection when handling hot materials. Hot plates, hot glassware, or hot water can cause burns. Do not touch hot objects with your bare hands.

Heating Use a clamp or tongs to pick up hot glassware. Do not touch hot objects with your bare hands.

Sharp Object Pointed-tip scissors, scalpels, knives, needles, pins, or tacks are sharp. They can cut or puncture your skin. Always direct a sharp edge or point away from yourself and others. Use sharp instruments only as instructed.

Electric Shock Avoid the possibility of electric shock. Never use electrical equipment around water, or when the equipment is wet or your hands are wet. Be sure cords are untangled and cannot trip anyone. Disconnect the equipment when it is not in use.

Corrosive Chemical You are working with an acid or another corrosive chemical. Avoid getting it on your skin or clothing, or in your eyes. Do not inhale the vapors. Wash your hands when you are finished with the activity.

Poison Do not let any poisonous chemical come in contact with your skin, and do not inhale its vapors. Wash your hands when you are finished with the activity.

Physical Safety When an experiment involves physical activity, take precautions to avoid injuring yourself or others. Follow instructions from your teacher. Alert your teacher if there is any reason you should not participate in the activity.

Animal Safety Treat live animals with care to avoid harming the animals or yourself. Working with animal parts or preserved animals also may require caution. Wash your hands when you are finished with the activity.

Plant Safety Handle plants in the laboratory or during field work only as directed by your teacher. If you are allergic to certain plants, tell your teacher before doing an activity in which those plants are used. Avoid touching harmful plants such as poison ivy, poison oak, or poison sumac, or plants with thorns. Wash your hands when you are finished with the activity.

Flames You may be working with flames from a lab burner, candle, or matches. Tie back loose hair and clothing. Follow instructions from your teacher about lighting and extinguishing flames.

No Flames Flammable materials may be present. Make sure there are no flames, sparks, or other exposed heat sources present.

Fumes When poisonous or unpleasant vapors may be involved, work in a ventilated area. Avoid inhaling vapors directly. Only test an odor when directed to do so by your teacher, and use a wafting motion to direct the vapor toward your nose.

Disposal Chemicals and other laboratory materials used in the activity must be disposed of safely. Follow the instructions from your teacher.

Hand Washing Wash your hands thoroughly when finished with the activity. Use antibacterial soap and warm water. Lather both sides of your hands and between your fingers. Rinse well.

General Safety Awareness You may see this symbol when none of the symbols described earlier appears. In this case, follow the specific instructions provided. You may also see this symbol when you are asked to develop your own procedure in a lab. Have your teacher approve your plan before you go further.

Science Safety Rules

To prepare yourself to work safely in the laboratory, read over the following safety rules. Then read them a second time. Make sure you understand and follow each rule. Ask your teacher to explain any rules you do not understand.

Dress Code

1. To protect yourself from injuring your eyes, wear safety goggles whenever you work with chemicals, burners, glassware, or any substance that might get into your eyes. If you wear contact lenses, notify your teacher.
2. Wear a lab apron or coat whenever you work with corrosive chemicals or substances that can stain.
3. Tie back long hair to keep it away from any chemicals, flames, or equipment.
4. Remove or tie back any article of clothing or jewelry that can hang down and touch chemicals, flames, or equipment. Roll up or secure long sleeves.
5. Never wear open shoes or sandals.

General Precautions

6. Read all directions for an experiment several times before beginning the activity. Carefully follow all written and oral instructions. If you are in doubt about any part of the experiment, ask your teacher for assistance.
7. Never perform activities that are not assigned or authorized by your teacher. Obtain permission before "experimenting" on your own. Never handle any equipment unless you have specific permission.
8. Never perform lab activities without direct supervision.
9. Never eat or drink in the laboratory.
10. Keep work areas clean and tidy at all times. Bring only notebooks and lab manuals or written lab procedures to the work area. All other items, such as purses and backpacks, should be left in a designated area.
11. Do not engage in horseplay.

First Aid

12. Always report all accidents or injuries to your teacher, no matter how minor. Notify your teacher immediately about any fires.
13. Learn what to do in case of specific accidents, such as getting acid in your eyes or on your skin. (Rinse acids from your body with lots of water.)
14. Be aware of the location of the first-aid kit, but do not use it unless instructed by your teacher. In case of injury, your teacher should administer first aid. Your teacher may also send you to the school nurse or call a physician.
15. Know the location of emergency equipment, such as the fire extinguisher and fire blanket, and know how to use it.
16. Know the location of the nearest telephone and whom to contact in an emergency.

Heating and Fire Safety

17. Never use a heat source, such as a candle, burner, or hot plate, without wearing safety goggles.
18. Never heat anything unless instructed to do so. A chemical that is harmless when cool may be dangerous when heated.
19. Keep all combustible materials away from flames. Never use a flame or spark near a combustible chemical.
20. Never reach across a flame.
21. Before using a laboratory burner, make sure you know proper procedures for lighting and adjusting the burner, as demonstrated by your teacher. Do not touch the burner. It may be hot. And never leave a lighted burner unattended!
22. Chemicals can splash or boil out of a heated test tube. When heating a substance in a test tube, make sure that the mouth of the tube is not pointed at you or anyone else.
23. Never heat a liquid in a closed container. The expanding gases produced may blow the container apart.
24. Before picking up a container that has been heated, hold the back of your hand near it. If you can feel heat on the back of your hand, the container is too hot to handle. Use an oven mitt to pick up a container that has been heated.

Using Chemicals Safely

25. Never mix chemicals "for the fun of it." You might produce a dangerous, possibly explosive substance.

26. Never put your face near the mouth of a container that holds chemicals. Many chemicals are poisonous. Never touch, taste, or smell a chemical unless you are instructed by your teacher to do so.

27. Use only those chemicals needed in the activity. Read and double-check labels on supply bottles before removing any chemicals. Take only as much as you need. Keep all containers closed when chemicals are not being used.

28. Dispose of all chemicals as instructed by your teacher. To avoid contamination, never return chemicals to their original containers. Never simply pour chemicals or other substances into the sink or trash containers.

29. Be extra careful when working with acids or bases. Pour all chemicals over the sink or a container, not over your work surface.

30. If you are instructed to test for odors, use a wafting motion to direct the odors to your nose. Do not inhale the fumes directly from the container.

31. When mixing an acid and water, always pour the water into the container first and then add the acid to the water. Never pour water into an acid.

32. Take extreme care not to spill any material in the laboratory. Wash chemical spills and splashes immediately with plenty of water. Immediately begin rinsing with water any acids that get on your skin or clothing, and notify your teacher of any acid spill at the same time.

Using Glassware Safely

33. Never force glass tubing or thermometers into a rubber stopper or rubber tubing. Have your teacher insert the glass tubing or thermometer if required for an activity.

34. If you are using a laboratory burner, use a wire screen to protect glassware from any flame. Never heat glassware that is not thoroughly dry on the outside.

35. Keep in mind that hot glassware looks cool. Never pick up glassware without first checking to see if it is hot. Use an oven mitt. See rule 24.

36. Never use broken or chipped glassware. If glassware breaks, notify your teacher and dispose of the glassware in the proper broken-glassware container. Never handle broken glass with your bare hands.

37. Never eat or drink from lab glassware.

38. Thoroughly clean glassware before putting it away.

Using Sharp Instruments

39. Handle scalpels or other sharp instruments with extreme care. Never cut material toward you; cut away from you.

40. Immediately notify your teacher if you cut your skin when working in the laboratory.

Animal and Plant Safety

41. Never perform experiments that cause pain, discomfort, or harm to animals. This rule applies at home as well as in the classroom.

42. Animals should be handled only if absolutely necessary. Your teacher will instruct you as to how to handle each animal species brought into the classroom.

43. If you know that you are allergic to certain plants, molds, or animals, tell your teacher before doing an activity in which these are used.

44. During field work, protect your skin by wearing long pants, long sleeves, socks, and closed shoes. Know how to recognize the poisonous plants and fungi in your area, as well as plants with thorns, and avoid contact with them. Never eat any part of a plant or fungus.

45. Wash your hands thoroughly after handling animals or a cage containing animals. Wash your hands when you are finished with any activity involving animal parts, plants, or soil.

End-of-Experiment Rules

46. After an experiment has been completed, turn off all burners or hot plates. If you used a gas burner, check that the gas-line valve to the burner is off. Unplug hot plates.

47. Turn off and unplug any other electrical equipment that you used.

48. Clean up your work area and return all equipment to its proper place.

49. Dispose of waste materials as instructed by your teacher.

50. Wash your hands after every experiment.

Glossary

A

absolute zero The temperature at which no more energy can be removed from matter. (p. 170)

acceleration The rate at which velocity changes. (p. 34)

actual mechanical advantage The mechanical advantage that a machine provides in a real situation. (p. 115)

air resistance The fluid friction experienced by objects falling through the air. (p. 59)

Archimedes' principle The rule that the buoyant force on an object is equal to the weight of the fluid displaced by that object. (p. 91)

B

balanced forces Equal forces acting on an object in opposite directions. (p. 46)

Bernoulli's principle The rule that a stream of fast-moving fluid exerts less pressure than the surrounding fluid. (p. 98)

bimetallic strip A strip made of two different metals that expand at different rates. (p. 186)

boiling Vaporization that occurs on and below the surface of a liquid. (p. 184)

boiling point The temperature at which a liquid substance boils. (p. 184)

buoyant force The upward force exerted by a fluid on a submerged object. (p. 91)

C

Celsius scale The temperature scale on which zero and 100 are the temperatures at which water freezes and boils. (p. 169)

centripetal force A force that causes an object to move in a circle. (p. 71)

change of state The physical change of matter from one state to another. (p. 182)

chemical energy The potential energy stored in chemical bonds. (p. 144)

combustion The process of burning a fuel to produce thermal energy. (p. 187)

compound machine A device that combines two or more simple machines. (p. 128)

condensation The change from the gaseous to the liquid form of matter. (p. 185)

conduction The transfer of heat between particles within a substance. (p. 172)

conductor A material that easily transfers heat between its particles. (p. 175)

controlled experiment An experiment in which all factors except one are kept constant. (p. 207)

convection The transfer of heat by the movement of currents within a fluid. (p. 173)

convection current A current caused by the rising of heated fluid and sinking of cooled fluid. (p. 173)

D

density The mass of a substance contained in a unit of volume. (p. 94)

E

efficiency The percentage of the input work that is converted to output work. (p. 114)

elastic potential energy The energy of stretched or compressed objects. (p. 143)

electrical energy The energy of moving electric charges. (p. 145)

electromagnetic energy The energy of light and other forms of radiation. (p. 145)

energy The ability to do work or cause change. (p. 140)

energy conversion The process of changing one form of energy into another. (p. 149)

evaporation Vaporization that occurs at the surface of a liquid. (p. 184)

external combustion engine An engine powered by fuel burned outside the engine. (p. 188)

F

Fahrenheit scale The temperature scale on which 32 and 212 are the temperatures at which water freezes and boils. (p. 169)

fluid A substance that can easily change shape. (p. 80)

fluid friction Friction that occurs as an object moves through a fluid. (p. 57)

force A push or pull exerted on an object. (p. 44)

fossil fuels Materials such as coal that are burned to release their chemical energy. (p. 155)

free fall The motion of a falling object when the only force acting on it is gravity. (p. 58)

freezing The change from the liquid to the solid form of matter. (p. 184)

freezing point The temperature at which a substance freezes. (p. 184)

friction The force that one surface exerts on another when the two rub against each other. (p. 56)

fulcrum The fixed point around which a lever pivots. (p. 121)

G

gears Two or more wheels linked together by interlocking teeth. (p. 128)

gravitational potential energy Potential energy that depends on the height of an object. (p. 143)

gravity The force that pulls objects toward each other. (p. 58)

H

heat Thermal energy that is transferred from one substance to another. (p. 171)

heat engine A device that converts thermal energy into mechanical energy. (p. 187)

hydraulic system A system that multiplies force by transmitting pressure from a small surface area through a confined fluid to a larger surface area. (p. 88)

hypothesis A possible explanation for a set of observations or answer to a scientific question; must be testable. (p. 206)

I

ideal mechanical advantage The mechanical advantage that a machine would have without friction. (p. 115)

inclined plane A flat surface with one end higher than the other. (p. 119)

inertia The tendency of an object to resist any change in its motion. (p. 48)

input force The force exerted on a machine. (p. 111)

insulator A material that does not easily transfer heat between its particles. (p. 175)

internal combustion engine An engine that burns fuel inside cylinders within the engine. (p. 188)

International System of Units (SI) A system of measurement based on multiples of ten and on established measures of mass, length, and time. (p. 19)

J

joule A unit of work equal to one newton-meter. (p. 109)

K

Kelvin scale The temperature scale on which zero is the temperature at which no more energy can be removed from matter. (p. 169)

kinetic energy Energy that an object has due to its motion. (p. 141)

L

law of conservation of energy The rule that energy cannot be created or destroyed. (p. 152)

law of conservation of momentum The rule that the total momentum of objects in an interaction does not change. (p. 68)

lever A rigid object that pivots about a fixed point. (p. 121)

M

machine A device that changes the amount of force exerted or the direction in which force is exerted. (p. 110)

manipulated variable The one factor that a scientist changes during an experiment. (p. 207)

mass The amount of matter in an object. (p. 49)

mechanical advantage The number of times the force exerted on a machine is multiplied by the machine. (p. 113)

mechanical energy Kinetic or potential energy associated with the motion or position of an object. (p. 144)

melting The change from the solid to the liquid form of matter. (p. 183)

melting point The temperature at which a substance melts. (p. 183)

meter The basic SI unit of length. (p. 19)

momentum The product of an object's mass and velocity. (p. 67)

motion The state in [illegible]'s distance from anot[illegible]

net f[illegible]

th[illegible]

newton A unit of measure that equals the force required to accelerate one kilogram of mass at 1 meter per second per second. (p. 53)

nuclear energy The potential energy stored in the nucleus of an atom. (p. 145)

O

operational definition A statement that describes how a variable is to be measured or a term is to be defined. (p. 207)

output force The force exerted on an object by a machine. (p. 111)

P

pascal A unit of pressure equal to one newton per square meter. (p. 79)

Pascal's principle The rule that when force is applied to a confined fluid, the increase in pressure is transmitted equally to all parts of the fluid. (p. 87)

plate One of the major pieces that make up Earth's upper layer. (p. 28)

potential energy Energy that is stored and held in readiness. (p. 142)

power The rate at which work is done. (p. 158)

pressure The force exerted on a surface divided by the total area over which the force is exerted. (p. 79)

projectile An object that is thrown. (p. 58)

pulley A grooved wheel around which is wrapped a rope, chain, or cable. (p. 126)

R

radiation The transfer of energy by electromagnetic waves. (p. 174)

reference point A place or object used for comparison to determine if an object is in motion. (p. 18)

responding variable The factor that changes as a result of chang[illegible] to the manipulated variable in an experime[illegible]

rolling fric[illegible] s when an [illegible]

[illegible] r

screw An inclined plane wrapped around a central cylinder to form a spiral. (p. 121)

sliding friction Friction that occurs when one solid surface slides over another. (p. 57)

specific heat The amount of heat required to raise the temperature of one kilogram of a substance by one kelvin. (p. 176)

speed The distance an object travels in one unit of time. (p. 20)

states The three forms (solid, liquid, and gas) in which matter exists. (p. 182)

T

temperature The measure of the average kinetic energy of the particles in a substance. (p. 168)

tendon A band of connective tissue that attaches a muscle to a bone. (p. 132)

terminal velocity The maximum velocity a falling object can achieve. (p. 59)

thermal energy The total energy of the particles in a substance or material. (p. 144)

thermal expansion The expansion of matter when it is heated. (p. 185)

thermostat A device that regulates temperature. (p. 186)

U

unbalanced force A nonzero net force, which changes an object's motion. (p. 46)

V

vaporization The change from the liquid to the gaseous form of matter. (p. 184)

variable Any factor that can change in an experiment. (p. 207)

velocity Speed in a given direction. (p. 23)

W

wedge An inclined plane that moves. (p. 120)

weight The force of gravity on an object at the surface of a planet. (p. 59)

wheel and axle Two circular or cylindrical objects that are fastened together and rotate about a common axis. (p. 124)

work Force exerted on an object that causes it to move. (p. 106)

Index

Acknowledgments

Staff Credits

The people who made up the **Science Explorer** team—representing design services, editorial, editorial services, electronic publishing technology, manufacturing & inventory planning, marketing, marketing services, market research, online services & multimedia development, production services, product planning, project office, and publishing processes—are listed below.

Carolyn Belanger, Barbara A. Bertell, Suzanne Biron, Peggy Bliss, Peter W. Brooks, Christopher R. Brown, Greg Cantone, Jonathan Cheney, Todd Christy, Lisa J. Clark, Patrick Finbarr Connolly, Edward Cordero, Robert Craton, Patricia Cully, Patricia M. Dambry, Kathleen J. Dempsey, Judy Elgin, Gayle Connolly Fedele, Frederick Fellows, Barbara Foster, Paula Foye, Loree Franz, Donald P. Gagnon Jr., Paul J. Gagnon, Joel Gendler, Elizabeth Good, Robert M. Graham, Kerri Hoar, Joanne Hudson, Linda D. Johnson, Anne Jones, Toby Klang, Carolyn Langley, Russ Lappa, Carolyn Lock, Cheryl Mahan, Dotti Marshall, Meredith Mascola, Jeanne Y. Maurand, Karen McHugh, Eve Melnechuk, Natania Mlawer, Paul W. Murphy, Cindy A. Noftle, Julia F. Osborne, Judi Pinkham, Caroline M. Power, Robin L. Santel; Suzanne J. Schineller, Emily Soltanoff, Kira Thaler-Marbit, Mark Tricca, Diane Walsh, Pearl Weinstein, Merce Wilczek, Helen Young.

Illustration

John Edwards & Associates: 68–69, 72, 81, 88 t, 142, 149, 188, 189
GeoSystems Global Corporation: 29
Andrea Golden: 10, 194
Martucci Design: 24, 38, 79, 96
Matt Mayerchak: 39, 101, 163, 191
Morgan Cain & Associates: 41, 60, 71, 75 top, 80, 84, 87, 88 b, 91, 94, 100, 103, 111, 120, 121, 126, 127, 137, 168, 169, 173, 176, 182, 183, 186, 190, 193, 195, 196
Ortelius Design Inc.: 30–31, 124–125
Matthew Pippin: 156
Rob Schuster: 99
J/B Woolsey Associates: 11, 13, 41, 59, 65, 75 bottom, 89, 99 insets, 103, 137, 165

Photography

Photo Research: Sue McDermott
Cover Image: Judy White/Picture Perfect

Nature of Science
Page 10, Brian Smale/Discover Magazine; **11,** Stephen G. Maka/DRK Photo; **12,** Brian Smale/Discover Magazine; **12 inset,** Helen Ghiradella/Discover Magazine.

Chapter 1
Pages 14–15, Frans Lanting/Minden Pictures; **16 t,** Richard Haynes; **16 bl,** Bob Abraham/The Stock Market; **16 br,** Roy Morsch/The Stock Market; **17 t,** D. Roundtree/The Image Bank; **17 b,** Steve Maslowshi/Photo Researchers; **18,** NASA; **19 l,** Chuck Zsymanski/International Stock; **19 r,** Robert Maier/Animals Animals; **20,** Mike Agliolo/International Stock; **21,** John Kelly/The Image Bank; **22,** National Motor Museum, Beaulieu, England; **23 t,** Topham/The Image Works; **23 b,** David Barnes/The Stock Market; **24,** Marc Romanelli/The Image Bank; **25,** A.T. Willet/The Image Bank; **27,** Richard Haynes; **28 t,** Russ Lappa; **28 b,** Image Makers/The Image Bank; **31,** Richard Haynes; **32,** Richard Haynes; **33,** Lou Jones/The Image Bank; **34 t,** Richard Haynes; **34 b,** Mike Hewitt/Allsport; **35 l,** Tracy Frankel/The Image Bank; **35 m,** Tim DeFrisco/Allsport; **35 r,** Yann Guichaoua/Agence Vandystadt/ Allsport; **36 t,** Addison Geary/Stock Boston; **36 inset,** Corel Corp.; **37,** Corel Corp.; **39,** Mike Agliolo/International Stock.

Chapter 2
Pages 42–43, David Stoecklein/The Stock Market; **44 t,** Russ Lappa; **44 bl,** Calimberti/Liaison International; **44 br,** Alain Ernoult/The Image Bank; **45,** Richard Thom/Visuals Unlimited; **46,** Elisabeth Weiland/Photo Researchers; **47 all,** Richard Haynes; **48,** Bilderberg/The Stock Market; **49 t,** Russ Lappa; **49 b, 51, 52,** Richard Haynes; **54,** Richard Haynes; **55,** Russ Lappa; **56 t,** Jan Hinsch/Science Photo Library/Photo Researchers; **56 b,** B & C Alexander/Photo Researchers; **57 tl,** The Photo Works/Photo Researchers; **57 tr,** Welzenbach/The Stock Market; **57 b,** Russ Lappa; **58 t,** Jack Novak/Superstock; **58 bl,** Megna/Peticolas/Fundamental Photographs; **58br,** Richard Megna/ Fundamental Photographs; **61,** NASA; **62,** Richard Haynes; **63,** Ken O'Donaghue; **64 t,** Richard Haynes; **64 b,** Ed Young/Science Photo Library/Photo Researchers; **65,** Bob Woodward/The Stock Market; **66 l,** Syracuse/Dick Blume/The Image Works; **66 r,** Michael Devin Daly/The Stock Market; **68,** Russ Lappa; **70 t,** Richard Haynes; **70 b,** Corel Corp.; **71,** Jeff Hunter/The Image Bank.

Chapter 3
Pages 76–77, Rana Clamitans/Visuals Unlimited; **78 t,** Richard Haynes; **78 bl,** Chlaus Lotscher/ Stock Boston; **78 br,** Milton Feinberg/Stock Boston; **82 l, 82 r,** Richard Megna/Fundamental Photographs; **83,** Russ Lappa; **84,** Benn Mitchell/The Image Bank; **85,** Russ Lappa; **86 t,** Richard Haynes; **86 b,** Chris Sheridan/ Monkmeyer; **89 l,** Stuart Westmorland/Photo Researchers; **89 inset,** Andrew Mertiner/Photo Researchers; **90 t,** Russ Lappa; **90 b,** Ken Marshall/Madison Press Limited; **91,** Russ Lappa; **93,** Richard Haynes; **94,** Russ Lappa; **95,** Runk/Schoenberger/Grant Heilman Photography, Inc.; **97 t,** Richard Haynes; **97 b,** Mercury Archives/The Image Bank; **98 t,** Richard Haynes; **98 b,** Patti McConville/The Image Bank; **100 t,** Russ Lappa; **100 b,** Richard Haynes; **101 bl,** Chlaus Lotscher/ Stock Boston; **101 br,** Milton Feinberg/Stock Boston.

Chapter 4
Pages 104–105, Belinda Banks/Tony Stone Images; **106 all,** Richard Haynes; **107 t,** David A. Jentz/Photo Network; **107 b,** Fotopic/Omni-Photo Communications; **109,** Stephen McBrady/Photo Edit; **110 t,** Richard Haynes; **110 b,** Skjold/Photo Edit; **111,** Skjold/Photo Edit; **112,** Siegfried Tauquer/Leo De Wys; **113 t,** David Young-Wolff/Photo Edit; **113 b,** Richard Haynes; **114,** Russ Lappa; **117,** Richard Haynes; **118 t,** Richard Haynes; **118 b,** Russ Lappa; **119,** John Akhtar/Vivid Images Phtg., Inc.; **120 t,** Tony Freeman/Photo Edit; **120 b, 121,** Russ Lappa; **122 t,** Museum of Modern Art, New York/©FPG International 1991; **123 t,** Russ Lappa; **123 l,** Jerry Wachter/Photo Researchers; **123 r,** Elliot Smith/International Stock; **124 t,** Sylvain Grandadam/Tony Stone Images; **124 b,** Gerard Champion/The Image Bank; **125 t,** Jeffrey Aaronson/Network Aspen; **125 r,** G.B. Archives/Sygma; **126,** John Elk/Stock Boston; **128 t,** David R. Frazier; **128 b,** Tony Freeman/Photo Edit; **129,** Jeff Smith/The Image Bank; **130,** Cleo Freelance Photo/New England Stock; **131,** Richard Haynes; **132,** Russ Lappa; **133 all,** Richard Haynes; **134 t,** Ken Karp; **134 m, b,** Richard Haynes.

Chapter 5
Pages 138–139, Chris Rogers/The Stock Market; **140 t,** Richard Haynes; **140 b,** Charles Doswell III/Tony Stone Images; **141,** Zigy Kaluzny/Tony Stone Images; **143,** J. MacPherson/The Stock Market; **144 l,** John Shaw/Tom Stack & Associates; **144 m,** Paul Silverman/Fundamental Photographs; **144 r,** Daniel Cox/Allstock/PNI; **144–145,** James Balog/Tony Stone Images; **145 t,** William L. Wantland/Tom Stack & Associates; **145 b,** Howard Sochurek/The Stock Market; **146, 147, 148 t,** Richard Haynes; **148 b,** Ken Straiton/The Stock Market; **150 t,** Dr. Harold E. Edgerton/The Harold E. Edgerton 1992 Trust; **150 b,** Jon Chomitz; **151 l,** Richard Megna/Fundamental Photographs; **151 r,** Russ Lappa; **152,** "Waterfall" by M. C. Escher, ©1998, Cordon Art-Baarn-Holland, All Rights Reserved; **153,** Courtesy of the Archives, California Institute of Technology; **154 t,** Russ Lappa; **154 b,** Ludek Pesek/Photo Researchers; **155,** Bryan Peterson/The Stock Market; **158,** Russ Lappa; **159,** Bill Bachmann/Photo Researchers; **161,** Richard Haynes; **162,** The Granger Collection, NY; **163,** Dr. Harold E. Edgerton/The Harold E. Edgerton 1992 Trust; **165,** Globus, Holway & Lobel/The Stock Market.

Chapter 6
Pages 166–167, Alfred Pasieka/Peter Arnold; **168, 170, 171 t,** Russ Lappa; **171 b,** Michael Mancuso/Omni-Photo Communications; **172,** Stephen L. Saks/Photo Researchers; **173,** Ken O'Donaghue; **174 t,** Tom Campbell/Gamma-Liaison; **174 b,** Richard Haynes; **175 l,** Wayne Lynch/DRK Photo; **175 r,** Gay Bumgarner/TSI; **177,** Mike Mazzaschi/Stock Boston; **179,** Richard Haynes; **180,** Andy Sacks/TSI; **181 t,** Richard Haynes; **181 b,** Wayne Eastep/TSI; **182 tl,** Runk/Schoenberger/Grant Heilman Photography; **182 tr,** Jack Reznicki/The Stock Market; **182 bl,** Jan Halaska/Photo Researchers; **184,** R. Knolan Benfield, Jr./Visuals Unlimited; **185,** Richard Choy/Peter Arnold, Inc.; **187 t,** Richard Haynes; **187 b,** Larry Ulrich/DRK Photo; **189,** Xenophon A. Beake/The Stock Market; **191,** Wayne Lynch/DRK Photo.

Interdisciplinary Exploration
Page 194 t, IFA/Peter Arnold; **194–195 m,** John Higginson/TSI; **194–195 b** Chris Warren /International Stock; **196–197,** Bob Kramer/Stock Boston; **197 t,** Joseph Pobereskin/TSI; **197 b,** Richard Haynes; **198 tl, 198 b,** Corbis-Bettmann; **198 tm, 198 tr,** The Granger Collection, NY; **199,** Corbis-Bettmann; **200–201,** Richard Weiss/Peter Arnold.

Skills Handbook
Page 202, Mike Moreland/Photo Network; **203 t,** Foodpix; **203 m,** Richard Haynes; **203 b,** Russ Lappa; **206,** Richard Haynes; **208,** Ron Kimball; **209,** Renee Lynn/Photo Researchers.